Eternal Life

Eternal Life

A QUESTION OF HONOR

Michael O'Buck

Copyright © Michael O'Buck.

All rights reserved. No part of this book may be reproduced in any form or by any electronic or mechanical means, including information storage and retrieval systems, without permission in writing from the publisher, except by reviewers, who may quote brief passages in a review.

ISBN: 978-1-64826-975-2   (Paperback Edition)
ISBN: 978-1-64826-976-9   (Hardcover Edition)
ISBN: 978-1-64826-973-8   (E-book Edition)

Some characters and events in this book are fictitious. Any similarity to real persons, living or dead, is coincidental and not intended by the author.

Book Ordering Information

Phone Number: 347-901-4929 or 347-901-4920
Email: info@globalsummithouse.com
Global Summit House
www.globalsummithouse.com

Printed in the United States of America

Dedicating this work to those who helped me search for answers to questons no one wanted to answer would be like trying to praise myself and others for doing what anyone else would do under the same circumstances. Instead, I would like to dedicate this work to the untold numbers who have questions that no one wants to answer and have nowhere else to turn. May your desire to know the truth lead you to the same place we were led.

INTRODUCTION

How does anyone introduce a book that is designed to make anyone that reads it take a long, deep look at himself? Do I explain that before I even began writing the book, I had to look very deeply at myself? Do I claim that it really changed my life? Do I hype it as the best thing since homemade biscuits? Or, do I just say . . . Get ready—here it comes?

If I tried any of these approaches, regardless of my most sincere intentions, I would dishonor the work itself. This book is a written record of progressive revelations and inspirations that I have personally experienced. Yet this book is not all about me. This book is to and about each one of us, including me. Even though this book may be classified as a 'Christian' work, it is written for anyone and everyone to read and question. Honor requires that you question until you understand what you are being shown and told. The very same honor requires the person showing and telling to accept that there will be questions that must be resolved so understanding may be achieved.

Eternal Life is therefore a question of honor. To honor this work and all that it entails, you must first determine if the work itself is true. After that, you must decide whether you can accept your own decision. In the end you will discover that you will live or die by the words that come from your very own mouth. Most of us have never realized the power of the words we speak. Once we learn the power of the spoken word; however, we realize that we have an awesome responsibility to honor the words we utter. That little piece of information will itself change your life.

It is my greatest hope that each one of you who reads these words will come to realize who you are, what you want, and why you are here. Learning these things can be and is a difficult task, but, with patience and understanding, the task can be accomplished by anyone who is willing to accept the challenge.

12/04/08

ETERNAL LIFE

Where does one begin when discussing something that literally has no end at all? I suppose you could start at the beginning, if you could determine when or where it began. Maybe you could start at the middle, if you could even guess when or where that might be. Perhaps the best place to start is the focal point of eternal life itself and just go where it leads you from there.

CHAPTER 1

1 John 1

1. That which was from the beginning, which we have heard, which we have seen with our eyes, which we have looked upon, and our hands have handled, of the Word of life;
2. (For the life was manifested, and we have seen it, and bear witness, and shew unto you that eternal life, which was with the Father, and was manifested unto us;)
3. That which we have seen and heard declare we unto you, that ye also may have fellowship with us: and truly our fellowship is with the Father, and with his Son Jesus Christ.
4. And these things write we unto you, that your joy may be full.

This is the most incredible eyewitness account that has ever been recorded about anything on this earth. John just claimed that he and others had seen, gazed intently at, and carefully touched a real person who had eternal life in himself. Paul noted that this same person appeared to over 500 followers at one time. This could not have been mass hysteria or delusional episodes for that many different people to have seen that exact same man, and be willing to risk their reputations and their whole lives by telling others about it.

John also said that this eternal life was clearly demonstrated to them. He was declaring what they had all seen to others so they could share in the fellowship that these eyewitnesses had with the Father and with his Son Jesus Christ. He wrote this to others in order for their joy to be full.

At this point, I could simply define eternal life, but, if I did, all you would have is a definition that would make no real sense. What I will do, instead, is show you what Christ himself taught about eternal life, what he witnessed to his followers like John, and what Christ's followers taught. You will then have both a definition and the understanding to go with it. That way you will be able to share this eternal life with anyone who wants to know what it is and how to have it.

Matthew 7

13. Enter ye in at the strait gate: for wide is the gate, and broad is the way, that leadeth to destruction, and many there be which go in thereat:
14. Because strait is the gate, and narrow is the way, which leadeth unto life, and few there be that find it.

Jesus illustrates two different paths that people can choose during their lifetime. One path has a wide gate and a broad way, is well traveled, and leads to destruction. There are lots of rest stops, places to get burgers, fries, and a shake, plenty of entertainment, plenty of people, and there is always something new going on just a little farther down the road. You can't see the end, but it has to be better than where you are now.

The second path, however, has to be entered at the strait gate. This path is not so well traveled, it's narrow, and it's hard to stay on without tripping or even falling sometimes. There are fewer people there, not as many rest stops, but you can take your time and enjoy the company you have, and the food is always filling because 'man does not live by bread alone, but by every word that proceedeth out of the mouth of God'.

Sometimes you may stray off the path and get lost or bogged down in a mess. Once you realize that you are bogged down, you have to get back to the path and continue. This is what the psalmist was saying when he said, "Thy word is a lamp unto my feet and a light unto my path.". You will have friends on the path with you who will be more than happy to help you.

In the end, this path leads to life. This is the very same eternal life John said he and others saw in the resurrected Jesus Christ. There are very few that ever find this path or the life that it leads to because it is a very narrow path.

Matthew 13

> 24. Another parable put he forth unto them, saying, The kingdom of heaven is likened unto a man which sowed good seed in his field:
> 25. But while men slept, his enemy came and sowed tares among the wheat, and went his way.
> 26. But when the blade was sprung up, and brought forth fruit, then appeared the tares also.
> 27. So the servants of the householder came and said unto him, Sir, didst not thou sow good seed in thy field? from whence then hath it tares?
> 28. He said unto them, An enemy hath done this. The servants said unto him, Wilt thou then that we go and gather them up?
> 29. But he said, Nay; lest while ye gather up the tares, ye root up also the wheat with them.
> 30. Let both grow together until the harvest: and in the time of harvest I will say to the reapers, Gather ye together first the tares, and bind them in bundles to burn them: but gather the wheat into my barn . . .
> 36. Then Jesus sent the multitude away, and went into the house: and his disciples came unto him, saying, Declare unto us the parable of the tares of the field.
> 37. He answered and said unto them, He that soweth the good seed is the Son of man;

> 38. The field is the world; the good seed are the children of the kingdom; but the tares are the children of the wicked one;
> 39. The enemy that sowed them is the devil; the harvest is the end of the world; and the reapers are the angels.
> 40. As therefore the tares are gathered and burned in the fire; so shall it be in the end of this world.
> 41. The Son of man shall send forth his angels, and they shall gather out of his kingdom all things that offend, and them which do iniquity;
> 42. And shall cast them into a furnace of fire: there shall be wailing and gnashing of teeth.
> 43. Then shall the righteous shine forth as the sun in the kingdom of their Father. Who hath ears to hear, let him hear.

During the time Jesus was teaching the multitudes, he spoke this parable about the kingdom of heaven. Unlike the previous parable he had told about seed that fell on different types of ground, the good seed was planted only in good, fertile ground. However, an enemy came in under the cover of darkness and planted another seed that is called 'tares'. This name does not do the seed justice. The seed was darnel. This plant resembled the wheat so much that it was very difficult—almost impossible—to tell each plant apart. The decision was to allow both to grow side by side in the good ground until maturity and then separate the two. Wheat went to the barn and darnel was bound to be burned.

But, why was darnel such a big deal? If you took wheat and made bread, you could eat it for food and nourishment. However, if you ate darnel, you would die because darnel is poisonous.

When Jesus interpreted this parable, he was prophesying about his coming reign in Jerusalem that the old testament prophets had spoken of. He was not talking about the church at all.

To understand this, you must look at what Jesus said, what Isaiah said, and what Paul said.

Luke 4

16. And he came to Nazareth, where he had been brought up: and, as his custom was, he went into the synagogue on the sabbath day, and stood up for to read.
17. And there was delivered unto him the book of the prophet Esaias. And when he had opened the book, he found the place where it was written,
18. The Spirit of the Lord is upon me, because he hath anointed me to preach the gospel to the poor; he hath sent me to heal the brokenhearted, to preach deliverance to the captives, and recovering of sight to the blind, to set at liberty them that are bruised,
19. To preach the acceptable year of the Lord.
20. And he closed the book, and he gave it again to the minister, and sat down. And the eyes of all them that were in the synagogue were fastened on him.
21. And he began to say unto them, This day is this scripture fulfilled in your ears.

When Jesus was in Nazareth, he went into the synagogue on one particular sabbath and, as he was accustomed to doing, stood up to read from the scriptures. He was handed the scroll of Isaiah. He opened the rolled up scroll and went to a certain point and read a short passage. The scriptures were not like today. There were no chapter divisions, no verse divisions, and no punctuation of any kind.

These scrolls were of two basic types. Either in all capital letters with no spacing between words or all lower case letters with no spacing between words—just one letter after another—from beginning to end. He had to search to find the passage he wanted to quote. He read exactly the part that described what he was doing and stopped exactly when he had finished. Then he handed the scroll back, sat down, and told the people that the prophecy he had quoted was fulfilled that very day in their presence. In order to appreciate how difficult it was for Jesus to be so exact, we need to go to Isaiah and see what he wrote.

Isaiah 61

1. The Spirit of the Lord God is upon me; because the Lord hath anointed me to preach good tidings unto the meek; he hath sent me to bind up the brokenhearted, to proclaim liberty to the captives, and the opening of the prison to them that are bound;
2. To proclaim the acceptable year of the Lord, and the day of vengeance of our God; to comfort all that mourn;
3. To appoint unto them that mourn in Zion, to give unto them beauty for ashes, the oil of joy for mourning, the garment of praise for the spirit of heaviness; that they might be called trees of righteousness, the planting of the Lord, that he might be glorified.

What Isaiah prophesied was that one man would do all these things and more. What Jesus quoted was only the part he was doing at the time. Note here that when Isaiah lived, the prophecies only covered the Jews and the Gentiles because the church of God did not exist. Note that when Jesus quoted Isaiah, the only people that existed were the Jews and the Gentiles—there was no church of God. This is very important.

Ephesians 3

1. For this cause I Paul, the prisoner of Jesus Christ for you Gentiles,
2. If ye have heard of the dispensation of the grace of God which is given me to you-ward:
3. How that by revelation he made known unto me the mystery; (as I wrote afore in few words,
4. Whereby, when ye read, ye may understand my knowledge in the mystery of Christ)
5. Which in other ages was not made known unto the sons of men, as it is now revealed unto his holy apostles and prophets by the Spirit;

> 6. That the Gentiles should be fellowheirs, and of the same body, and partakers of his promise in Christ by the gospel:
> 7. Whereof I was made a minister, according to the gift of the grace of God given unto me by the effectual working of his power.

Paul told the Ephesians that the mystery of Christ was revealed to him. This was after the death and resurrection of Christ Jesus. This was after the day of Pentecost when the spirit of God filled the apostles. This was after Peter witnessed the spirit of God manifested in the Gentiles in Caesarea. Paul said that God never revealed this to anyone before He revealed it to Paul himself.

This means Isaiah didn't know about the church of God. It means that none of the prophets knew about the church of God. It means Jesus himself didn't know about the church of God.

It also means that for Christ to fulfill the rest of Isaiah's prophecy, the church of God cannot exist on the earth at all. It is extremely important then that the church of God know exactly what eternal life is. Each of our lives depend on knowing exactly what is truth and what is error. With truth, we have the promise of eternal life. With error, we have only death.

Matthew 18

> 7. Woe unto the world because of offences! for it must needs be that offences come; but woe to that man by whom the offence cometh!
> 8. Wherefore if thy hand or thy foot offend thee, cut them off, and cast them from thee: it is better for thee to enter into life halt or maimed, rather than having two hands or two feet to be cast into everlasting fire.
> 9. And if thine eye offend thee, pluck it out, and cast it from thee: it is better for thee to enter into life with one eye, rather than having two eyes to be cast into hell fire.

> **10.** Take heed that ye despise not one of these little ones; for I say unto you, That in heaven their angels do always behold the face of my Father which is in heaven.
> **11.** For the Son of man is come to save that which was lost.

People have struggled to understand this passage for a long time. It means a lot more than anyone could imagine. Jesus is talking about two things here—offenses and eternal life. He is saying that offenses will keep you from having eternal life.

In order to have eternal life, you must do away with anything and everything that is offensive to God. You must be totally committed to doing away with all offenses, not just improving yourself and 'being a better person'.

He illustrates the commitment by saying that if your hand or your foot causes you to be offensive to God, you should cut them off and cast them away from you yourself—not have someone else do it for you. If your eye causes you to be offensive, you should pluck out your own eye and throw it away yourself. If you are not willing to be that committed, you will compromise and not receive eternal life.

He didn't literally mean to maim or cripple your body to prove your desire to receive eternal life. He meant that your commitment to doing away with any and all offenses would have to be as strong as the commitment it would take for you to cut off your own hand or foot, or to pluck out your own eye.

Matthew 19

> **16.** And, behold, one came and said unto him, Good Master, what good thing shall I do, that I may have eternal life?
> **17.** And he said unto him, Why callest thou me good? there is none good but one, that is, God: but if thou wilt enter into life, keep the commandments.
> **18.** He saith unto him, Which? Jesus said, Thou shalt do no murder, Thou shalt not commit adultery, Thou shalt not steal, Thou shalt not bear false witness,

19. Honour thy father and thy mother: and, Thou shalt love thy neighbour as thyself.
20. The young man saith unto him, All these things have I kept from my youth up: what lack I yet?
21. Jesus said unto him, If thou wilt be perfect, go and sell that thou hast, and give to the poor, and thou shalt have treasure in heaven: and come and follow me.
22. But when the young man heard that saying, he went away sorrowful: for he had great possessions.
23. Then said Jesus unto his disciples, Verily I say unto you, That a rich man shall hardly enter into the kingdom of heaven.
24. And again I say unto you, It is easier for a camel to go through the eye of a needle, than for a rich man to enter into the kingdom of God.
25. When his disciples heard it, they were exceedingly amazed, saying, Who then can be saved?
26. But Jesus beheld them, and said unto them, With men this is impossible; but with God all things are possible.

Jesus was teaching about eternal life and was approached by a rich young man. The young man asked Jesus what he had to do personally to enter into eternal life. Jesus told him to obey the commandments. When he questioned Jesus about which ones, he told Jesus he had done those things from his youth up. What else was there for him to do?

When Jesus told him to sell all he had, give it to the poor, and come and follow Jesus, the man left filled with sorrow because he was very rich. Jesus told his disciples how difficult it is for a rich man to enter the kingdom of heaven.

When his disciples had difficulty seeing how anyone could enter the kingdom of heaven, Jesus said, though it is impossible with men, with God all things are possible.

We will come back to this same man in Luke and look at this again. There is more to this story than Matthew revealed.

Luke 3

21. Now when all the people were baptized, it came to pass, that Jesus also being baptized, and praying, the heaven was opened,
22. And the Holy Ghost descended in a bodily shape like a dove upon him, and a voice came from heaven, which said, Thou art my beloved Son; in thee I am well pleased.

Luke 4

1. And Jesus being full of the Holy Ghost returned from Jordan, and was led by the Spirit into the wilderness,
2. Being forty days tempted of the devil. And in those days he did eat nothing: and when they were ended, he afterward hungered.
14. And Jesus returned in the power of the Spirit into Galilee: and there went out a fame of him through all the region round about.
15. And he taught in their synagogues, being glorified of all.

Matthew also records these events as well, but Luke provides a summary without going into great detail. Jesus' baptism by John occurred before Jesus began teaching anywhere at all. After he left the river and went into the wilderness, he returned to Galilee in the full power of the spirit of God and began to teach.

I took the time to stop here and say that, in order that everyone knows that Jesus didn't teach anything—not even eternal life—until after he was filled with the spirit of God. This will become very important to remember as we progress through this book.

Luke 10

25. And, behold, a certain lawyer stood up, and tempted him, saying, Master, what shall I do to inherit eternal life?

> 26. He said unto him, What is written in the law? how readest thou?
> 27. And he answering said, Thou shalt love the Lord thy God with all thy heart, and with all thy soul, and with all thy strength, and with all thy mind; and thy neighbour as thyself.
> 28. And he said unto him, Thou hast answered right: this do, and thou shalt live.

A lawyer stood up and deliberately tempted Jesus in front of everyone by asking what he—a man of the law—should do to inherit eternal life. Knowing this, Jesus asked the teacher of the law what the law said to him—a man of the law. His answer proved that he knew the intent of the law.

Jesus told him to go and follow the intent of the law that he himself had just spoken to everyone and he would have eternal life. The lawyer, however, was so determined to find a way around the intent by following the letter of the law, that he could not accept his own answer. Too many people are the same way today.

Luke 12

> 13. And one of the company said unto him, Master, speak to my brother, that he divide the inheritance with me.
> 14. And he said unto him, Man, who made me a judge or a divider over you?
> 15. And he said unto them, Take heed, and beware of covetousness: for a man's life consisteth not in the abundance of the things which he possesseth.
> 16. And he spake a parable unto them, saying, The ground of a certain rich man brought forth plentifully:
> 17. And he thought within himself, saying, What shall I do, because I have no room where to bestow my fruits?
> 18. And he said, This will I do: I will pull down my barns, and build greater; and there will I bestow all my fruits and my goods.

> 19. And I will say to my soul, Soul, thou hast much goods laid up for many years; take thine ease, eat, drink, and be merry.
> 20. But God said unto him, Thou fool, this night thy soul shall be required of thee: then whose shall those things be, which thou hast provided?
> 21. So is he that layeth up treasure for himself, and is not rich toward God.
> 22. And he said unto his disciples, Therefore I say unto you, Take no thought for your life, what ye shall eat; neither for the body, what ye shall put on.
> 23. The life is more than meat, and the body is more than raiment.

Jesus was teaching eternal life when two men came to him to settle an inheritance dispute. He told them right up front that eternal life does not consist of material possessions period. He went on to tell them with a parable that even your breath life—your soul—is not determined, defined by, nor consists of material possessions. Greedy desire for what someone has or may get will stop you from receiving eternal life. That path keeps getting narrower and narrower.

Christians do not realize that eternal life itself does not consist of, nor is defined or determined by material possessions. If they did, they wouldn't try to tie their Christian life to things in their life.

Luke 18

> 18. And a certain ruler asked him, saying, Good Master, what shall I do to inherit eternal life?
> 19. And Jesus said unto him, Why callest thou me good? none is good, save one, that is, God.
> 20. Thou knowest the commandments, Do not commit adultery, Do not kill, Do not steal, Do not bear false witness, Honour thy father and thy mother.
> 21. And he said, All these have I kept from my youth up.

> **22. Now when Jesus heard these things, he said unto him, Yet lackest thou one thing: sell all that thou hast, and distribute unto the poor, and thou shalt have treasure in heaven: and come, follow me.**
> **23. And when he heard this, he was very sorrowful: for he was very rich.**
> **24. And when Jesus saw that he was very sorrowful, he said, How hardly shall they that have riches enter into the kingdom of God!**

Now we are going to look at Luke and Matthew together to see the story of this young man who asked Jesus how to inherit eternal life.

According to Matthew, this man was a young man. According to Luke, this man was a ruler or a judge over people. This means he was well known and his judgements were respected. Matthew said he had great wealth. Luke said he was very rich.

Both of them said that this young man had kept the commandments from his childhood through adulthood. He obeyed willingly and not for appearance sake. Yet, when Jesus told him to sell everything, give it to the poor, and come and follow with the disciples, the young man was very sorrowful and went away because he was very wealthy, very well known, and very well respected.

All that he had was the result of blessings from God because he was obedient to God's commandments. It was too much for him to have to give up the blessings from God just to have eternal life.

This young man was not some rich powerful pagan gentile. This man was the ancient equivalent to today's strong, powerful, standing, believing, believer who can do all things through Christ Jesus.

Christians today have somehow developed the notion that material possessions prove how good a Christian you are. The more obedient you are, the more blessings you receive—especially if you live in an affluent society like we have here.

Sadly, a great many of today's Christians would react the same way this young man did. The things they have, the respect they have, the name they have, are all the results of their obedience. To ask them to give all that up and simply follow Christ would be more than they could do.

I say these things not to judge, but to warn. I say these things with a breaking heart and I pray every day that we as Christians will return to the simplicity that is in Christ Jesus.

The gospel of John deals more with the teachings about eternal life than the other gospels. His record is more detailed concerning the teaching of eternal life than the others.

CHAPTER 2

John 3

14. And as Moses lifted up the serpent in the wilderness, even so must the Son of man be lifted up:
15. That whosoever believeth in him should not perish, but have eternal life.
16. For God so loved the world, that he gave his only begotten Son, that whosoever believeth in him should not perish, but have everlasting life.
17. For God sent not his Son into the world to condemn the world; but that the world through him might be saved.
18. He that believeth on him is not condemned: but he that believeth not is condemned already, because he hath not believed in the name of the only begotten Son of God.
19. And this is the condemnation, that light is come into the world, and men loved darkness rather than light, because their deeds were evil.
20. For every one that doeth evil hateth the light, neither cometh to the light, lest his deeds should be reproved.
21. But he that doeth truth cometh to the light, that his deeds may be made manifest, that they are wrought in God.
22. After these things came Jesus and his disciples into the land of Judaea; and there he tarried with them, and baptized . . .

> **35. The Father loveth the Son, and hath given all things into his hand.**
> **36. He that believeth on the Son hath everlasting life: and he that believeth not the Son shall not see life; but the wrath of God abideth on him.**

This passage is from a conversation Jesus had with Nicodemus. Nicodemus was a Pharisee who was on the ruling council of the temple. He came to Jesus by night for two reasons. First, the Pharisees were following Jesus around by day trying to find some way to discredit him or trap him in his own words. Second, Nicodemus had the chance to talk to Jesus privately and ask him direct questions to find out exactly who Jesus really was.

Jesus understood his intent and treated Nicodemus with the respect he deserved. Jesus told Nicodemus that he was the only begotten son of God and whoever believed in him would have everlasting life. He also told Nicodemus that he would be lifted up just as Moses had lifted up the serpent in the wilderness for the children of Israel.

Jesus didn't come to condemn the world, rather he came to save the world through what he himself would do. Anyone who believed on Jesus wasn't condemned; however, anyone who didn't believe on Jesus was condemned simply because he didn't believe in the name of the only begotten son of God.

The condemnation was that light had come into the world and people wouldn't come to it because they did wicked and evil things. They would rather be in darkness to hide the things they did.

People who were truthful would come to the light to show that their deeds were worked through the inspiration of God.

After talking to Nicodemus, Jesus and his disciples left and went to Judea and stayed for a while and baptized people.

John closed the account by saying that God loved the son and gave all things into his hand. He then said that anyone having the son has everlasting life. He also said anyone not having the son will not even see everlasting life, but had the wrath of God abiding on him instead.

John 4

1. When therefore the Lord knew how the Pharisees had heard that Jesus made and baptized more disciples than John,
2. (Though Jesus himself baptized not, but his disciples,)
3. He left Judaea, and departed again into Galilee.
4. And he must needs go through Samaria.
5. Then cometh he to a city of Samaria, which is called Sychar, near to the parcel of ground that Jacob gave to his son Joseph.
6. Now Jacob's well was there. Jesus therefore, being wearied with his journey, sat thus on the well: and it was about the sixth hour.
7. There cometh a woman of Samaria to draw water: Jesus saith unto her, Give me to drink.
8. (For his disciples were gone away unto the city to buy meat.)
9. Then saith the woman of Samaria unto him, How is it that thou, being a Jew, askest drink of me, which am a woman of Samaria? for the Jews have no dealings with the Samaritans.
10. Jesus answered and said unto her, If thou knewest the gift of God, and who it is that saith to thee, Give me to drink; thou wouldest have asked of him, and he would have given thee living water.
11. The woman saith unto him, Sir, thou hast nothing to draw with, and the well is deep: from whence then hast thou that living water?
12. Art thou greater than our father Jacob, which gave us the well, and drank thereof himself, and his children, and his cattle?
13. Jesus answered and said unto her, Whosoever drinketh of this water shall thirst again:
14. But whosoever drinketh of the water that I shall give him shall never thirst; but the water that I shall give

> him shall be in him a well of water springing up into everlasting life.
> 15. The woman saith unto him, Sir, give me this water, that I thirst not, neither come hither to draw . . .
> 23. But the hour cometh, and now is, when the true worshippers shall worship the Father in spirit and in truth: for the Father seeketh such to worship him.
> 24. God is a Spirit: and they that worship him must worship him in spirit and in truth.

Jesus was near where John the Baptist was and many people were coming to him. He never baptized a single person himself, but his disciples did. When he found out the Pharisees were looking for him, he left for Galilee and went by way of Samaria.

Jesus went into Samaria because he knew that the most righteous and right reverend Pharisees were too pure to go anywhere near unclean people. He got to a town called Sychar during the hot part of the day and sat down by a well while his disciples went into town to buy food.

A woman came to draw water and Jesus broke custom by simply asking her to give him a drink. She immediately reminded him of two things. First, he was a Jew and she was a Samaritan. Jews would not have anything to do with Samaritans at all—not even speak to them. Second, he was an unaccompanied man and she was an unaccompanied woman. It was totally against custom for him to even speak to her—especially if they didn't know one another.

Jesus responded by telling her that if she knew the gift of God, and who was talking to her, she would be the one asking for a drink. If she did, he would give her living water to drink. Being the astute woman that she was, she immediately noted that he had nothing to draw water with and that the well was a deep well.

She then asked him if he was greater than Jacob, the man who gave them the well to begin with—Jacob—the man who drank from the well himself as well as his family and his livestock.

Jesus told her that whoever drank from Jacob's well would get thirsty and have to drink again. Whoever drank the water he gave them would never be thirsty again because that water would become a well in each of them springing up into everlasting life.

It was then that the woman asked for the water because she didn't want to be thirsty any more and she didn't want to keep coming to the well to draw water. Their conversation continued and she determined that Jesus was a prophet of God. Eventually, she wanted to know where the proper place to worship was.

Jesus told her God wa s not interested in wh ere he wa s worshipped—only how he was worshipped. His true worshipers would worship in spirit and truth because that was what God was looking for.

Jesus told her that God himself is a spirit and that the only true way to worship him is in spirit and truth—no matter where you are.

John 5

24. Verily, verily, I say unto you, He that heareth my word, and believeth on him that sent me, hath everlasting life, and shall not come into condemnation; but is passed from death unto life.
25. Verily, verily, I say unto you, The hour is coming, and now is, when the dead shall hear the voice of the Son of God: and they that hear shall live.
26. For as the Father hath life in himself; so hath he given to the Son to have life in himself;
27. And hath given him authority to execute judgment also, because he is the Son of man.
28. Marvel not at this: for the hour is coming, in the which all that are in the graves shall hear his voice,
29. And shall come forth; they that have done good, unto the resurrection of life; and they that have done evil, unto the resurrection of damnation.
30. I can of mine own self do nothing: as I hear, I judge: and my judgment is just; because I seek not mine own will, but the will of the Father which hath sent me.
31. If I bear witness of myself, my witness is not true.

32. There is another that beareth witness of me; and I know that the witness which he witnesseth of me is true.

33. Ye sent unto John, and he bare witness unto the truth.

34. But I receive not testimony from man: but these things I say, that ye might be saved.

35. He was a burning and a shining light: and ye were willing for a season to rejoice in his light.

36. But I have greater witness than that of John: for the works which the Father hath given me to finish, the same works that I do, bear witness of me, that the Father hath sent me.

37. And the Father himself, which hath sent me, hath borne witness of me. Ye have neither heard his voice at any time, nor seen his shape.

38. And ye have not his word abiding in you: for whom he hath sent, him ye believe not.

39. Search the scriptures; for in them ye think ye have eternal life: and they are they which testify of me.

40. And ye will not come to me, that ye might have life.

Jesus was in the temple during one of the feasts and the Pharisees began attacking him for what he was teaching the people. He wasn't as nice to the Pharisees as he was to the people. He revealed a lot in these passages that we haven't even noticed today.

Jesus told the Pharisees that whoever heard his word and believed on the one who sent him would have everlasting life. They would skip past judgment and go right into everlasting life.

He then told them that now was the time that the dead would hear the voice of the son of God and those hearing his voice would have eternal life—they would live.

He then said that the Father—God himself—had eternal life (life in himself). God is the only being specifically declared to have eternal life. This same God that Jesus told the Samaritan woman is a spirit has life totally in himself. There is no outside source for this unique life. It then by definition is completely self contained, self generating, and self perpetuating. It cannot under any circumstances or conditions grow old, weaken, diminish, hunger, thirst, or die—ever.

Not only that, but this same God had promised Jesus that he too would have this very same eternal life. He just didn't tell Jesus when he would have it or how he would get it.

When Jesus was speaking to the Pharisees, he was filled with the spirit of God because it was after he had been baptized by John and before he was crucified. The fullness of God himself dwelt in Jesus Christ and was tabernacled in his body, yet Jesus did not have eternal life. He still got thirsty, hungry, tired, felt pain, etc. Jesus only had the promise of eternal life.

God gave Jesus the authority to execute judgment also because he is the Son of man. As such, he could give this same promise of eternal life to as many as heard his words. This is why he said that then was the time that the dead would hear the voice of the son of God and those that heard would have eternal life. His judgment was that we are dead already, and only those who hear the voice of the son of God will live.

Jesus said that, in the future, all who were in the grave would hear his voice and come forth. Some would receive eternal life and others would face judgment.

He told the Pharisees that if he bore witness of himself, his witness wouldn't be true. He told them that John witnessed about him and for a while they were willing to listen to him. He also said he didn't need the witness of men because he had greater witness than that.

The works he did themselves proved he had been sent by God. God even bore witness to him when John baptized him. He then told the Pharisees that they had never heard God's voice or seen him at any time. They didn't have God's word abiding in them at all because they refused to believe the one God himself had sent to them.

He told them to search the scriptures because they thought that they would have eternal life for knowing them. The scriptures testified of Jesus, yet the Pharisees refused to come to the very man that the scriptures spoke of to have eternal life.

John 10

7. Then said Jesus unto them again, Verily, verily, I say unto you, I am the door of the sheep.
8. All that ever came before me are thieves and robbers: but the sheep did not hear them.
9. I am the door: by me if any man enter in, he shall be saved, and shall go in and out, and find pasture.
10. The thief cometh not, but for to steal, and to kill, and to destroy: I am come that they might have life, and that they might have it more abundantly.
11. I am the good shepherd: the good shepherd giveth his life for the sheep.
12. But he that is an hireling, and not the shepherd, whose own the sheep are not, seeth the wolf coming, and leaveth the sheep, and fleeth: and the wolf catcheth them, and scattereth the sheep.
13. The hireling fleeth, because he is an hireling, and careth not for the sheep.
14. I am the good shepherd, and know my sheep, and am known of mine.
15. As the Father knoweth me, even so I know the Father: and I lay down my life for the sheep.
16. And other sheep I have, which are not of this fold: them also I must bring, and they shall hear my voice; and there shall be one fold, and one shepherd.
17. Therefore doth my Father love me, because I lay down my life, that I might take it again.
18. No man taketh it from me, but I lay it down of myself. I have power to lay it down, and I have power to take it again. This commandment have I received of my Father.
19. There was a division therefore again among the Jews for these sayings.
20. And many of them said, He hath a devil, and is mad; why hear ye him?

21. Others said, These are not the words of him that hath a devil. Can a devil open the eyes of the blind?
22. And it was at Jerusalem the feast of the dedication, and it was winter.
23. And Jesus walked in the temple in Solomon's porch.
24. Then came the Jews round about him, and said unto him, How long dost thou make us to doubt? If thou be the Christ, tell us plainly.
25. Jesus answered them, I told you, and ye believed not: the works that I do in my Father's name, they bear witness of me.
26. But ye believe not, because ye are not of my sheep, as I said unto you.
27. My sheep hear my voice, and I know them, and they follow me:
28. And I give unto them eternal life; and they shall never perish, neither shall any man pluck them out of my hand.
29. My Father, which gave them me, is greater than all; and no man is able to pluck them out of my Father's hand.
30. I and my Father are one.
31. Then the Jews took up stones again to stone him.
32. Jesus answered them, Many good works have I shewed you from my Father; for which of those works do ye stone me?
33. The Jews answered him, saying, For a good work we stone thee not; but for blasphemy; and because that thou, being a man, makest thyself God.
34. Jesus answered them, Is it not written in your law, I said, Ye are gods?
35. If he called them gods, unto whom the word of God came, and the scripture cannot be broken;
36. Say ye of him, whom the Father hath sanctified, and sent into the world, Thou blasphemest; because I said, I am the Son of God?

Jesus spoke another parable to illustrate his relationship to those who followed him. He compared himself to a shepherd and his followers to sheep that the shepherd actually owned.

By saying he was the door of the sheep, he told them he was their protector. When sheep were in a pen, there was only one way in or out. The shepherd would guard the entrance to protect the sheep from any predator. He would even sleep across the entrance at night to keep predators and thieves out.

Anyone coming before him who made such a claim was a thief and a robber, but the sheep wouldn't listen to his voice.

The thief's purpose was to steal, kill, and destroy the flock of sheep. Jesus came to give his sheep eternal life beyond anything that could measure it. This life does not consist of, nor can be defined by, nor measured by material things at all—ever.

He declared himself to be the good shepherd that would give his life—his soul—his last breath—for his sheep to have eternal life.

He wasn't a hireling who watched other people's sheep. When a hireling sees a predator or robber, he will save his own life first. He will leave the sheep unprotected to be killed and scattered by the predator or robber.

He knew his sheep and his sheep knew him. He knew his Father the same way his Father knew him. No man could take his life because God had given him the authority to give his own life and take it again.

The things he said caused a serious division among the Jews. These were the leaders of the people and they were the ones who followed him around trying to trap in his words. These were the ones Nicodemus avoided by coming to Jesus by night.

Some of them said he was mad and had a devil. Others said that it was impossible for anyone with a devil to heal a man that was blind from birth. That was one of the signs of God's chosen one.

These events occurred during the Feast of Tabernacles when Jesus was at the temple in Jerusalem. Later, during the winter, Jesus was at the feast of dedication and was walking in Solomon's porch. These same leaders surrounded him again demanded that he tell them plainly if he was really Messiah—the Christ-the anointed one—or not. They were tired of the doubts among themselves, of following him around trying to accuse him of anything, of trying to trick him or trap him in his own words,—just exactly who was he?

He said he told them who he was, and they wouldn't believe him. He said that the works he did in his Father's name and not his own name proved who he was, and they wouldn't believe that either. He said they were not of his sheep because they wouldn't hear what he said and come to him.

His sheep heard his voice, he knew them, and they followed him. His gift to them was eternal life and they would never die. No man could take them from him because his Father gave them to him. His Father is greater than all, and no man can take them from his Father—ever.

Then Jesus said I and my Father are one.

When he said that the leaders began picking up stones to kill him. He asked them just exactly which one of the good works from his Father did they plan to stone him for. They immediately accused him of blasphemy, a very serious charge. They twisted what he said to say he was a man who by that single statement was trying to make himself God in the flesh. If that is what he was actually doing, it would be blasphemy and they would be justified in their charge. His next answer would determine what they did.

He said that in their own scriptures God himself had said "ye are gods". If God said this to men that he had given his word to, and the scriptures cannot be broken, why were these men accusing the one God himself had set apart, and sent to them, of blasphemy just because he said he was the son of God?

He left after that and stayed away for a while, but the people kept coming to him to hear the words of eternal life.

CHAPTER 3

While Jesus was teaching, the time was growing closer to observe Passover, the next time Jesus was required to be in the temple. During this time before preparation for Passover, Jesus received a message that Lazarus, the brother of Mary and Martha was sick. His only comment was that the sickness wasn't unto death. He then stayed where he was for two more days before he decided it was time to go to Bethany where Lazarus and his sisters lived.

John 11

11. These things said he: and after that he saith unto them, Our friend Lazarus sleepeth; but I go, that I may awake him out of sleep.
12. Then said his disciples, Lord, if he sleep, he shall do well.
13. Howbeit Jesus spake of his death: but they thought that he had spoken of taking of rest in sleep.
14. Then said Jesus unto them plainly, Lazarus is dead.
15. And I am glad for your sakes that I was not there, to the intent ye may believe; nevertheless let us go unto him.
16. Then said Thomas, which is called Didymus, unto his fellowdisciples, Let us also go, that we may die with him.
17. Then when Jesus came, he found that he had lain in the grave four days already.
18. Now Bethany was nigh unto Jerusalem, about fifteen furlongs off:

19. And many of the Jews came to Martha and Mary, to comfort them concerning their brother.
20. Then Martha, as soon as she heard that Jesus was coming, went and met him: but Mary sat still in the house.
21. Then said Martha unto Jesus, Lord, if thou hadst been here, my brother had not died.
22. But I know, that even now, whatsoever thou wilt ask of God, God will give it thee.
23. Jesus saith unto her, Thy brother shall rise again.
24. Martha saith unto him, I know that he shall rise again in the resurrection at the last day.
25. Jesus said unto her, I am the resurrection, and the life: he that believeth in me, though he were dead, yet shall he live:
26. And whosoever liveth and believeth in me shall never die. Believest thou this?
27. She saith unto him, Yea, Lord: I believe that thou art the Christ, the Son of God, which should come into the world.
28. And when she had so said, she went her way, and called Mary her sister secretly, saying, The Master is come, and calleth for thee.
29. As soon as she heard that, she arose quickly, and came unto him.
30. Now Jesus was not yet come into the town, but was in that place where Martha met him.
31. The Jews then which were with her in the house, and comforted her, when they saw Mary, that she rose up hastily and went out, followed her, saying, She goeth unto the grave to weep there.
32. Then when Mary was come where Jesus was, and saw him, she fell down at his feet, saying unto him, Lord, if thou hadst been here, my brother had not died.

33. When Jesus therefore saw her weeping, and the Jews also weeping which came with her, he groaned in the spirit, and was troubled.
34. And said, Where have ye laid him? They said unto him, Lord, come and see.
35. Jesus wept.
36. Then said the Jews, Behold how he loved him!
37. And some of them said, Could not this man, which opened the eyes of the blind, have caused that even this man should not have died?
38. Jesus therefore again groaning in himself cometh to the grave. It was a cave, and a stone lay upon it.
39. Jesus said, Take ye away the stone. Martha, the sister of him that was dead, saith unto him, Lord, by this time he stinketh: for he hath been dead four days.
40. Jesus saith unto her, Said I not unto thee, that, if thou wouldest believe, thou shouldest see the glory of God?
41. Then they took away the stone from the place where the dead was laid. And Jesus lifted up his eyes, and said, Father, I thank thee that thou hast heard me.
42. And I knew that thou hearest me always: but because of the people which stand by I said it, that they may believe that thou hast sent me.
43. And when he thus had spoken, he cried with a loud voice, Lazarus, come forth.
44. And he that was dead came forth, bound hand and foot with graveclothes: and his face was bound about with a napkin. Jesus saith unto them, Loose him, and let him go.
45. Then many of the Jews which came to Mary, and had seen the things which Jesus did, believed on him.
46. But some of them went their ways to the Pharisees, and told them what things Jesus had done.

Jesus first told his disciples that Lazarus was asleep and he was going to awaken him. When his disciples thought Lazarus was just asleep, they figured the rest would be good for him. Then Jesus told his disciples that Lazarus was dead.

He told them that he was glad for their sakes to the extent they may believe all the things he had been teaching them. Thomas said they should go and they could die with him.

When Jesus came to Bethany, he found that Lazarus had already been buried for 4 days. Since Jerusalem was very close by, many people had come to comfort Mary and Martha for the loss of their brother.

As soon as Martha heard Jesus was coming, she left to go meet him, but Mary stayed home with the guests.

When Martha saw Jesus, she told him that her brother wouldn't have died if he had been there as if to say Jesus should have come when they first sent for him.

Jesus told her that Lazarus would rise again. Martha understood Lazarus would rise in the resurrection at the last day. The next thing Jesus said would rock the world if people understood him. The tragic thing is that most Christians don't understand it well enough to explain it to others.

When Jesus asked Martha if she believed that he was the resurrection and the life and that anyone who believed in him, even if he were dead, would live and anyone who was alive and believed in him would never die, she answered yes. She told Jesus she believed he was Messiah, the Christ who was to come into the world.

Martha then left and told Mary secretly that the Master was there and wanted to see her. Mary got up and went to see him where he waited. The people visiting and comforting her thought she was going to the tomb to weep, so they followed her.

When Mary saw Jesus, she told him that, he had just been there, Lazarus wouldn't have died. She also was telling Jesus that he should have come when they sent for him.

When Jesus saw her and the others with her crying, he groaned in the spirit and was troubled. After all that he had told and shown them—after they followed him—they still did not understand about eternal life.

Jesus then asked to be taken to where the body was laid, and as he went, he openly wept. Some of the Jews there commented about how much Jesus loved Lazarus because Jesus wept openly. Others openly questioned how a man who could open the eyes of the blind couldn't keep Lazarus from dying.

This caused Jesus to groan within himself at their unbelief. When they came to the cave Lazarus was in, Jesus told them to remove the stone. Martha said Lazarus would be stinking after having been buried four days already.

Jesus reminded Martha that, if she would just believe, she would see the glory of God. He then prayed the strangest prayer—he never prayed to God for the strength or for permission to restore life to Lazarus. Jesus just thanked God for always hearing him and prayed for the sake of the people there to actually believe that Jesus was sent from God.

After that prayer, Jesus called Lazarus personally to come forth. When Lazarus came forth, Jesus ordered that he be unwrapped from his grave clothes. Lazarus was buried according to custom. He was wrapped in strips of cloth and bound together like an Egyptian mummy. The children of Israel had learned this burial procedure while they were still in Egypt. Joseph had been mummified by the Egyptians to honor what he had done for Egypt. This is why Jesus ordered Lazarus to be loosed.

Many of those who came to comfort Mary believed Jesus when they saw him raise Lazarus from the dead. However, those who wondered why a man who could restore sight to the blind couldn't keep a man from dying went to the priests and told them the things Jesus did. From that day on, the priests decided to find a way to kill him.

Knowing the turmoil around him, Jesus went with his disciples near the wilderness to a city called Ephraim and stayed until it was time to go and prepare for Passover at Jerusalem.

Jesus did not come back to the temple again until the time of preparation for Passover. He only came into the area amid large crowds of people and totally frustrated the priests, who wanted to take him quietly and in secret. They weren't sure where he was staying, but they knew he wasn't in Jerusalem.

The last night he was with his disciples, he spoke to them more of eternal life after Judas Iscariot left to tell the priest where Jesus would be later on that night. It is here that we again pick up and continue this chapter.

John 14

1. Let not your heart be troubled: ye believe in God, believe also in me.
2. In my Father's house are many mansions: if it were not so, I would have told you. I go to prepare a place for you.
3. And if I go and prepare a place for you, I will come again, and receive you unto myself; that where I am, there ye may be also.
4. And whither I go ye know, and the way ye know.
5. Thomas saith unto him, Lord, we know not whither thou goest; and how can we know the way?
6. Jesus saith unto him, I am the way, the truth, and the life: no man cometh unto the Father, but by me.
7. If ye had known me, ye should have known my Father also: and from henceforth ye know him, and have seen him.
8. Philip saith unto him, Lord, shew us the Father, and it sufficeth us.
9. Jesus saith unto him, have I been so long time with you, and yet hast thou not known me, Philip? he that hath seen me hath seen the Father; and how sayest thou then, Shew us the Father?
10. Believest thou not that I am in the Father, and the Father in me? the words that I speak unto you I speak not of myself: but the Father that dwelleth in me, he doeth the works.
11. Believe me that I am in the Father, and the Father in me: or else believe me for the very works' sake.

> 12. Verily, verily, I say unto you, He that believeth on me, the works that I do shall he do also; and greater works than these shall he do; because I go unto my Father.
> 13. And whatsoever ye shall ask in my name, that will I do, that the Father may be glorified in the Son.
> 14. If ye shall ask any thing in my name, I will do it.
> 15. If ye love me, keep my commandments.
> 16. And I will pray the Father, and he shall give you another Comforter, that he may abide with you for ever;
> 17. Even the Spirit of truth; whom the world cannot receive, because it seeth him not, neither knoweth him: but ye know him; for he dwelleth with you, and shall be in you.
> 18. I will not leave you comfortless: I will come to you.
> 19. Yet a little while, and the world seeth me no more; but ye see me: because I live, ye shall live also.
> 20. At that day ye shall know that I am in my Father, and ye in me, and I in you.

After Judas Iscariot left, Jesus began to prepare his disciples for the hardest time of their lives. He knew he was going to die. He knew they would be afraid for their own lives. He also knew that they would understand all he revealed to them after everything unfolded. He had to give them final instructions before he was taken from them.

He told them that, since they believed God's words, they should believe his words also. He told them that his Father's house had many mansions, and that he was going to prepare a place for them. He also said that he would come back for them so they could be with him—he just didn't say when he would come back for them.

He then told them that they knew where he was going and they knew how to get there. Thomas told him they had no idea where he was going, much less the way to get there.

Next Jesus said, "I am the way, the truth, and the life: no man cometh to the Father, but by me.". He was telling them that it was his obedience to the Father that the promises of God were sealed by. He told them he was the physical embodiment of truth itself—the very living fiber of the word of God—for them to walk with, learn from, and follow. He was the herald of eternal life from God to all men. He was the true shepherd that would give his own life for his sheep to have eternal life. There could be no other way to the Father but by him.

Philip said it would be enough if Jesus would just show them the Father. Jesus then asked Philip how long he had been with Jesus and could not see the Father in everything he did. Jesus told Philip that none of the things he said or did were of himself. Everything that Jesus did or said was from the Father who dwelled in him. He dwelled in the Father the same way because he was perfectly obedient to the Father.

He told the disciples to believe that the Father dwelled in him and he in the Father, or else believe for the very works' sake themselves. No man could do the things he did in and of himself.

He then went on to say that whoever believed on him would do the works he did, and even greater works, because he was going to the Father. If they asked anything in his name he would do it for the Father to be glorified in the son. These are very powerful statements and require an obedience to God that people don't naturally have from birth. This is why Paul later told Christians to bring every thought captive to the obedience of Christ—our obedience to God must be as his was—even to death.

He wanted his followers to keep his commandments out of love for him, not to prove to others that they were his followers. He said he would pray for the Father to send them a comforter that the world could not receive because it was something the world did not know. This was the spirit of truth, the same spirit that was already with them. It would be with them forever because it would be in them like it was in Jesus himself.

He also promised to come to them personally himself so they would not be without comfort during the trying days to come. He said shortly, the world would not see him again, but his disciples would. On that day, they would know he was in the Father and the Father was in him this whole time. On that day they would see for themselves that, because he had eternal life, they would have eternal life also.

He spoke a few more things to them while sitting with them and then said it was time to go. As they were walking along toward the mount of Olives, he told them many more things. One of the things he told them was that they would be witnesses of him because they had been with him from the beginning—the very same beginning John refers to in 1st John.

He offered a prayer just before entering the garden he customarily went to at night. The prayer included what he wanted for his followers. He spoke in front of his disciples so they themselves would be assured of his promises to them.

John 17

1. These words spake Jesus, and lifted up his eyes to heaven, and said, Father, the hour is come; glorify thy Son, that thy Son also may glorify thee:
2. As thou hast given him power over all flesh, that he should give eternal life to as many as thou hast given him.
3. And this is life eternal, that they might know thee the only true God, and Jesus Christ, whom thou hast sent . . .
9. I pray for them: I pray not for the world, but for them which thou hast given me; for they are thine.
10. And all mine are thine, and thine are mine; and I am glorified in them.
11. And now I am no more in the world, but these are in the world, and I come to thee. Holy Father, keep through thine own name those whom thou hast given me, that they may be one, as we are.
12. While I was with them in the world, I kept them in thy name: those that thou gavest me I have kept, and none of them is lost, but the son of perdition; that the scripture might be fulfilled.

13. And now come I to thee; and these things I speak in the world, that they might have my joy fulfilled in themselves.
14. I have given them thy word; and the world hath hated them, because they are not of the world, even as I am not of the world.
15. I pray not that thou shouldest take them out of the world, but that thou shouldest keep them from the evil.
16. They are not of the world, even as I am not of the world.
17. Sanctify them through thy truth: thy word is truth.
18. As thou hast sent me into the world, even so have I also sent them into the world.
19. And for their sakes I sanctify myself, that they also might be sanctified through the truth.
20. Neither pray I for these alone, but for them also which shall believe on me through their word;
21. That they all may be one; as thou, Father, art in me, and I in thee, that they also may be one in us: that the world may believe that thou hast sent me.
22. And the glory which thou gavest me I have given them; that they may be one, even as we are one:
23. I in them, and thou in me, that they may be made perfect in one; and that the world may know that thou hast sent me, and hast loved them, as thou hast loved me.

He declared the time is come. He asked God to glorify him so he could glorify God. God had given him power over all flesh to give eternal life to all that God sent him. Eternal life was to know without doubt the only true God and his son Jesus Christ, whom God himself had sent to them.

As he continued praying, he let it be known that he wasn't praying for the world at all. He was only praying for the ones God had sent him because they belonged to God. He then said that all his were God's and all God's were his and that he was glorified in his disciples.

He was no longer in the world, but was coming to the Father; however, his disciples were still in the world. He asked God to protect the disciples through his own name that they could themselves be one with God the very same way Jesus was one with God.

This takes us back to John 10:30 when Jesus said "I and my Father are one.". The Jewish leaders falsely accused him of making himself God and wanted to stone him for blasphemy. His final response to them was that he was declaring himself to be the son of God.

Now, we have to choose. If the leaders were right and Jesus declared himself to be God, then his prayer is for his followers to be God as well by being one with God. However, if Jesus is the son of God as he declared, then his prayer is for his followers to be begotten sons of God and be one with God the same way Jesus is.

Jesus then said that he had kept all those God had given him except one—the son of perdition—whom the scriptures had foretold. He spoke these things in their presence for them to have his joy fulfilled in themselves.

He gave his disciples the word of God and the world hated them for it. They weren't of the world even as Jesus himself wasn't of the world. He didn't want them taken out of the world, but he wanted them protected from the evil of the world.

He wanted them to be set apart by the truth of God—by his very word itself. He sent his disciples out into the world the same way God sent him into the world. He was setting himself apart for their sakes so they themselves could be set apart by the truth.

The last four verses of this passage bring the most exciting news. History becomes present and future all at once. Jesus prayed not only that his disciples would be one the same way he was one with God, but also anyone who heard their word and believed Jesus was the only begotten son of God would also be one with God as well. This was every person for all time.

Now, it's time to go back to John 10:30 again. We each now have to make an individual choice about ourself. If we claim that Jesus declared himself to be God, then we must also claim that we too are God because we are one with God the same way Jesus is. However, if we claim that Jesus declared himself to be the son of God, then we must also claim that we too are sons of God because we are one with God the same way Jesus is.

Christians, it's time. We either accept the word of God for exactly what it says it is, or we believe whatever we want to believe and call it Christian. God himself is calling us from the depths of his word. The next step is up to each one of us.

The next chapter deals with what Jesus witnessed to his disciples after he was resurrected.

CHAPTER 4

The next events are some of the most exciting events recorded, yet outside the scriptures themselves there are no records anywhere that indicate any of these sightings actually happened. There are people today in certain fields of 'medicine' who claim that these events never took place at all. These 'events' were merely the result of delusional episodes among a specific group of people. Some of these 'medical' professionals also claim that people who believe these things today are mentally ill and delusional themselves.

I am not going to cover every one of them. I am going to speak about enough of these things for you to see that these weren't isolated delusional episodes or attacks of mass hysteria. The other events, I leave for you to read yourself and see whether or not these things actually happened.

John 14

> 18. I will not leave you comfortless: I will come to you.
> 19. Yet a little while, and the world seeth me no more; but ye see me: because I live, ye shall live also.
> 20. At that day ye shall know that I am in my Father, and ye in me, and I in you.
> 21. He that hath my commandments, and keepeth them, he it is that loveth me: and he that loveth me shall be loved of my Father, and I will love him, and will manifest myself to him.

> 22. Judas saith unto him, not Iscariot, Lord, how is it that thou wilt manifest thyself unto us, and not unto the world?
> 23. Jesus answered and said unto him, If a man love me, he will keep my words: and my Father will love him, and we will come unto him, and make our abode with him.
> 24. He that loveth me not keepeth not my sayings: and the word which ye hear is not mine, but the Father's which sent me.

Here Jesus is talking to those that were with him at dinner the night he was taken prisoner and eventually killed. He promised them that he would personally come to them to comfort them.

He told them that soon the world would see him no more, yet they would. He also told them that, because he had eternal life, they would have eternal life as well.

He did not have eternal life when he told them this because he had not been taken prisoner and killed yet.

Therefore, he was referring to what the disciples would see when he manifested himself to them again.

A different man named Judas asked how it would be possible for Jesus to show himself to the disciples without the rest of the world seeing him as well. Jesus said he would appear to those who loved him and kept his words. Those who didn't love him wouldn't keep his words and would not see him at all. He then told his disciples that the words he told them were not his words, but were from the Father himself.

John 15

> 26. But when the Comforter is come, whom I will send unto you from the Father, even the Spirit of truth, which proceedeth from the Father, he shall testify of me:
> 27. And ye also shall bear witness, because ye have been with me from the beginning.

That same night, Jesus told his disciples that the Father would send his own spirit—the spirit of truth itself—to comfort them. The spirit of truth will testify of Jesus himself. They themselves would bear witness because they had been with him from the beginning.

Luke 1

1. Forasmuch as many have taken in hand to set forth in order a declaration of those things which are most surely believed among us,
2. Even as they delivered them unto us, which from the beginning were eyewitnesses, and ministers of the word;
3. It seemed good to me also, having had perfect understanding of all things from the very first, to write unto thee in order, most excellent Theophilus,
4. That thou mightest know the certainty of those things, wherein thou hast been instructed.

Luke said in his opening that he was taught by people who were from the beginning eyewitnesses to everything Jesus said and did. He said many had written accounts of the events. He also said that he had an exact understanding of their eyewitness testimony. That meant he had to question them and listen to their answers. He also had to search the scriptures to see if what they were saying was true or not.

After he had done this, it seemed good for him to write an ordered account to Theophilus in order for him to have the very same exact understanding of the things he had been taught. The beginning Luke referred to is the same beginning Jesus referred to when he told his disciples they would bear witness themselves.

Acts 1

1. The former treatise have I made, O Theophilus, of all that Jesus began both to do and teach,

> 2. Until the day in which he was taken up, after that he through the Holy Ghost had given commandments unto the apostles whom he had chosen:
> 3. To whom also he shewed himself alive after his passion by many infallible proofs, being seen of them forty days, and speaking of the things pertaining to the kingdom of God:

In his second book, Luke refers Theophilus to his first book. He said that it was a record of all that Jesus did and taught in the presence of these witnesses from the day he first started until the day he was taken up. He showed himself with eternal life after his death and was with the apostles for forty days. During that time, Jesus showed them many infallible proofs and spoke to them concerning the kingdom of God. This is the time period Jesus referred to with his disciples the night that he was taken and eventually killed.

1 John 1

> 1. That which was from the beginning, which we have heard, which we have seen with our eyes, which we have looked upon, and our hands have handled, of the Word of life;
> 2. (For the life was manifested, and we have seen it, and bear witness, and shew unto you that eternal life, which was with the Father, and was manifested unto us;)
> 3. That which we have seen and heard declare we unto you, that ye also may have fellowship with us: and truly our fellowship is with the Father, and with his Son Jesus Christ.
> 4. And these things write we unto you, that your joy may be full.

The apostle John refers to the same time period that Luke referred to. This is the same period Jesus told his disciples they would bear witness of to others.

1 Corinthians 15

1. Moreover, brethren, I declare unto you the gospel which I preached unto you, which also ye have received, and wherein ye stand;
2. By which also ye are saved, if ye keep in memory what I preached unto you, unless ye have believed in vain.
3. For I delivered unto you first of all that which I also received, how that Christ died for our sins according to the scriptures;
4. And that he was buried, and that he rose again the third day according to the scriptures:
5. And that he was seen of Cephas, then of the twelve:
6. After that, he was seen of above five hundred brethren at once; of whom the greater part remain unto this present, but some are fallen asleep.
7. After that, he was seen of James; then of all the apostles.
8. And last of all he was seen of me also, as of one born out of due time.
9. For I am the least of the apostles, that am not meet to be called an apostle, because I persecuted the church of God.
10. But by the grace of God I am what I am: and his grace which was bestowed upon me was not in vain; but I laboured more abundantly than they all: yet not I, but the grace of God which was with me.
11. Therefore whether it were I or they, so we preach, and so ye believed.

The case of Paul is a special case. Paul was not one of the original twelve nor was he one of the followers when Jesus was teaching. Paul came along much later. He was present at the stoning of Stephen, which occurred some time after Jesus had ascended from the mount of Olives. Paul didn't stone Stephen, but he held the cloaks for the men who did stone Stephen.

Eternal Life

As Paul progressed, he was convinced that the Christians were perverting the true worship of the God of Abraham. He obtained letters of authority from the temple to seize the Christians in Damascus, imprison them, sell them into slavery, take their property, whatever it took to wipe them out. He had a life changing experience on the road to Damascus while his name was Saul and became the man later known as Paul.

In this letter to Christians in Corinth, Paul lists some of the appearances of Christ to his followers. Paul lists the appearances to Peter, the twelve, over five hundred brethren at once, James, all of the apostles, and finally to Paul himself. Paul declared that he himself had seen the risen Jesus the same way John declared the he and the others had seen the risen Jesus.

First, we are going to check Paul's experience with what Jesus told his disciples the night he was taken prisoner, then we will examine Paul's account of Christ's appearances a little closer.

Acts 9

1. **And Saul, yet breathing out threatenings and slaughter against the disciples of the Lord, went unto the high priest,**
2. **And desired of him letters to Damascus to the synagogues, that if he found any of this way, whether they were men or women, he might bring them bound unto Jerusalem.**
3. **And as he journeyed, he came near Damascus: and suddenly there shined round about him a light from heaven:**
4. **And he fell to the earth, and heard a voice saying unto him, Saul, Saul, why persecutest thou me?**
5. **And he said, Who art thou, Lord? And the Lord said, I am Jesus whom thou persecutest: it is hard for thee to kick against the pricks.**
6. **And he trembling and astonished said, Lord, what wilt thou have me to do? And the Lord said unto him,**

> Arise, and go into the city, and it shall be told thee what thou must do.
> 7. And the men which journeyed with him stood speechless, hearing a voice, but seeing no man.
> 8. And Saul arose from the earth; and when his eyes were opened, he saw no man: but they led him by the hand, and brought him into Damascus.
> 9. And he was three days without sight, and neither did eat nor drink.

Saul went to the high priest himself for letters of authority to the synagogues in Damascus giving him the right to take these radical people prisoner and bring them as captives to Jerusalem. As he neared Damascus, he was suddenly enveloped in a bright light and fell to the ground. He heard a voice that engaged him in conversation. The voice identified himself as Jesus, the one Saul was persecuting.

Saul trembled and was astonished because he actually saw and gazed at the very same Jesus that John, Peter, Andrew, the twelve, and over five hundred brethren had seen and gazed at themselves. When he asked what Jesus would have him to do, Jesus told him to go into the city and he would be told what to do.

There were others who were travelling with him. These men heard the voice that Saul heard and heard the conversation Saul had with Jesus, yet they didn't see anyone or anything at all. This brings us back to John chapter 14 where Jesus made a distinction between those who would see him and those who would not see him. It also tells volumes about Saul. The words of God were abiding in Saul's heart, or Jesus would never have manifested himself to Saul. The men with Saul did not have the words of God abiding in their heart, or they would have seen Jesus themselves.

Saul actually believed he was doing the work of the God of Abraham by getting rid of this radical group of people who were subverting the worship of the true God of Abraham. When Saul stood up, he couldn't see anything at all. The men led him into the city and he stayed three days without being able to see anything at all. His eyes weren't welded shut. He simply could not see at all. He didn't eat or drink at all during that time. As a Pharisee, he would have spent that time of fasting in prayer and waiting for God to reveal what he was to do next.

This is the event Paul was describing to the churches in Corinth. This is a life changing event. When Paul listed Christ's appearances to the others, he included himself at the end because he saw the very same thing they did. The record of the appearances is confusing enough if you don't pay attention very closely; however, traditional teachings have entered that will cause people to argue about what happened. As a result people only tend to look at the parts that support their particular doctrinal position.

For example, how many of the apostles actually saw Jesus after he was resurrected? Paul says Jesus appeared to the twelve and again he says Jesus appeared to all the apostles. Did he appear to all twelve or did he only appear to eleven? The scriptures say twelve, but the churches teach only eleven. The churches go out of the way not to look at any scriptures that might make anyone question "church doctrine'.

Let's begin with 1 Corinthians 15:5 where Paul specifically says Jesus appeared to the twelve. The new testament version translated from the Latin Vulgate says Jesus appeared to the Eleven. A footnote at the bottom of the page explains why.

"15,5: *Eleven:* the correct reading is probably that of most Greek MSS, "the Twelve." In fact there were only eleven Apostles after the loss of Judas, but "the Twelve" had become the title of the group irrespective of the actual number."

For a thousand years there was only one church, but that one church finally began to split over doctrinal questions. Once people were taught to read again, and the printing press was invented, bibles began appearing in other languages besides Latin. The translators went to the Greek and Latin texts they had plus any copies of Hebrew texts they had to translate the scriptures into other common languages. These translations all say Paul said "the Twelve" but the churches using these translations said it was only eleven. Even today churches still teach the very same thing. We are about to find out what the scriptures say themselves about this, but, be warned—not everyone will want to see this or want anyone else to see it either.

Mark 16

9. Now when Jesus was risen early the first day of the week, he appeared first to Mary Magdalene, out of whom he had cast seven devils.
10. And she went and told them that had been with him, as they mourned and wept.
11. And they, when they had heard that he was alive, and had been seen of her, believed not.
12. After that he appeared in another form unto two of them, as they walked, and went into the country.
13. And they went and told it unto the residue: neither believed they them.
14. Afterward he appeared unto the eleven as they sat at meat, and upbraided them with their unbelief and hardness of heart, because they believed not them which had seen him after he was risen.

Mark's account begins early on the first day of the week—after Jesus had already risen. He appeared to Mary Magdalene and allowed her to look at him closely, but not to touch him at all. She went back and told them he was alive, but they did not believe her report.

Later, Jesus appeared to two disciples as they were walking in the country. They immediately went back to tell the apostles, but their report was not believed either.

Later, as they were eating, Jesus appeared to the eleven and scolded them for not believing the reports of the others who had already seen him that day.

Luke 24

33. And they rose up the same hour, and returned to Jerusalem, and found the eleven gathered together, and them that were with them,
34. Saying, The Lord is risen indeed, and hath appeared to Simon.

35. And they told what things were done in the way, and how he was known of them in breaking of bread.
36. And as they thus spake, Jesus himself stood in the midst of them, and saith unto them, Peace be unto you.
37. But they were terrified and affrighted, and supposed that they had seen a spirit.
38. And he said unto them, Why are ye troubled? and why do thoughts arise in your hearts?
39. Behold my hands and my feet, that it is I myself: handle me, and see; for a spirit hath not flesh and bones, as ye see me have.
40. And when he had thus spoken, he shewed them his hands and his feet.
41. And while they yet believed not for joy, and wondered, he said unto them, Have ye here any meat?
42. And they gave him a piece of a broiled fish, and of an honeycomb.
43. And he took it, and did eat before them.
44. And he said unto them, These are the words which I spake unto you, while I was yet with you, that all things must be fulfilled, which were written in the law of Moses, and in the prophets, and in the psalms, concerning me.
45. Then opened he their understanding, that they might understand the scriptures,
46. And said unto them, Thus it is written, and thus it behoved Christ to suffer, and to rise from the dead the third day:
47. And that repentance and remission of sins should be preached in his name among all nations, beginning at Jerusalem.
48. And ye are witnesses of these things.

Luke starts his narrative on the first day of the week just like Mark, but Luke adds details that expand what Mark said. For instance, Mark said that Jesus appeared to two disciples as they were walking in the countryside. Luke tells the story of the men, where they were going, the conversation they had with an apparent stranger, and their final recognition of Jesus himself. Luke adds that, when these two arrived, the eleven and others with them were discussing Jesus appearing to Simon Peter.

Luke went on to say that these men added their account, but Mark says the apostles didn't believe them. It was during this time that the eleven were preparing to eat their evening meal after a long day of steady news updates which they refused to believe.

This is when Jesus suddenly stood in their midst and said "Peace be unto you". These men were behind locked doors for fear that they too would be taken as Jesus was. Jesus didn't call out and ask to enter. He didn't knock or beat on a locked door. Suddenly, he was simply standing in their midst. These men were terrified and supposed they were seeing a spirit and not a man at all.

He immediately questioned them as to why they would even think that way. He told them to look at his hands and feet—to touch him—see for themselves—a spirit did not have flesh and bones the way he had flesh and bones. He denied being spirit in any way, shape, or form at all. He wasn't part spirit and part anything else at all. He declared he was flesh and bone. Note he did not say he was flesh and blood—he said flesh and bone.

The apostles believed him, but they still had doubts, so Jesus asked them for something to eat. He ate a piece of broiled fish and a honeycomb in front of them to prove he wasn't a spirit. Spirits can not eat flesh because that which is born of spirit is spirit and that which is born of flesh is flesh.

Jesus told them that these were the things he had told them before he died, that all the things written in the law of Moses, the prophets, and the psalms concerning him must be fulfilled. He then opened their understanding of the scriptures and told them it was necessary for him to suffer, die, and rise again the third day. Repentance and remission of sins were to be preached in all nations, beginning at Jerusalem. These men were to be the eyewitnesses to these things.

Again, in Luke we see the group of apostles being referred to as the eleven to distinguish them from the others with them. Let's go to John now and see the same record again.

John 20

> **19. Then the same day at evening, being the first day of the week, when the doors were shut where the disciples were assembled for fear of the Jews, came Jesus and stood in the midst, and saith unto them, Peace be unto you.**
> **20. And when he had so said, he shewed unto them his hands and his side. Then were the disciples glad, when they saw the Lord.**
> **21. Then said Jesus to them again, Peace be unto you: as my Father hath sent me, even so send I you.**
> **22. And when he had said this, he breathed on them, and saith unto them, Receive ye the Holy Ghost:**
> **23. Whose soever sins ye remit, they are remitted unto them; and whose soever sins ye retain, they are retained.**
> **24. But Thomas, one of the twelve, called Didymus, was not with them when Jesus came.**

John starts on the first day just like Mark and Luke did. At the end of the same first day of the week, John says the disciples were behind closed doors because they were afraid that they would be taken the way Jesus was. Jesus stood in their midst and showed them his hands and his side. They were glad after they saw him, but they still had doubts and did not have the joy Jesus had promised them.

Jesus then gave them a mission—as he was sent from the Father, even so he was sending them to be his eyewitnesses. He told them to receive the Holy Ghost and whoever they remitted sins for would be remitted; however, whoever they retained sins for would be retained. John also notes that Thomas, one of the twelve, called Didymus, was not there when Jesus came that evening.

Let's put everything together. At one time Jesus had a group of disciples. From that group he personally chose twelve men, whom he personally called apostles, to be with him and learn from him directly. These men were to be his eyewitnesses. There were many others who followed him closely as well, but there were only twelve personally appointed by Jesus himself to be apostles. Therefore, all the apostles were disciples, but only twelve of the disciples were apostles.

John said that everybody there when Jesus appeared was a disciple. He made no distinction at all between any of them, nor did he say how many were there. He then made a distinction between Thomas and the other disciples. Thomas was one of the twelve apostles and Thomas wasn't there that night. Mark made a distinction between the eleven who were apostles and the other disciples with them that night. Luke made a distinction between the eleven who were apostles and the other disciples who were there with them that night. It appears that the eleven refers to the number of apostles there and not to the name of the group just as one of the twelve refers to Thomas specifically.

How can we be sure that this is actually the case? After all, it has been taught and accepted without question for so long that Judas went out and hanged himself before Jesus was ever crucified based on the reference in Matthew. In order to see which is true, we must look deeper in the scriptures.

Mark 3

13. And he goeth up into a mountain, and calleth unto him whom he would: and they came unto him.
14. And he ordained twelve, that they should be with him, and that he might send them forth to preach,
15. And to have power to heal sicknesses, and to cast out devils:
16. And Simon he surnamed Peter;
17. And James the son of Zebedee, and John the brother of James; and he surnamed them Boanerges, which is, The sons of thunder:

> 18. And Andrew, and Philip, and Bartholomew, and Matthew, and Thomas, and James the son of Alphaeus, and Thaddaeus, and Simon the Canaanite,
> 19. And Judas Iscariot, which also betrayed him: and they went into an house.

Mark states that Jesus picked twelve men specifically from a group to be with him personally and to go out and preach as he sent them. He also gave them power to heal sicknesses and to cast out devils. This power he gave them was the very same power that he himself had. Whatever happened to anyone in that specific group of men called apostles was of direct concern to Jesus because he chose a specific number of them for a specific purpose.

Luke 24

> 44. And he said unto them, These are the words which I spake unto you, while I was yet with you, that all things must be fulfilled, which were written in the law of Moses, and in the prophets, and in the psalms, concerning me.
> 45. Then opened he their understanding, that they might understand the scriptures,
> 46. And said unto them, Thus it is written, and thus it behoved Christ to suffer, and to rise from the dead the third day:
> 47. And that repentance and remission of sins should be preached in his name among all nations, beginning at Jerusalem.
> 48. And ye are witnesses of these things.
> 49. And, behold, I send the promise of my Father upon you: but tarry ye in the city of Jerusalem, until ye be endued with power from on high.

The evening Jesus appeared to the apostles and disciples who were gathered together, Jesus told them that ALL things written in the law of Moses, in the prophets, and in the psalms concerning him MUST be fulfilled. Then he opened their understanding so they could understand the scriptures themselves. He also told them that they were eyewitness to all the things that had happened.

Acts 1

15. And in those days Peter stood up in the midst of the disciples, and said, (the number of names together were about an hundred and twenty,)
16. Men and brethren, this scripture must needs have been fulfilled, which the Holy Ghost by the mouth of David spake before concerning Judas, which was guide to them that took Jesus.
17. For he was numbered with us, and had obtained part of this ministry.
18. Now this man purchased a field with the reward of iniquity; and falling headlong, he burst asunder in the midst, and all his bowels gushed out.
19. And it was known unto all the dwellers at Jerusalem; insomuch as that field is called in their proper tongue, Aceldama, that is to say, The field of blood.
20. For it is written in the book of Psalms, Let his habitation be desolate, and let no man dwell therein: and his bishoprick let another take.
21. Wherefore of these men which have companied with us all the time that the Lord Jesus went in and out among us,
22. Beginning from the baptism of John, unto that same day that he was taken up from us, must one be ordained to be a witness with us of his resurrection.
23. And they appointed two, Joseph called Barsabas, who was surnamed Justus, and Matthias.
24. And they prayed, and said, Thou, Lord, which knowest the hearts of all men, shew whether of these two thou hast chosen,

> 25. That he may take part of this ministry and apostleship, from which Judas by transgression fell, that he might go to his own place.
> 26. And they gave forth their lots; and the lot fell upon Matthias; and he was numbered with the eleven apostles.

In the period of time from Jesus' ascent until the day of Pentecost, it suddenly became necessary for Peter to replace one of the apostles. The whole forty day period before the ascent, it wasn't necessary for Jesus himself to replace any of the apostles.

When Peter addressed the approximately 120 disciples, he referred to, but didn't quote, Psalms 69:25, and applied the passage directly to Judas because he had been one of the twelve specifically appointed to be with Jesus and to be eyewitnesses of all the events from the baptism of John until the day Jesus himself was taken up from among them. He then said that one of those disciples who had gone in and out among them from the beginning MUST be appointed to be an eyewitness to the resurrection of Jesus. In other words, there MUST be 12 eyewitnesses. Jesus appointed 12 to be eyewitnesses of all these things.

The psalm of David concerned Peter greatly because one of the TWELVE eyewitnesses was dead. Had one of the TWELVE eyewitnesses been dead when Jesus appeared to the ones he had chosen himself, it would have concerned him as well. After all, he told the apostles that ALL the things written in the law of Moses, and in the prophets, and in the Psalms concerning himself MUST be fulfilled. Judas' death would have concerned Jesus greatly, because he personally appointed Judas to be an eyewitness of these things.

This means that Judas was alive when Jesus appeared the first day and was alive the whole forty days Jesus was with them and instructing them more fully in the scriptures. This whole conflict in teaching has resulted from a misunderstanding of what Matthew said about Judas. That misunderstanding has become "church doctrine" and every effort has been made by the church itself to keep anyone from saying any different thing. Even people who read this will not accept it because these scriptures contradict accepted "church doctrine", yet it is written right there in the bible for all to see.

What does it matter when Judas died? This book is about Eternal Life. If we have made such a small error in understanding what the scriptures say about this particular event, how many more errors have we made? Worse yet, if we have accepted this error as the word of God and made it "church doctrine", how many more errors have we made "church doctrine" and called that the word of God as well? The only sure way to understand the scriptures is to compare one scripture with another. We cannot depend on others to tell us what they think it means. Our lives depend on how we handle the things that are written right in front of our eyes.

The tragedy of Judas' death lies not in that he killed himself. The tragedy lies in that AFTER he saw Eternal Life in Jesus, AFTER he walked with Jesus for forty days, and AFTER he saw Jesus ascend, Judas killed himself. Jesus had already forgiven Judas—God had already forgiven Judas—that's why Jesus died and was resurrected in the first place. The tragedy is that Judas could not forgive himself for what he did and convinced himself that he could never be forgiven. Too many people today think the same way Judas did.

CHAPTER 5

Acts 3

1. Now Peter and John went up together into the temple at the hour of prayer, being the ninth hour.
2. And a certain man lame from his mother's womb was carried, whom they laid daily at the gate of the temple which is called Beautiful, to ask alms of them that entered into the temple;
3. Who seeing Peter and John about to go into the temple asked an alms.
4. And Peter, fastening his eyes upon him with John, said, Look on us.
5. And he gave heed unto them, expecting to receive something of them.
6. Then Peter said, Silver and gold have I none; but such as I have give I thee: In the name of Jesus Christ of Nazareth rise up and walk.
7. And he took him by the right hand, and lifted him up: and immediately his feet and ancle bones received strength.
8. And he leaping up stood, and walked, and entered with them into the temple, walking, and leaping, and praising God.
9. And all the people saw him walking and praising God:
10. And they knew that it was he which sat for alms at the Beautiful gate of the temple: and they were filled with

wonder and amazement at that which had happened unto him.

11. And as the lame man which was healed held Peter and John, all the people ran together unto them in the porch that is called Solomon's, greatly wondering.
12. And when Peter saw it, he answered unto the people, Ye men of Israel, why marvel ye at this? or why look ye so earnestly on us, as though by our own power or holiness we had made this man to walk?
13. The God of Abraham, and of Isaac, and of Jacob, the God of our fathers, hath glorified his Son Jesus; whom ye delivered up, and denied him in the presence of Pilate, when he was determined to let him go.
14. But ye denied the Holy One and the Just, and desired a murderer to be granted unto you;
15. And killed the Prince of life, whom God hath raised from the dead; whereof we are witnesses.
16. And his name through faith in his name hath made this man strong, whom ye see and know: yea, the faith which is by him hath given him this perfect soundness in the presence of you all.

This account begins with Peter and John going into the temple to pray during the ninth hour of the day, which would be around 3:00 in the afternoon. As they entered, they went past a lame man who was begging for alms at the gate called Beautiful. They stopped and had the man look at them, and he did. Of course, he was expecting some charitable gift from them. The only way this man could live was to accept charitable gifts from the worshippers who came through the gate to worship.

Peter told the man they had no money to give him, but they would give him what they had. He commanded the man in the Name of Jesus Christ of Nazareth to rise up and walk. He took the man by the right hand and lifted him up. The man's feet and ankles were immediately filled with strength and he began walking, jumping around, and praising God for this gift as he entered the temple. The people were amazed because they knew this man was lame and had been laying at the gate for years, and now he was walking, jumping around, and praising God.

Before we continue, let's look a little closer at this story. As it unfolds, the story tells us that the man was over 40 years old and had been brought to that gate and had lain there begging every single day of his life. That means this man had lain at the temple gate from the day Jesus was born and throughout Jesus' life. Every single time Jesus came into the temple or left the temple by that gate, he walked past that lame man. Every single time Jesus' disciples and apostles entered or left the temple through that gate, they walked past the very same man. Jesus, the man who healed men blind from birth, the man who healed all manner of sicknesses, the man who cast out demons, the man who raised Lazarus from the dead, Jesus completely ignored this lame man at the temple gate. So did his apostles and his disciples.

Jesus told his disciples that the things he saw and heard from his Father were the things he said and did. That means God never told Jesus to heal the lame man at the temple gate, or he would have healed him. It also means that the day Peter healed the lame man, God told him to stop and do it and Peter saw that he could do just that. Peter had the very same power in himself that Jesus Christ of Nazareth had when he walked the earth. Like Jesus Christ, Peter used that power as he was shown and told to do so. Like Jesus Christ, Peter sought no reputation for himself at all.

The lame man told the people that Peter and John stopped, and Peter had healed him. The people immediately surrounded Peter and John on Solomon's porch of the temple and looked at them in awe. Peter was a fisherman, and as such, he never had a chance to go to the Roman college of political correctness or to the Temple of God school of homiletics to learn how to preach to people without offending them. The man Peter learned from was a carpenter who never had a chance to go to any of these schools either. When these people surrounded Peter and John with these worshipful gazes, Peter unloaded on them. He wasn't trying to establish the First Apostolic Church of Peter and John.

Peter asked the people why they would even think that he and John could heal a man through their own personal power or their own personal holiness. He told them that the God of Abraham, and Isaac, and Jacob had glorified his son Jesus—the same Jesus these people had delivered up to be killed and had denied in the presence of Pilate, the Roman governor who could find no fault in him at all and wanted to let him go. Instead, they wanted a murderer to be released and, as a result, were directly responsible for killing the Prince of Eternal Life.

However, the God of Abraham, and Isaac, and Jacob raised his son from the dead and gave him Eternal Life. Peter and John as well as many others were eyewitnesses to these events. It is through faith in the name of Jesus Christ of Nazareth that the lame man they all knew stood before them completely whole.

This singular event late in the evening set off a series of events that led to Peter and John being held overnight and having to appear before the council headed by the high priest and his relatives. After having appeared before the council, Peter and John were sent out while the council deliberated. It is here that we look at the record again.

Acts 4

> 13. Now when they saw the boldness of Peter and John, and perceived that they were unlearned and ignorant men, they marvelled; and they took knowledge of them, that they had been with Jesus.
> 14. And beholding the man which was healed standing with them, they could say nothing against it.
> 15. But when they had commanded them to go aside out of the council, they conferred among themselves,
> 16. Saying, What shall we do to these men? for that indeed a notable miracle hath been done by them is manifest to all them that dwell in Jerusalem; and we cannot deny it.

> **17.** But that it spread no further among the people, let us straitly threaten them, that they speak henceforth to no man in this name.
>
> **18.** And they called them, and commanded them not to speak at all nor teach in the name of Jesus.
>
> **19.** But Peter and John answered and said unto them, Whether it be right in the sight of God to hearken unto you more than unto God, judge ye.
>
> **20.** For we cannot but speak the things which we have seen and heard.
>
> **21.** So when they had further threatened them, they let them go, finding nothing how they might punish them, because of the people: for all men glorified God for that which was done.
>
> **22.** For the man was above forty years old, on whom this miracle of healing was shewed.

When Peter and John answered the council, the priests knew that they were unlearned and ignorant men. They also knew these men had been with Jesus. Yet, there was no way to openly discredit them with lack of proper credentials because the man who was lame before was standing right beside them in the council. They sent these men outside to confer among themselves to devise a proper way to handle this situation.

The priests admitted that the healing of this lame man was a miracle. They knew there was no way to deny it or claim fakery because everybody knew this man and news of this event was all over Jerusalem. The only option was to stop the spread of this was to threaten Peter and John and see that they didn't teach the name of Jesus any more.

When they called Peter and John back in, the council immediately commanded them not to ever speak or teach the name of Jesus again. Peter's response was for them to judge whether it was right in the sight of God to listen to what men said or to what God said. They could only speak the things that they themselves had seen and heard, no matter what anyone else wanted them to do.

This calls to mind what Jesus himself told his apostles and disciples. He told them that the things he saw and heard from his Father were the things he said and did. He did or said nothing in and of himself because he sought no reputation for himself at all.

The only thing left for the council to do was to threaten them and let them go. The healed lame man standing with Peter and John was over 40 years old. Even the priests ignored him as they passed by going in and out of the temple. They could not deny what had happened because they knew the man as well.

Acts 4

32. And the multitude of them that believed were of one heart and of one soul: neither said any of them that ought of the things which he possessed was his own; but they had all things common.

33. And with great power gave the apostles witness of the resurrection of the Lord Jesus: and great grace was upon them all.

34. Neither was there any among them that lacked: for as many as were possessors of lands or houses sold them, and brought the prices of the things that were sold,

35. And laid them down at the apostles' feet: and distribution was made unto every man according as he had need.

36. And Joses, who by the apostles was surnamed Barnabas, (which is, being interpreted, the son of consolation,) a Levite, and of the country of Cyprus,

37. Having land, sold it, and brought the money, and laid it at the apostles' feet.

A phenomenal event occurred at this point. The people who believed what the apostles were teaching underwent a transformation. They were united as though they were one person. They did not seek their own possessions above others. They openly and willingly shared whatever they had with one another.

The apostles witnessed the resurrection of Jesus Christ with great power. Their words weren't just meaningless babble. There was no lack among the people, because those who had great excess sold off the excess and brought the gain to the apostles to help those who were in need. Joses, whom the apostles called Barnabas, sold his land in Cyprus and brought the money to the apostles.

This wasn't a Christian welfare state, or a Christian communist society where the rich forfeit their wealth to support the poor to make everyone equal. This was designed to help those in need as needed. Everyone goes through times of need, but need is not supposed to be an ongoing state. This is why it states that there was not any among them that lacked.

Acts 5

1. **But a certain man named Ananias, with Sapphira his wife, sold a possession,**
2. **And kept back part of the price, his wife also being privy to it, and brought a certain part, and laid it at the apostles' feet.**
3. **But Peter said, Ananias, why hath Satan filled thine heart to lie to the Holy Ghost, and to keep back part of the price of the land?**
4. **Whiles it remained, was it not thine own? and after it was sold, was it not in thine own power? why hast thou conceived this thing in thine heart? thou hast not lied unto men, but unto God.**
5. **And Ananias hearing these words fell down, and gave up the ghost: and great fear came on all them that heard these things.**
6. **And the young men arose, wound him up, and carried him out, and buried him.**
7. **And it was about the space of three hours after, when his wife, not knowing what was done, came in.**
8. **And Peter answered unto her, Tell me whether ye sold the land for so much? And she said, Yea, for so much.**

> 9. Then Peter said unto her, How is it that ye have agreed together to tempt the Spirit of the Lord? behold, the feet of them which have buried thy husband are at the door, and shall carry thee out.
> 10. Then fell she down straightway at his feet, and yielded up the ghost: and the young men came in, and found her dead, and, carrying her forth, buried her by her husband.
> 11. And great fear came upon all the church, and upon as many as heard these things.
> 12. And by the hands of the apostles were many signs and wonders wrought among the people; (and they were all with one accord in Solomon's porch.

This event takes place after Barnabas brought his money to the apostles. While most people look at this event as tragic and go on, there is much more here than first meets the eye. Ananias and his wife Sapphira had some extra property. They decided together to sell the property and to keep some of the money for themselves without telling anyone.

What kind of person thinks this way? One kind would be the person who had a need for part of the money at the time. Of course such a person would make it clear from the beginning that he was planning to do so. Are there people like this today? Of course there are.

The second kind, however, is the kind that wants to be known of others as a great benefactor, a giver, a generous humanitarian, someone who really cares about the needs of others. This is the kind of person looking for the plaque on the reserved pew dedicated to him and his family for their giving nature toward the church and its members. This is the kind of person who desires the stained glass window in his honor for his dedication to the church and its membership. Such a person makes an open display publicly, but behind the scenes other things are going on that never surface. Ananias and his wife were of the second kind. Are there people like this today? Of course there are.

When Ananias came in, he went up to the apostles and laid the money down and never spoke a word. However, the spirit in Peter revealed to him the thoughts and intentions of Ananias' heart the same way the very same spirit had revealed to Christ the thoughts and intention of men's hearts. Peter immediately asked Ananias why Satan had filled his heart to lie to the Holy Spirit himself.

After all, while Ananias owned the land, the land was under his control. Once he sold the land, the money was under his control to do with as he wished. Why did he lie by keeping part of the money? Peter then told Ananias that he wasn't lying to men, but to God himself. As soon as Peter said this, Ananias fell down and died on the spot.

Some of the young men there immediately rose up, wound him with cloth, carried him out, and buried him. About three hours later, Ananias' wife Sapphira came in and didn't have any idea what had happened to her husband. Peter asked her if they had sold the land for a certain price and she told him yes. Peter then asked her how it was that both of them had conspired together to tempt the spirit of the Lord.

Peter then told her that the same men who had just buried her husband were at the door, and would carry her out too. She immediately fell down at his feet and died on the spot. The same men came in, found her dead, carried her out, and buried her by her husband. If you think healing a lame man got people's attention, what do you think this did?

The apostles worked many signs and wonders among the people and they were all of one accord in Solomon's porch at the temple. These things and others led to Peter and John being thrown into prison again. This time, however, an angel brought them out and told them to go back to the temple and teach all the words of Eternal Life.

When the high priest and his company came the next day, Peter and John were not in the prison even though the doors were locked and the guard was still standing watch. When the high priest heard that Peter and John were teaching in the temple, he sent for them without violence because the crowd might rise up and stone the temple leaders.

Acts 5

27. And when they had brought them, they set them before the council: and the high priest asked them,

> 28. Saying, Did not we straitly command you that ye should not teach in this name? and, behold, ye have filled Jerusalem with your doctrine, and intend to bring this man's blood upon us.
> 29. Then Peter and the other apostles answered and said, We ought to obey God rather than men.
> 30. The God of our fathers raised up Jesus, whom ye slew and hanged on a tree.
> 31. Him hath God exalted with his right hand to be a Prince and a Saviour, for to give repentance to Israel, and forgiveness of sins.
> 32. And we are his witnesses of these things; and so is also the Holy Ghost, whom God hath given to them that obey him.

Once the temple guards brought Peter and John before the high priest, he immediately asked them why they were still teaching in the name they had been forbidden to use. Then Peter, John, and the other apostles with them said they ought to obey God and not men. They declared Jesus to be a prince and savior to give repentance to Israel and forgiveness of sin. Then they declared themselves witnesses of these things along with the holy ghost that God gives those who obey him.

Not only were these apostles eyewitnesses but also this holy ghost that God gives anyone who obeys him is a witness to Christ as well. Therefore, the witness didn't die with the apostles. The things they did didn't die with them either, because the spirit from God that was in them as a witness didn't die when the apostles died.

These things angered the high priest and he wanted these men dead; however, a noted Pharisee named Gamaliel stood up and had these apostles removed for a short time and advised the council against rash action.

His advice was to leave them alone. If what they did was of their own, it would die out on its own. If it was of God, then the council would be on the wrong side and fighting against God.

After hearing Gamaliel's reasonings, the council called in these men, threatened them again, beat them, and let them go. The apostles' defiance of the council stirred up the leaders, but Gamaliel was wise enough to get them to see they they should make no hasty decision when dealing with this situation in the temple.

Some time after this, the voice of reason began to fade and the council started to attack and kill members of this new movement in Jerusalem, starting with a notable disciple named Stephen. A man named Saul of Tarsus was present at the stoning and gave his consent to the action, even though he didn't participate directly.

As the council stretched forth it's hand more fiercely, the members of this new movement scattered into areas all around and taught the death and resurrection of Jesus Christ wherever they went. One such was Philip.

Acts 8

> **26. And the angel of the Lord spake unto Philip, saying, Arise, and go toward the south unto the way that goeth down from Jerusalem unto Gaza, which is desert.**
>
> **27. And he arose and went: and, behold, a man of Ethiopia, an eunuch of great authority under Candace queen of the Ethiopians, who had the charge of all her treasure, and had come to Jerusalem for to worship,**
>
> **28. Was returning, and sitting in his chariot read Esaias the prophet.**
>
> **29. Then the Spirit said unto Philip, Go near, and join thyself to this chariot.**
>
> **30. And Philip ran thither to him, and heard him read the prophet Esaias, and said, Understandest thou what thou readest?**
>
> **31. And he said, How can I, except some man should guide me? And he desired Philip that he would come up and sit with him.**
>
> **32. The place of the scripture which he read was this, He was led as a sheep to the slaughter; and like a lamb dumb before his shearer, so opened he not his mouth:**

33. In his humiliation his judgment was taken away: and who shall declare his generation? for his life is taken from the earth.
34. And the eunuch answered Philip, and said, I pray thee, of whom speaketh the prophet this? of himself, or of some other man?
35. Then Philip opened his mouth, and began at the same scripture, and preached unto him Jesus.
36. And as they went on their way, they came unto a certain water: and the eunuch said, See, here is water; what doth hinder me to be baptized?
37. And Philip said, If thou believest with all thine heart, thou mayest. And he answered and said, I believe that Jesus Christ is the Son of God.
38. And he commanded the chariot to stand still: and they went down both into the water, both Philip and the eunuch; and he baptized him.
39. And when they were come up out of the water, the Spirit of the Lord caught away Philip, that the eunuch saw him no more: and he went on his way rejoicing.
40. But Philip was found at Azotus: and passing through he preached in all the cities, till he came to Caesarea.

Philip was told by an angel to go south on the road from Jerusalem into the desert area of Gaza. There was an Ethiopian eunuch who was in charge of queen Candace's treasury returning to Ethiopia after worshipping at the temple in Jerusalem. He was riding along in his chariot and reading from the scroll of Isaiah. A man of his importance had a driver, so the eunuch was sitting and reading aloud from Isaiah when the spirit told Philip to go and join himself to the chariot.

Philip ran along beside the eunuch and asked him if he understood what he was reading aloud. He answered that what he was reading was impossible to understand without someone to explain it to him. The eunuch didn't know if Isaiah was talking about himself or someone else. He wasn't sure what the prophet meant. Philip started at the same scripture in Isaiah and explained to the eunuch about Jesus Christ. Philip explained actually seeing Christ with Eternal Life and then watching him ascend from the mount of Olives.

As they traveled, they came upon some water and the eunuch asked Philip to baptize him. Philip told him he had to believe the witness with all his heart. The eunuch said he believed Jesus Christ was the son of God and ordered his driver to stop. Philip got into the water with the eunuch and baptized him. Immediately, Philip vanished and was next seen in Azotus. He went from there through all the cities around until he got to Caesarea. The eunuch went home rejoicing.

Philip had the same power in himself that Christ had. He simply disappeared and reappeared in another place. When Jesus told his apostles they would be endued with power from on high and they would do the things he did and even greater things, he meant exactly what he said.

Acts 9

1. **And Saul, yet breathing out threatenings and slaughter against the disciples of the Lord, went unto the high priest,**
2. **And desired of him letters to Damascus to the synagogues, that if he found any of this way, whether they were men or women, he might bring them bound unto Jerusalem.**
3. **And as he journeyed, he came near Damascus: and suddenly there shined round about him a light from heaven:**
4. **And he fell to the earth, and heard a voice saying unto him, Saul, Saul, why persecutest thou me?**
5. **And he said, Who art thou, Lord? And the Lord said, I am Jesus whom thou persecutest: it is hard for thee to kick against the pricks.**
6. **And he trembling and astonished said, Lord, what wilt thou have me to do? And the Lord said unto him,**

Arise, and go into the city, and it shall be told thee what thou must do.

7. And the men which journeyed with him stood speechless, hearing a voice, but seeing no man.

8. And Saul arose from the earth; and when his eyes were opened, he saw no man: but they led him by the hand, and brought him into Damascus.

9. And he was three days without sight, and neither did eat nor drink.

10. And there was a certain disciple at Damascus, named Ananias; and to him said the Lord in a vision, Ananias. And he said, Behold, I am here, Lord.

11. And the Lord said unto him, Arise, and go into the street which is called Straight, and inquire in the house of Judas for one called Saul, of Tarsus: for, behold, he prayeth,

12. And hath seen in a vision a man named Ananias coming in, and putting his hand on him, that he might receive his sight.

13. Then Ananias answered, Lord, I have heard by many of this man, how much evil he hath done to thy saints at Jerusalem:

14. And here he hath authority from the chief priests to bind all that call on thy name.

15. But the Lord said unto him, Go thy way: for he is a chosen vessel unto me, to bear my name before the Gentiles, and kings, and the children of Israel:

16. For I will shew him how great things he must suffer for my name's sake.

17. And Ananias went his way, and entered into the house; and putting his hands on him said, Brother Saul, the Lord, even Jesus, that appeared unto thee in the way as thou camest, hath sent me, that thou mightest receive thy sight, and be filled with the Holy Ghost.

18. And immediately there fell from his eyes as it had been scales: and he received sight forthwith, and arose, and was baptized.
19. And when he had received meat, he was strengthened. Then was Saul certain days with the disciples which were at Damascus.
20. And straightway he preached Christ in the synagogues, that he is the Son of God.
21. But all that heard him were amazed, and said; Is not this he that destroyed them which called on this name in Jerusalem, and came hither for that intent, that he might bring them bound unto the chief priests?
22. But Saul increased the more in strength, and confounded the Jews which dwelt at Damascus, proving that this is very Christ.
23. And after that many days were fulfilled, the Jews took counsel to kill him:
24. But their laying await was known of Saul. And they watched the gates day and night to kill him.
25. Then the disciples took him by night, and let him down by the wall in a basket.
26. And when Saul was come to Jerusalem, he assayed to join himself to the disciples: but they were all afraid of him, and believed not that he was a disciple.
27. But Barnabas took him, and brought him to the apostles, and declared unto them how he had seen the Lord in the way, and that he had spoken to him, and how he had preached boldly at Damascus in the name of Jesus.
28. And he was with them coming in and going out at Jerusalem.
29. And he spake boldly in the name of the Lord Jesus, and disputed against the Grecians: but they went about to slay him.
30. Which when the brethren knew, they brought him down to Caesarea, and sent him forth to Tarsus.

This is the same Saul of Tarsus that was at the stoning of Stephen. This Saul became a Pharisee under the teaching and guidance of a respected doctor of the law named Gamaliel—the same Gamaliel that spoke to the temple leaders about Peter, John, and the other apostles. Gamaliel was, for a little while, a voice of reason to the council who advised against taking any action against these apostles.

While Saul didn't personally hate followers of this way of Christ, he did see this new way as a threat that would pervert the worship of the true God of Abraham, and Isaac, and Jacob. He went to the high priest and received letters of authority from the temple to go to Damascus and root out these followers, bind them, and bring them before the temple council in Jerusalem.

As he neared Damascus, Saul was suddenly surrounded by a flashing bright light from the heavens. He fell to the ground and heard a voice asking him why was he persecuting the person speaking. When Saul asked who it was speaking, the voice said it was Jesus.

Saul then asked what he should do and Jesus told him to go to Damascus and wait for instructions. The men with him heard the entire conversation, yet they saw no man. This event was not the result of a psychotic episode or some delusional mental disturbance. The other men present actually heard the whole conversation themselves, though they didn't understand what was said.

When Saul arose, he could not see at all. The men led him to a house in Damascus and he fasted for three full days.

Then a disciple named Ananias had a vision in which he was told to go to the house of Judas on Strait street and ask to see Saul of Tarsus because Saul was fasting and praying. He was told that Saul had seen a man named Ananias coming to him and restoring his sight to him.

Ananias responded by saying that Saul had done much evil against the followers of Christ in Jerusalem and, even then, was in Damascus to imprison the followers and take them back to Jerusalem. In other words, Ananias wasn't too sure this was the wisest course of action to take on his part. Ananias was then told to go ahead because Saul was a specially chosen person to speak of Christ before Gentiles, kings, and the children of Israel.

Ananias then went to the house, put his hands on Saul, and told him that the same Jesus he saw on the way to Damascus had sent him there to restore Saul's eyesight and that he would be filled with the same power from on high that the others themselves had. As he said this, the darkness before Saul peeled away in layers like scales dropping off and his sight was fully restored. He was then baptized. He ate, regained his strength, and stayed for some days with the disciples in Damascus that he had gone to arrest.

Before going further, we should stop a minute and look at Saul's blindness. The scriptures don't say that his eyes had scales on them or that they were welded shut. The scriptures say the darkness fell away from his eyes as scales fall off. The darkness fell away in layers and his sight was fully restored. As he was filled with the power from on high, the darkness he saw fell away and was replaced by light. As time went on, Saul changed his name to Paul and wrote many letters to the Christian churches. From reading his letters, you can see his occasional reference to this darkness, but it is always mentioned in connection with one's heart.

With this knowledge, one can see that Saul's eyes weren't damaged at all. There would have been no way to physically examine him and find anything at all wrong with his eyesight. Saul could see perfectly; however, the only thing Saul could see for three days and three nights was darkness itself—the very darkness that was in his own heart. That's why he keeps mentioning the darkness in your hearts.

Saul, being a Pharisee, knew all the scriptures in the law of Moses, the prophets, and in the psalms concerning Jesus. For three days, he went over those scriptures from memory and Jesus opened his understanding of them the same way he did to his apostles and disciples during the forty days he was with them before he ascended. By the time Ananias arrived, Saul was convinced that Jesus of Nazareth was the son of God and the promised Messiah. Saul was convinced by no man, rather by the word of God itself that he already knew that had been covered by the darkness in his own heart.

While in Damascus, Saul immediately began going to the synagogues and preaching that Christ was the son of God. The leaders were amazed because they knew his reputation from what he had done in Jerusalem and they knew he came to Damascus to arrest the followers of this new way and take them back to Jerusalem. Saul's strength and power grew and confounded them even more. Here was a Pharisee who could prove from the scriptures that Jesus was the very Christ—the Messiah—the risen son of God himself. This wasn't some uneducated fisherman, farmer, or laborer. This was a man of letters and a force to be reckoned with. His words had power.

The leaders took counsel to kill Saul, but he was aware of their plan. Even though the leaders had the gates watched day and night to take him and kill him, the disciples managed to let Saul over the city wall in a basket and he got away.

When Saul got back to Jerusalem, he tried to join the disciples but they wanted no part of him. They were afraid of him and didn't believe he had really become a follower. However Barnabas took him to the apostles—the same Barnabas that had sold his property in Cyprus—and told them about Saul. He told them that Christ had appeared to Saul on the way to Damascus, that Christ had spoken to Saul, and that Saul had been boldly preaching the name of Jesus in Damascus.

Saul stayed with the apostles and came and went with them for some time. In their comings and goings, Saul began disputing with the Grecians so much so that they decided to kill him. The brethren got Saul away to Caesarea and then sent him home to Tarsus.

Acts 11

1. **And the apostles and brethren that were in Judaea heard that the Gentiles had also received the word of God.**
2. **And when Peter was come up to Jerusalem, they that were of the circumcision contended with him,**

3. Saying, Thou wentest in to men uncircumcised, and didst eat with them.

4. But Peter rehearsed the matter from the beginning, and expounded it by order unto them, saying,

5. I was in the city of Joppa praying: and in a trance I saw a vision, A certain vessel descend, as it had been a great sheet, let down from heaven by four corners; and it came even to me:

6. Upon the which when I had fastened mine eyes, I considered, and saw fourfooted beasts of the earth, and wild beasts, and creeping things, and fowls of the air.

7. And I heard a voice saying unto me, Arise, Peter; slay and eat.

8. But I said, Not so, Lord: for nothing common or unclean hath at any time entered into my mouth.

9. But the voice answered me again from heaven, What God hath cleansed, that call not thou common.

10. And this was done three times: and all were drawn up again into heaven.

11. And, behold, immediately there were three men already come unto the house where I was, sent from Caesarea unto me.

12. And the spirit bade me go with them, nothing doubting. Moreover these six brethren accompanied me, and we entered into the man's house:

13. And he shewed us how he had seen an angel in his house, which stood and said unto him, Send men to Joppa, and call for Simon, whose surname is Peter;

14. Who shall tell thee words, whereby thou and all thy house shall be saved.

15. And as I began to speak, the Holy Ghost fell on them, as on us at the beginning.

16. Then remembered I the word of the Lord, how that he said, John indeed baptized with water; but ye shall be baptized with the Holy Ghost.

> 17. Forasmuch then as God gave them the like gift as he did unto us, who believed on the Lord Jesus Christ; what was I, that I could withstand God?
> 18. When they heard these things, they held their peace, and glorified God, saying, Then hath God also to the Gentiles granted repentance unto life.

Peter had gone to Caesarea and preached the words of Eternal Life to Cornelius and his family and the followers in Jerusalem had heard about it. Peter knew he would have to explain his actions when he got back, so he prepared himself. Sure enough there were some followers of the circumcision who contended with him because he sat and ate with uncircumcised Gentiles.

It's difficult today to see the impact of this question, so maybe we should bring this into today's light and look for a minute. It would be like a man or a small group of men who were to found the Church of the Almighty Dollar. No one could become a member of this church unless they had a minimum income of at least $500,000 per year. Then one of the founders leaves for a while and, all of a sudden, everyone hears that Trailer Park USA heard the word of God from this founder. When he returned, some of the respectable members would be horrified and angry that this founding member and great leader had gone to a backyard barbecue with several families and friends, the kids, hunting dogs, and pickup trucks, and had actually sat down and eaten with "trailer trash".

While no such church actually exists, people who think that way do exist. This is the same way those of the circumcision thought. Uncircumcised people didn't know God, couldn't know God, and were unclean people. They didn't even deserve the chance to hear about God unless they became circumcised and agreed to keep all the law of Moses first. Peter was their leader. Peter thought that way himself, until he went to Caesarea.

When Peter answered these men, he told them how he had a vision in Joppa. He was hungry and a sheet came down from heaven with all manner of four footed beasts, wild beasts, creeping things, and birds in the sky. He was told to kill and eat. He flatly refused because nothing unclean or common had ever entered his mouth. The man was a true paragon of circumcised virtue, a great leader with high moral standards. He was then told not to call anything God had cleansed unclean or common—ever. This happened three times before the vision was over.

As soon as the vision was over, three men came and asked for Peter. He was told by the spirit to go with them without question. He did, and took six other brethren with him as witnesses to everything that was to be said and done. Upon entering the man's house, Peter and the others were shown the place where an angel had stood and told the man to send to Joppa for Peter. When Peter came, he would tell them how this man and all his household would be saved.

As Peter began to speak of the death and resurrection of Jesus Christ, the same holy ghost—this power from on high—that had filled the apostles on the day of Pentecost suddenly filled the people in Cornelius' house the same way it did to the apostles on the day of Pentecost. Now the same power that was in Christ, and in the apostles, and in the disciples was in the Gentiles as well. It was then that Peter remembered that Jesus had told them that John baptized with water, but they would be baptized with the holy ghost—this power from on high.

Peter's only conclusion was that, since the Gentiles received the very same gift from God that the apostles themselves received, who was he to withstand God? When the men heard this account, they held their peace and glorified God because repentance unto Eternal Life had been given to the Gentiles as well.

Acts 13

44. **And the next sabbath day came almost the whole city together to hear the word of God.**
45. **But when the Jews saw the multitudes, they were filled with envy, and spake against those things which were spoken by Paul, contradicting and blaspheming.**

> **46. Then Paul and Barnabas waxed bold, and said, It was necessary that the word of God should first have been spoken to you: but seeing ye put it from you, and judge yourselves unworthy of everlasting life, lo, we turn to the Gentiles.**
> **47. For so hath the Lord commanded us, saying, I have set thee to be a light of the Gentiles, that thou shouldest be for salvation unto the ends of the earth.**
> **48. And when the Gentiles heard this, they were glad, and glorified the word of the Lord: and as many as were ordained to eternal life believed.**

Paul and Barnabas were in Antioch preaching in the synagogues about the death and resurrection of Jesus Christ. One sabbath nearly the whole city turned out to hear the word of God. This made the Jewish leaders jealous of Paul, so they spoke against the things Paul was saying. They were contradicting his words and blaspheming God. Paul and Barnabas told them that, by necessity, the word of God should have been spoken to them first because they were of the children of Israel. However, by refusing the word of God, they judged themselves unworthy to receive Eternal Life. Instead, Paul and Barnabas would go to the Gentiles.

God had commanded them to be a light to the Gentiles and for salvation unto the ends of the earth. When the Gentiles heard this, they glorified the word of God, and those that were ordained to Eternal Life believed what Paul and Barnabas taught them.

This concludes the second section of this book. The third and final section deals with the church itself. It deals with the things written specifically to the church and not to the world at large. However, anyone may read and learn from the materials that will be covered.

CHAPTER 6

Church, this part of the book is written specifically to you. Others can read it for understanding, but the things said from this point on apply directly to you. Sadly, some of you will mock these things. Be forewarned, there are very controversial things that will be discussed, and your actions will reveal to the whole world the true intentions of your hearts.

The next two passages were written by two different men to the church. In order to see clearly what each means, they must be taken together and read as a whole thought.

> **2 Peter 1**
>
> **20. Knowing this first, that no prophecy of the scripture is of any private interpretation.**
> **21. For the prophecy came not in old time by the will of man: but holy men of God spake as they were moved by the Holy Ghost.**
>
> **2 Timothy 3**
>
> **16. All scripture is given by inspiration of God, and is profitable for doctrine, for reproof, for correction, for instruction in righteousness:**
> **17. That the man of God may be perfect, throughly furnished unto all good works.**

Peter and Paul were both apostles of Christ to the church. Peter dealt primarily with those in the church who were of the circumcision and had been taught the scriptures from childhood. Paul, however, was primarily dealing with the Gentiles who had never known God and were without God and without hope in this world. Since they were dealing with people from different backgrounds, they each spoke the word of God in a different form. However, they did not contradict one another because each man was speaking the very same word of God.

Peter said that the very first thing the church needs to know and understand is that there is not nor can there ever be any private or personal interpretation of any scripture at all. He wasn't just talking about the prophets who uttered these words, he was talking about anyone. He said that these men did not just decide to say something that sounded good to them. He said these men spoke as they were moved by the Holy Ghost—the spirit of God himself. This spirit didn't possess them, put them in a trance, and utter through some ethereal voice or write something through some sort of 'automatic writing'.

This spirit didn't drag them along, kicking and screaming, with no control over the words they spoke. It inspired them and revealed the words of God himself to them. They spoke and did the things that God told them and showed them. They used their own vocabulary to express what they themselves saw and heard from God. Look at the psalms. They differ from one another in style because different men wrote them, but none of them contradict one another at all. Look at the prophets. These books differ from one another in vocabulary and style, yet they don't contradict each other at all. These men had control over their own faculties when they uttered the things they spoke themselves from their own mouths.

Paul said that all scripture is given by the inspiration of God—the exact same thing Peter said when he referred to the prophets being moved by the Holy Ghost—exactly the same thing Christ himself said when he told his disciples that he spoke and did the things he saw and heard from his Father. Paul further stated that, as such, the scriptures were profitable for doctrine—knowing how to make right judgment and live accordingly. Also, they are profitable for reproof—showing how an error in judgment has been made. Finally, for correction—showing how to correct error in judgment so a person can again make right judgment and live accordingly. These three things constitute instruction in righteousness—the ability to judge rightly and to live life accordingly.

The purpose for this is that the man of God—not the man of this world—may be perfect. This is not perfect as in without flaw, but rather in the sense of being perfected from within to the point the the man of God may be completely prepared for all good works—good works that come from within and not just for the sake of outward show to others. Such works seek no reward, recognition, or reputation from others. The good works speak for themselves and seek only to glorify God and his son, the risen Christ Jesus. Any other kind of good work for any other reason at all smacks of self righteousness and is totally contrary to what the scriptures say right here.

Peter traced this spirit all the way back to the prophets. This was the same spirit that dwelt in Christ himself. This is the same power from on high that Christ promised his apostles they would be endued with. This is the same spirit that filled the apostles and disciples in the temple on the day of Pentecost. Peter witnessed the very same spirit fill the Gentiles in the house of Cornelius as Peter spoke the words of life to them. This is the same spirit that Paul was filled with as Ananias healed him in Damascus. This is the same spirit that Christ prayed would not only be given to his apostles, but also to anyone who believed their word.

Church, if the scriptures are true, and this same power existed and was manifested even before the apostles were born, why do some of you insist that the things the apostles did through this power died when they died? Why do you insist that these men were special and their power was only for a sign until the church became fully established? Why do you insist that once the bible was completed, this power was done away with because that which was perfect has come? Do you do these things out of ignorance, the way Paul did when he persecuted the church of God? Or do you do these things deliberately, knowing that you are not teaching the truth that is in the scriptures? Church, I cannot answer these questions, only you can and then only individually.

2 Corinthians 5

1. For we know that if our earthly house of this tabernacle were dissolved, we have a building of God, an house not made with hands, eternal in the heavens.
2. For in this we groan, earnestly desiring to be clothed upon with our house which is from heaven:
3. If so be that being clothed we shall not be found naked.
4. For we that are in this tabernacle do groan, being burdened: not for that we would be unclothed, but clothed upon, that mortality might be swallowed up of life.
5. Now he that hath wrought us for the selfsame thing is God, who also hath given unto us the earnest of the Spirit.

Paul wrote this to the church—the body of people whose head is Christ himself—at Corinth. He did not write this to the city council, the Roman procurator, or to the trade guilds. This is to the church itself. Paul was talking to them about their body. We as Christians earnestly desire to have this new body that is eternal and from God himself. We also know that as long as we live here in our present body, we cannot have this new body. We therefore groan, not that we should be released from this body, but rather that we should have this new body and death itself would no longer exist because we would then have Eternal Life. He said that God has given us this spirit as an earnest—a down payment—to assure us that we will have this new body with Eternal Life.

1 Corinthians 15

39. All flesh is not the same flesh: but there is one kind of flesh of men, another flesh of beasts, another of fishes, and another of birds.
40. There are also celestial bodies, and bodies terrestrial: but the glory of the celestial is one, and the glory of the terrestrial is another.

41. There is one glory of the sun, and another glory of the moon, and another glory of the stars: for one star differeth from another star in glory.
42. So also is the resurrection of the dead. It is sown in corruption; it is raised in incorruption:
43. It is sown in dishonour; it is raised in glory: it is sown in weakness; it is raised in power:
44. It is sown a natural body; it is raised a spiritual body. There is a natural body, and there is a spiritual body.
45. And so it is written, The first man Adam was made a living soul; the last Adam was made a quickening spirit.
46. Howbeit that was not first which is spiritual, but that which is natural; and afterward that which is spiritual.
47. The first man is of the earth, earthy: the second man is the Lord from heaven.
48. As is the earthy, such are they also that are earthy: and as is the heavenly, such are they also that are heavenly.
49. And as we have borne the image of the earthy, we shall also bear the image of the heavenly.
50. Now this I say, brethren, that flesh and blood cannot inherit the kingdom of God; neither doth corruption inherit incorruption.
51. Behold, I shew you a mystery; We shall not all sleep, but we shall all be changed,
52. In a moment, in the twinkling of an eye, at the last trump: for the trumpet shall sound, and the dead shall be raised incorruptible, and we shall be changed.
53. For this corruptible must put on incorruption, and this mortal must put on immortality.
54. So when this corruptible shall have put on incorruption, and this mortal shall have put on immortality, then shall be brought to pass the saying that is written, Death is swallowed up in victory.
55. O death, where is thy sting? O grave, where is thy victory?

In this earlier letter to this same church at Corinth, Paul was discussing this same body because a question had arisen about this in the church. Paul starts out by telling them that not all flesh is the same. There are different kinds of flesh—one of man, a different one of beasts, a different kind for fish, yet a different kind for birds—therefore not all flesh is the same flesh. He said there are heavenly bodies and earthly bodies, each one differing from the other with its own glory.

He stated these things because he was addressing the resurrection of the dead. The body dies and decays. It is raised in a form that never gets tired, hungry, sick, never grows old, and never dies. The body is sown in dishonor and raised in glory—the glory of God himself. It is sown in weakness and raised in the power of God himself. Our body is sown as the natural body it is and raised as the spiritual body we are promised. Paul said that there is a natural body and there is a spiritual body.

Paul also says that the natural body came first through Adam and the spiritual body came later through the last Adam, Christ Jesus himself. The first Adam is of the earth—earthy. The last Adam is the lord FROM heaven—not the lord OF heaven. Those things that are of the earth are earthy, just as those things of heaven are heavenly. Paul also states that as we have borne the physical body that is the image of Adam, so shall we also bear the spiritual body that is the image of Christ himself. Paul then said that FLESH and BLOOD cannot inherit the kingdom of God, just as corruption cannot inherit incorruption.

Paul then revealed a mystery. All of us are not going to die (sleep), yet all of us will be changed. The corruptible must become incorruptible and the mortal must become immortal. When that happens, then the saying will come to pass, Death is swallowed up in victory. O death, where is thy sting? O grave, where is thy victory? Until that time, however, death and the grave will continue as they have ever done from the time of Adam.

Luke 24

36. And as they thus spake, Jesus himself stood in the midst of them, and saith unto them, Peace be unto you.
37. But they were terrified and affrighted, and supposed that they had seen a spirit.
38. And he said unto them, Why are ye troubled? and why do thoughts arise in your hearts?
39. Behold my hands and my feet, that it is I myself: handle me, and see; for a spirit hath not flesh and bones, as ye see me have.
40. And when he had thus spoken, he shewed them his hands and his feet.
41. And while they yet believed not for joy, and wondered, he said unto them, Have ye here any meat?
42. And they gave him a piece of a broiled fish, and of an honeycomb.
43. And he took it, and did eat before them.
44. And he said unto them, These are the words which I spake unto you, while I was yet with you, that all things must be fulfilled, which were written in the law of Moses, and in the prophets, and in the psalms, concerning me.
45. Then opened he their understanding, that they might understand the scriptures,
46. And said unto them, Thus it is written, and thus it behoved Christ to suffer, and to rise from the dead the third day:
47. And that repentance and remission of sins should be preached in his name among all nations, beginning at Jerusalem.
48. And ye are witnesses of these things.
49. And, behold, I send the promise of my Father upon you: but tarry ye in the city of Jerusalem, until ye be endued with power from on high.

The record in Luke 24 tells of Jesus' first appearance to the disciples and some of the apostles at the evening of the first day of the week after he was risen. They were discussing some of the earlier appearances when he suddenly was just standing in their midst and spoke to them. They were completely terrified and supposed they were seeing a spirit. Jesus then asked them why they were so troubled and why they would even think such thoughts.

Jesus then told those present to look at, examine closely, and touch his hands and feet for themselves. He said that a spirit did not have FLESH and BONES as he himself had. This is the same man that told the Samaritan woman that God is a spirit. Since they still didn't believe what he was saying, Jesus asked these men for some food and ate a piece of fish and a honeycomb in front of them.

The risen Christ Jesus in his new glorified spiritual body just denied and proved to his apostles that he was not a spirit in any way, shape, or form at all—not even part spirit at all. He then told them about the things written in the law of Moses, the prophets, and the pslams that concerned him directly. He made it possible for these men assembled there that night to understand everything the scriptures said.

He told them it was necessary for him to suffer and die, and rise again on the third day. He told them that repentance and remission of sins should be preached in all nations, beginning at Jerusalem. He told them that they themselves were eyewitnesses of these things. He also told them to wait in Jerusalem for the promise of the Father—the day when they would be endued (literally clothed from within) with power from on high. The record of this event is in the book of Acts on the day of Pentecost when the apostles suddenly were filled with holy spirit and began to speak in the languages of everyone present at the feast.

Church, these three references deal with the resurrected body and Eternal Life. These three references should give each of you an understanding of the kind of body we as Christians should expect to have. If these passages are indeed the inspired word of God, and as such, truth itself, why do some of you teach that Jesus has a spirit body? Why do some of you teach that Jesus only took on a physical form for his disciple and apostles to be able to see him? Why do some of you teach Jesus is part God (spirit) and part man (flesh) when Jesus denied and proved that he was not spirit in any way, shape, or form at all?

Church, Jesus Christ himself said the scriptures cannot be broken. Why do some of you teach that his reference to being FLESH and BONES is the same as Paul's reference to FLESH and BLOOD? Why do you ignore what John wrote of this same event in 1John 1:1-4 when he said that Eternal Life was manifested to them and they saw it for themselves in a person with a physical body. Granted, the physical body was no longer an earthy body, but a heavenly body. It was still a physical body according to the risen Christ Jesus himself. I cannot answer these questions for you. You must answer these questions for yourselves and you must answer as individuals, not as a group. The scriptures themselves require an answer.

1 Thessalonians 4

13. But I would not have you to be ignorant, brethren, concerning them which are asleep, that ye sorrow not, even as others which have no hope.
14. For if we believe that Jesus died and rose again, even so them also which sleep in Jesus will God bring with him.
15. For this we say unto you by the word of the Lord, that we which are alive and remain unto the coming of the Lord shall not prevent them which are asleep.
16. For the Lord himself shall descend from heaven with a shout, with the voice of the archangel, and with the trump of God: and the dead in Christ shall rise first:
17. Then we which are alive and remain shall be caught up together with them in the clouds, to meet the Lord in the air: and so shall we ever be with the Lord.
18. Wherefore comfort one another with these words.

Paul's words here were to encourage Christians not to sorrow at the death of fellow Christians as though there was no hope. He refers to the dead in Christ to be asleep in Christ. He says that those of us who are alive at the time the lord comes will not prevent, that is precede, those who are asleep in Christ. Christ himself shall descend from heaven with a shout, with the accompanying voice of the archangel, and with the trump of God. It is then and only then that the dead in Christ (and no one else except the dead in Christ) shall rise because the corruptible MUST put on incorruption (become incorruptible). They will have the same kind of body Christ himself has—the same kind of body Christ himself witnessed to his disciples and apostles after he was resurrected. Each one will have a new body of FLESH and BONES with Life in itself just like Christ has.

Immediately after that, those of us who are alive and have remained to this point will be forcefully snatched away from the earth. As this happens, our mortal bodies MUST put on immortality (become immortal). In our new bodies, will will meet Christ himself and the risen dead in Christ in the CLOUDS. Christ will not be on the earth when this happens. No one on the earth will be able to see any of this because this event occurs in the CLOUDS. It is at this point that God himself will bring those who are Christ's with him to the place that has been prepared for us by Christ himself. These are the words we should comfort one another with.

1 John 3

1. **Behold, what manner of love the Father hath bestowed upon us, that we should be called the sons of God: therefore the world knoweth us not, because it knew him not.**
2. **Beloved, now are we the sons of God, and it doth not yet appear what we shall be: but we know that, when he shall appear, we shall be like him; for we shall see him as he is.**
3. **And every man that hath this hope in him purifieth himself, even as he is pure.**

John declared the love of God is such that we, as Christians, should be called the sons of God just as Christ himself is the only begotten son of God. Who among us can even conceive of a love that deep or that strong? Yet, the scriptures tell us that we are to share that very same love one to another. Therefore, it is impossible for those of the world to know us because they didn't even know Christ.

We are sons of God right now—this very instant. We can't see what we shall be because we are still mortal and corruptible. Our nature is still flawed and selfish. We cannot have this new body because we are still of the earth—earthy. Yet we know that, when Christ does appear, whether dead in Christ or alive in Christ, we shall be like him. Our bodies will have the same nature as his. We shall be FLESH an BONES with Eternal Life, just like he is. We shall see him as he is right now. No one else except those that are Christ's will see this. This is why it takes place in the clouds.

With this hope, each of us seeks to purify ourself even as Christ is pure. By this, we are removing things from our hearts and minds that would come between this Eternal Life and the new body that will contain it. Will we ever be perfect? As long as we have the bodies we have now, we will by the nature of that body be selfish. We can learn to perfect ourselves from within by learning to think and live a different way. We can learn to be as obedient to God as Christ himself in spite of the flaws we naturally have. God has given us everything we need to do this. It is up to us who have this hope to do these things with the help of the spirit God has given us. It means we have to change our very nature from within. Our battle is within us and not with the world.

John 14

1. **Let not your heart be troubled: ye believe in God, believe also in me.**
2. **In my Father's house are many mansions: if it were not so, I would have told you. I go to prepare a place for you.**

> **3. And if I go and prepare a place for you, I will come again, and receive you unto myself; that where I am, there ye may be also.**

Jesus made this promise to his apostles before he was crucified. He said that there were many mansions in his Father's house and that he was going there specifically to prepare a place for them—those that were his. He then said that he would return for them and take them there to be with him. Paul and John described this very thing and didn't contradict a single word Jesus said.

Church, after having seen these things for yourselves, why do some of you teach that we go to heaven immediately when we die? Why do some of you teach that the dead are in heaven now with spirit bodies? Why do some of you substitute the teachings and philosophies of men for the words that are written in the scriptures? Why do some of you use men's philosophical definitions to explain what these scriptures say? The scriptures themselves are asking you these questions. Again, each of you must answer individually, not as a group.

1 Timothy 3

> **15. But if I tarry long, that thou mayest know how thou oughtest to behave thyself in the house of God, which is the church of the living God, the pillar and ground of the truth.**

Paul told Timothy that the house of God—the church of the living God—is the pillar and ground of the truth itself. The church is the immovable base for the truth. This is the same truth Paul told the Romans God himself would judge by. It is the same truth Christ declared was the word of God itself. It is the same truth that the psalmist said that God has magnified above even his own name. The church therefore has been given a great honor and an awesome responsibility as keeper, protector, and teacher of the truth that the scriptures speak of and define themselves.

Eternal Life

1 Peter 4

17. For the time is come that judgment must begin at the house of God: and if it first begin at us, what shall the end be of them that obey not the gospel of God?
18. And if the righteous scarcely be saved, where shall the ungodly and the sinner appear?

We are now approaching the time of God's judgment. Peter says that judgment MUST begin at the house of God. That is because the house of God is the pillar and ground of the truth itself. Now we as Christians must face the truth of the scriptures and decide individually whether to accept what has been said to us or to believe whatever we want to.

If judgment begins with us, what will happen to those who don't obey the gospel of God? In addition, if those of us found to be righteous are scarcely saved, what chance do the ungodly and sinners have?

Church, the scriptures are opening themselves to you. They are questioning you. You are the pillar and ground of the truth itself. You now have to face the truth. There is still time to change and show the whole world what God has given anyone who will accept it. Church you are about to be divided. Some of you will have the truth God has given you and some of you will have your own form of self-righteousness. Once the division is complete, Christ will come for those that are his. After that, there will be no repentance in the church at all. The church that is left will no longer be the church of God at all, their hearts being seared and hardened against God and his mercy. The whole world will witness these things and a great multitude will still turn to Christ at the cost of their own lives. The church that is left will be their executioner. These are terrible things, yet the scriptures tell of even greater horrors than this that are yet to come before Christ comes to personally rule himself.

I have not said these things to frighten you or to anger you. I have said these things to show you what each one of us must now face. As we continue in this book, the scriptures themselves will show you these and other things I as of yet have not discussed. Please do not dismiss these things as opinions. The scriptures speak plainly and now the scriptures must be explained just as plainly. There must be no doubt in anyone's mind about the decision each and every one of us must make. Once we have made and committed to our decision, there can be no turning back. Just as Pharaoh kept hardening his heart against the will of God until God would not allow him to repent, so shall it be in the church. Please consider the results of your decision before you make it and commit to it. God's judgment is according to the truth against those who do such things.

CHAPTER 7

We as Christians should know that we do not have Eternal Life in us right now. We also should know that the body we have cannot contain Eternal Life because it is mortal and corruptible. We also should know that when we accepted the death and resurrection of Christ Jesus, we were filled with power from on high—holy spirit—the very power of God Almighty himself. It wasn't for us to run around and prove we were better than anyone else or even each other. It was to give each one of us a personal guarantee that each of us would have the very same Eternal Life that Jesus Christ himself has right this very minute. Keeping these things in mind, we are now going to hear from Paul about this Life.

Colossians 3

1. If ye then be risen with Christ, seek those things which are above, where Christ sitteth on the right hand of God.
2. Set your affection on things above, not on things on the earth.
3. For ye are dead, and your life is hid with Christ in God.
4. When Christ, who is our life, shall appear, then shall ye also appear with him in glory.
5. Mortify therefore your members which are upon the earth; fornication, uncleanness, inordinate affection, evil concupiscence, and covetousness, which is idolatry:
6. For which things' sake the wrath of God cometh on the children of disobedience:

7. In the which ye also walked some time, when ye lived in them.
8. But now ye also put off all these; anger, wrath, malice, blasphemy, filthy communication out of your mouth.
9. Lie not one to another, seeing that ye have put off the old man with his deeds;
10. And have put on the new man, which is renewed in knowledge after the image of him that created him:
11. Where there is neither Greek nor Jew, circumcision nor uncircumcision, Barbarian, Scythian, bond nor free: but Christ is all, and in all.
12. Put on therefore, as the elect of God, holy and beloved, bowels of mercies, kindness, humbleness of mind, meekness, longsuffering;
13. Forbearing one another, and forgiving one another, if any man have a quarrel against any: even as Christ forgave you, so also do ye.
14. And above all these things put on charity, which is the bond of perfectness.
15. And let the peace of God rule in your hearts, to the which also ye are called in one body; and be ye thankful.
16. Let the word of Christ dwell in you richly in all wisdom; teaching and admonishing one another in psalms and hymns and spiritual songs, singing with grace in your hearts to the Lord.
17. And whatsoever ye do in word or deed, do all in the name of the Lord Jesus, giving thanks to God and the Father by him.

If we truly are Christian and risen with Christ, then we should seek things that are above—heavenly—where Christ sits at the right hand of God himself. Our hearts should be focused on heavenly things, not on the worldly things of this earth. When we were baptized into Christ, we died to the worldly things of this earth. The Eternal Life we have is hidden with Christ in God. That Life will be revealed in us with all its glory when Christ himself appears for us to share with him its glory and not one instant sooner.

Since this is the case, we should treat the things we used to do as though they were dead and never engage in that way of thinking again. These things are fornication (unlawful desire), uncleanness (any form of impurity), inordinate affection (uncontrollable desire), evil concupiscence (depravity), and covetousness (greediness). These things are all part of self gratification and self indulgence. As such, all are idolatrous to God. These are the things that bring the wrath of God on the children of disobedience, and there was a time when all of us have done these things as a matter of course in our lives.

In addition to these things, we are to do away with anger, wrath, malice, and filthy communication (not just "dirty words", but any type of communication that is disgraceful or shameful). Do not lie to one another or to anyone else for that matter. You have done away with your old nature and have been given a new nature that is like the nature of God himself. In this nature, there is neither Jew nor Gentile, circumcision nor uncircumcision, Barbarian, Scythian, bond nor free. In this nature Christ himself is all and in all of you.

Even though we are physically different in size, age, sex, color, places of birth, places of residence, education, skills, hobbies, etc., we all share the one and the selfsame spirit—the very same spirit that was in Christ himself—the power of God Himself—and it works all in all. It is what gives to each one of us the very nature of God Himself. That spirit is the personal guarantee from God Himself to each one of us that each of us will have the same Eternal Life that Jesus Christ has right now.

We should therefore develop genuine tender concern for one another, kindness, true humility, willingness to learn from one another, and great patience with one another. We should patiently endure the differences we have from one to the other. We should be forgiving of one another and not let our individual differences get in the way. If we do have a dispute with one another, we should remember that Christ forgave us, so we should likewise forgive one another.

Above all else, we should love one another the way Christ and the Father love each one of us. This doesn't mean throw money in the plate when it's passed. It means having a true genuine caring for one another and being willing to offer whatever help we can one to another.

Finally, we should allow the peace of God which passes all understanding live and govern the thoughts and actions of each of our hearts. We are called to be individual members of one body and we should be thankful for the chance to share this with one another.

Allow the words of Christ himself to live in us in their fullness with all their wisdom. We are to teach and admonish one another with psalms, hymns, and spiritual songs, singing with grace in our hearts to God himself.

Whatever we do or say should be done to honor Jesus himself and not to honor ourselves. Our thanks should be to God by the way we honor his son.

1 Corinthians 13

1. Though I speak with the tongues of men and of angels, and have not charity, I am become as sounding brass, or a tinkling cymbal.
2. And though I have the gift of prophecy, and understand all mysteries, and all knowledge; and though I have all faith, so that I could remove mountains, and have not charity, I am nothing.
3. And though I bestow all my goods to feed the poor, and though I give my body to be burned, and have not charity, it profiteth me nothing.
4. Charity suffereth long, and is kind; charity envieth not; charity vaunteth not itself, is not puffed up,
5. Doth not behave itself unseemly, seeketh not her own, is not easily provoked, thinketh no evil;
6. Rejoiceth not in iniquity, but rejoiceth in the truth;
7. Beareth all things, believeth all things, hopeth all things, endureth all things.

> 8. Charity never faileth: but whether there be prophecies, they shall fail; whether there be tongues, they shall cease; whether there be knowledge, it shall vanish away.
> 9. For we know in part, and we prophesy in part.
> 10. But when that which is perfect is come, then that which is in part shall be done away.
> 11. When I was a child, I spake as a child, I understood as a child, I thought as a child: but when I became a man, I put away childish things.
> 12. For now we see through a glass, darkly; but then face to face: now I know in part; but then shall I know even as also I am known.
> 13. And now abideth faith, hope, charity, these three; but the greatest of these is charity.

Before continuing, we should stop and look at this charity—this love—that God has given us. Paul explained it in detail here in 1 Corinthians chapter 13 and it deserves a closer look. He isn't talking about tossing coins in a collection plate or having $5,000 or $10,000 a plate fund-raisers for the rich and famous to show how much there really care about the poor or the environment. This charity—this love—is completely different than anyone has been led to believe.

Though we speak with the tongues of men and angels themselves, though we are most eloquent and polished, if we do not have this love in us, we are just in this for the big show. It looks and sounds impressive to others, but there is no substance to what we do at all.

Even though we have the gift of prophecy, can understand all mysteries, have all knowledge, and have faith to the point we can move mountains, if we do not have this love in us, we are nothing at all except on the surface. There is no depth to us and we have no substance.

If each of us were to give all that we have to feed the poor, or give up our life for others, if each of us does not have this love in our hearts, there is no real benefit in what we do.

The love that God has given us is patient and longsuffering, and is kind to others; it is not envious of the accomplishments of others;

it does not brag about its own accomplishments because it is humble and not proud. This love does not conduct itself in a shameful manner at all ever. It is not self seeking, nor can it be easily provoked to anger, nor does it think evil of or toward others.

This love finds pleasure in the truth. It finds no pleasure in bending or twisting the truth for any reason at all. This love patiently bears all things, trusts in all things, and endures all things. This love never stops. Prophecies will eventually cease, because they will no longer be necessary. Other tongues will eventually cease as well. Knowledge will eventually cease. The reason for this is that we only know in part and only prophecy in part. When that which is perfect is come, those things which are done in part will cease because they will no longer be necessary.

When we were children, we spoke, we understood, and we thought as children. When we became adults we put away the childish things in our lives. Now, we see as through a glass darkly, like seeing a reflection in a mirror. When that which is perfect is come, we shall truly see face to face and not one second sooner will that happen. Now we know in part, then and only then will we know even as we are known.

Now living in and through us are faith, hope, and this love God has given us. The greatest of these is the love God has given us.

1 Peter 1

22. Seeing ye have purified your souls in obeying the truth through the spirit unto unfeigned love of the brethren, see that ye love one another with a pure heart fervently:
23. Being born again, not of corruptible seed, but of incorruptible, by the word of God, which liveth and abideth for ever.
24. For all flesh is as grass, and all the glory of man as the flower of grass. The grass withereth, and the flower thereof falleth away:
25. But the word of the Lord endureth for ever. And this is the word which by the gospel is preached unto you.

Since you have purified yourselves by obeying the truth through the power God himself gave you, make sure you love one another with a pure heart fervently without any pretense at all. Do not love one another because you have to, rather because you want to from the depths of your own heart. You are reborn, not of corruptible seed which will die. You are born now by the incorruptible word of God himself which lives and abides forever.

All flesh of the earth is as grass, and the greatest accomplishments of man are as the flower of grass. Grass withers and its flower falls off. However, the word of the Lord that you are reborn with endures forever. That is the word which is preached to you by the gospel of the death and resurrection of Christ to Eternal Life.

It was necessary to spend some time defining this love that Paul was talking about. This love can be faked on the surface. However, when this love is present, there is no doubt what others see. It is totally unlike anything else. Its depth is beyond measure. Its patience, hope, endurance, forgiveness, humility, and kindness set it apart from anything else. It is totally beyond any emotional description, yet it can be portrayed on the surface as emotional. It can be expressed emotionally, but it is not based on emotion, nor is it an emotion.

This love is based upon obeying the truth God has given us. Our love of the truth brings us to the ability of sharing this love with others. This love is not unconditional. Only those who have the love of the truth in their hearts can have and develop this love within themselves. This love is part of the fruit produced in each of us through the power of God working in each of us individually. The presence of the spirit of God in us assures us of the promise of Eternal Life. The promise of Eternal life causes us to develop this love within ourselves and share it with others.

Church, does this love exist in your congregation? Has your congregation ever heard of this kind of love? It is time for some hard things that may show you the answer. Some of you may not like this, but the word of God is truth itself.

1 Corinthians 6

1. Dare any of you, having a matter against another, go to law before the unjust, and not before the saints?
2. Do ye not know that the saints shall judge the world? and if the world shall be judged by you, are ye unworthy to judge the smallest matters?
3. Know ye not that we shall judge angels? how much more things that pertain to this life?
4. If then ye have judgments of things pertaining to this life, set them to judge who are least esteemed in the church.
5. I speak to your shame. Is it so, that there is not a wise man among you? no, not one that shall be able to judge between his brethren?
6. But brother goeth to law with brother, and that before the unbelievers.
7. Now therefore there is utterly a fault among you, because ye go to law one with another. Why do ye not rather take wrong? why do ye not rather suffer yourselves to be defrauded?
8. Nay, ye do wrong, and defraud, and that your brethren.
9. Know ye not that the unrighteous shall not inherit the kingdom of God? Be not deceived: neither fornicators, nor idolaters, nor adulterers, nor effeminate, nor abusers of themselves with mankind,
10. Nor thieves, nor covetous, nor drunkards, nor revilers, nor extortioners, shall inherit the kingdom of God.
11. And such were some of you: but ye are washed, but ye are sanctified, but ye are justified in the name of the Lord Jesus, and by the Spirit of our God.
12. All things are lawful unto me, but all things are not expedient: all things are lawful for me, but I will not be brought under the power of any.

Why do you go to the courts to settle your disputes in the church? Instead of going before the brethren, why do you go publicly before wicked and unreasonable men to judge you? Why do righteous men make a laughingstock of themselves and their calling by appealing to the unrighteous for righteous judgement?

Do you realize that the saints will judge the world? If you shall judge the world, why can't you handle the smallest of matters within your own selves? Do you realize that you will judge even angels themselves? How much more should you be able to judge matters pertaining to this life we are presently living?

If there is a case where you must judge matters pertaining to this present life, then set those among you who you have the least regard for to be your judges. You should be ashamed of the way you treat one another. You act as though there is not one of you that has the wisdom to make a sound judgment between brothers. You have petty jealousies, envyings, contentions, and divisions because you either do not have the love of God in you or you will not listen to what it is telling you to do. You would rather take a brother to law before unbelievers. You will not let your word be your bond as God's word is his bond.

This is a terrible fault among you. Out of love, why not just take the wrong and suffer being defrauded? Out of love why would you want to defraud anyone in the first place, especially your own brother? You would rather defraud others, even your brothers.

Don't you understand? The unrighteous shall not inherit the kingdom of God. Do not deceive yourselves for even a second. Neither fornicators, nor idolators, nor adulterers, nor effeminate, nor abusers of themselves with mankind, nor thieves, nor covetous, nor drunkards, nor revilers, nor extortioners shall inherit the kingdom of God because they are self serving and self gratifying people.

There were times before you accepted the work of Christ that you did these things, but now you are washed, you are set apart from the world, you are justified in the name of the Lord Jesus and by the spirit of God that is in us. It is time for us to learn to live this way instead of the way the world lives. Each one of us should realize that all things are lawful unto us, but all things are not necessarily beneficial for us. We should also realize that, in this love, all things we do are lawful, but none of us should allow ourselves to be brought under the power of anyone else.

Galatians 5

13. For, brethren, ye have been called unto liberty; only use not liberty for an occasion to the flesh, but by love serve one another.
14. For all the law is fulfilled in one word, even in this; Thou shalt love thy neighbour as thyself.
15. But if ye bite and devour one another, take heed that ye be not consumed one of another.
16. This I say then, Walk in the Spirit, and ye shall not fulfil the lust of the flesh.
17. For the flesh lusteth against the Spirit, and the Spirit against the flesh: and these are contrary the one to the other: so that ye cannot do the things that ye would.
18. But if ye be led of the Spirit, ye are not under the law.
19. Now the works of the flesh are manifest, which are these; Adultery, fornication, uncleanness, lasciviousness,
20. Idolatry, witchcraft, hatred, variance, emulations, wrath, strife, seditions, heresies,
21. Envyings, murders, drunkenness, revellings, and such like: of the which I tell you before, as I have also told you in time past, that they which do such things shall not inherit the kingdom of God.
22. But the fruit of the Spirit is love , joy, peace , longsuffering, gentleness, goodness, faith,
23. Meekness, temperance: against such there is no law.
24. And they that are Christ's have crucified the flesh with the affections and lusts.
25. If we live in the Spirit, let us also walk in the Spirit.
26. Let us not be desirous of vain glory, provoking one another, envying one another.

Church, our calling is not one of rules and regulations to be followed to be righteous enough to be in the presence of God. Our calling is that we should realize that the obedience of Christ Jesus has already put us in the presence of God. This liberty and freedom from laws is like nothing mankind has ever seen before. We should not ever use this freedom to serve our own selfish desires. Rather, we should use this freedom to serve one another out of genuine love.

All the law can be fulfilled in us by one word; Thou shalt love thy neighbor as thyself. Technically (for the hair splitters among you) that is 7 words. However that is one thought—one goal. If we cease our self serving attitudes and love one another the way we learn to love ourselves (you know—the way Christ loves us so much that he himself died for our rebelliousness—the way God loves us so much that He himself raised Christ from the dead), we will fulfill all the law for righteousness from our own hearts. This love will flow out from each of us and will be seen by everyone. Do you see it in your life? Do you see it in anyone else? Do you see it in your congregations? WHY NOT?

If you still backbite and attack one another, you are still worldly and you are not following the spirit of God that is in you, if indeed you actually have the spirit of God in you at all. Be careful that you do not destroy one another, because you will if you don't have this love one toward another.

Walk in this spirit—this power—God has given you and you will not fulfill the selfish desires all of us have. The selfishness in us resists the power God gave us and the power God gave us resists the selfishness in us. They are two totally different things that are completely contrary to one another. It's the struggle we each have that keeps us from doing the things that we would do. However, if you allow the power of God to inspire, encourage, and strengthen you, then you are not under any law that governs righteous behaviors. You behave righteously from your heart without having to see what law you are following.

The works of the flesh (selfishness) are clearly shown by behavior. These are: adultery, fornication, uncleanness, lasciviousness, idolatry, witchcraft, hatred, variance, emulations, wrath, strife, seditions, heresies, envyings, murders, drunkenness, revellings, and things of such nature. People who live after this manner shall not inherit the kingdom of God at all because these things are self centered, self serving, and self gratifying.

In contrast, the result of following after the inspiration of the spirit of God is the love God has, true joy, the peace of God himself that passes all understanding, longsuffering—patience that allows you to keep your own actions under control when dealing with yourself and with others, gentleness, goodness, faith—thinking the same thoughts as God himself, meekness—willingness to learn and to be taught, temperance—moderation in all things. There is no law against any of these things. That's why we should not desire to live under any law to be righteous. Living this way fulfills the laws that would make us righteous before God if we could just obey them and not rebel against them.

Those who have accepted the works of Christ and are truly his in their hearts have turned away from selfish desires and treat them as dead things. Are any of us perfect? Do we still do unrighteous and selfish things from time to time? Very likely more often than we know. However, our goal is still to follow the inspiration of the spirit of God within us to develop the fruit in us that no law can condemn.

If we as Christians truly live in this spirit, then let us walk in such a way that we are constantly following the inspiration of God and not serving ourselves and calling what we do "Christian".

Let us not seek glory from others that is here today and gone tomorrow. Let us not provoke, judge, or antagonize one another. Let us not envy the accomplishments of others. This behavior only grieves the spirit in us and leads to much worse behavior.

1 John 5

9. If we receive the witness of men, the witness of God is greater: for this is the witness of God which he hath testified of his Son.

10. He that believeth on the Son of God hath the witness in himself: he that believeth not God hath made him

a liar; because he believeth not the record that God gave of his Son.

11. And this is the record, that God hath given to us eternal life, and this life is in his Son.
12. He that hath the Son hath life; and he that hath not the Son of God hath not life.
13. These things have I written unto you that believe on the name of the Son of God; that ye may know that ye have eternal life, and that ye may believe on the name of the Son of God.
14. And this is the confidence that we have in him, that, if we ask any thing according to his will, he heareth us:
15. And if we know that he hear us, whatsoever we ask, we know that we have the petitions that we desired of him.
16. If any man see his brother sin a sin which is not unto death, he shall ask, and he shall give him life for them that sin not unto death. There is a sin unto death: I do not say that he shall pray for it.
17. All unrighteousness is sin: and there is a sin not unto death.
18. We know that whosoever is born of God sinneth not; but he that is begotten of God keepeth himself, and that wicked one toucheth him not.
19. And we know that we are of God, and the whole world lieth in wickedness.
20. And we know that the Son of God is come, and hath given us an understanding, that we may know him that is true, and we are in him that is true, even in his Son Jesus Christ. This is the true God, and eternal life.
21. Little children, keep yourselves from idols. Amen.

Church, we put a lot of emphasis on the character and testimony of men, yet the witness of God is far greater than that of any man. God said that anyone who believes on the son of God carries the witness within himself. Anyone that doesn't believe God has made him a liar because he refuses to believe the record that God himself gave of his only begotten son. Here is the record. God himself has given us Eternal Life and this Life is in his only begotten son right now.

God has given us the very same promise he gave Jesus Christ himself before he was crucified. God fulfilled his promise to Jesus when he raised Jesus from the dead. Like Jesus, we have the promise of the very same Eternal Life that Jesus himself has right now. He will fulfill that same promise to us when Jesus comes for those that are his. Therefore, he that has accepted the death and resurrection of Christ has Eternal Life; and he that has not accepted the death and resurrection of Christ DOES NOT have Eternal Life.

These things are written for you to believe on the name of the son of God himself and know without any doubt at all that you have Eternal Life. This knowledge gives us the confidence to know that, if we ask anything according to the will of God, He himself hears us when we ask. We also know that, because God hears us, He will give us whatever we ask according to His will—not according to our own selfish desires.

If we see a brother overtaken in a sin that is not unto death, rather than judge him, we should pray and ask God to give Eternal Life for them that sin not unto death, and God will grant our petition. However, there is a sin that is unto death and we should not even pray for those who commit it.

All unrighteousness is sin, yet there is sin that is not unto death. If it were not so, we could not be told to pray for those who commit a sin that is not unto death.

We know that anyone born of God doesn't sin by nature because he has the spirit of God in himself. If he follows the inspiration of the spirit in himself, he protects himself and the wicked one can't touch him. Are we perfect? Do we always follow the guidance of the spirit in us? NO! That's why we are instructed to pray for those who sin a sin that is not unto death. This is a battle inside of us. We are gradually overcoming our shortcomings, so we are still making mistakes and doing things we shouldn't. It's a good thing we can pray for one another and help and encourage one another.

We know we are of God and the whole world around us lies in wickedness, whether those in the world realize it or not. We know that the son of God has come and has given us an understanding the world doesn't have. With this understanding, we know him that is true, and are in him that is true, because we are in his son Jesus Christ. We know the true God and he has given us Eternal Life. Stay away from idols. Anything that is self centered, self serving, or self gratifying is idolatrous to God.

It may seem odd that I would spend so much time talking about this love of God when I am writing a book about Eternal Life, but there is a strong relationship that needs to be understood. We have the promise of Eternal Life. We have in us power from on high, that God himself gave to each one of us. This power assures us that God himself will give each one of us the very same Eternal Life that he gave his only begotten son Jesus Christ. This love is part of the fruit produced in each one of us as we learn to use the power God has given us. This love binds us together and unifies us. It helps us to be complete and to walk worthy of the Eternal Life we are to receive from God himself.

Listen very carefully. If others don't see this love in us, or we don't see this love in others, something is terribly wrong. Either what we have in us is not the spirit of God himself, or we are not listening to the inspiration of the spirit of God in us. Before we can even think of looking at others, we must be certain within ourselves where we actually stand. This is why God gave us the holy spirit to begin with. It is crucial to understand these things—our very Life depends upon this. God gave us of his very own spirit in order for us to change ourselves so that we reflect the very image of the risen Christ Jesus in our lives—in spite of our shortcomings.

1 Corinthians 1

10. Now I beseech you, brethren, by the name of our Lord Jesus Christ, that ye all speak the same thing, and that there be no divisions among you; but that ye be perfectly joined together in the same mind and in the same judgment.

I beg you—that all—each and every single one of you—speak the same thing. Let there be no divisions of any kind among you for any reason at all—EVER. Instead be perfectly (completely) joined together in the same mind and in the same judgment. Divisions is an interesting term. It means splits. A modern word for this is denominations. Imagine that—let there be no denominations of any kind among you for any reason at all—EVER. Ouch! That's a mean thing to say! What narrow—minded person would say that? The word of God says it!

Church, listen carefully. Where there are divisions (denominations), there are strifes, commotions, emulations, variances, and confusion. In these things abide every evil work. Regardless of our intent, jealousies, hatreds, and spitefulness abound. I know the first thing anyone will say is that our division (denomination) isn't divided because we all believe the same thing. Let someone else from a different denomination come in among you and try to question your belief. You will treat him as an enemy of God and will not allow him to be a member until he accepts your doctrine. After all, you have to protect your doctrine which is, of course the word of God itself. But then, his questions about your doctrine are his attempt to protect his denominational doctrine, which is of course the word of God itself.

Church, there are over 50,000 recorded, verified, and catalogued denominations among you. These are the respectable ones. There are many others that are not so respectable ones called cults. Each of you will fight to the death if necessary to defend your respective denomination or cult, that is if you really are a true believer. You are proud of your divisions more so than you are of the promises of God. Each of you believes that your particular division is the keeper of the true word of God. Yet each and every single one of you stand in direct defiance of the word of God, and you are proud of it. I say these things with a breaking heart, not as one who would stand as a judge. I stand and speak a clear warning. Terrible things are about to happen—and it will begin with us because we, as the church, have been charged as the pillar and ground of truth itself. Church, God himself is about to judge us and cleanse his own house.

We need to look at ourselves from a completely different direction. It will be difficult for all of us; however, the spirit of God himself will reveal it to us and give us the strength to face what we see. We need to change ourselves—not the world. We have adopted so much of the worldly way that we have lost sight of our goal. We are to develop ourselves to the point that we can each individually reflect the very image of the risen son of God himself in our own lives in spite of our natural weaknesses. Then we will be as lights shining brightly in the darkness lighting the way for all to come who will hear the word of God. In the next chapter, we shall see the kind of mind God has given us to use and develop.

CHAPTER 8

This chapter of the book deals with the mind. The mind is an incredible thing. People wrongly assume that the mind and the brain are the same thing. The brain is an organ in our bodies that gathers, classifies, and sorts information. It also regulates the body. However, the mind is something totally different in that it doesn't limit itself to collecting, classifying, sorting, and regulating. The mind does things with the information around it the the brain as a physical organ is simply not designed to do. The mind takes information, makes comparisons, draws conclusions, and establishes links between things that may or may not be obviously connected. Any reference to the mind in this text is not to the brain. Please do not confuse this.

In order to grasp and understand Eternal Life, we must understand something about our own mind. The bible refers to the mind basically from three different and yet interrelated points. The scriptures refer to the center of intellect, the center of perception and understanding, and the actual thoughts themselves. Not knowing what is being discussed can cause tremendous confusion and strain in anyone. We are going to look at each one separately. When we put each part together, you will have a pleasant surprise waiting for you.

Romans 1

18. For the wrath of God is revealed from heaven against all ungodliness and unrighteousness of men, who hold the truth in unrighteousness;

19. Because that which may be known of God is manifest in them; for God hath shewed it unto them.
20. For the invisible things of him from the creation of the world are clearly seen, being understood by the things that are made, even his eternal power and Godhead; so that they are without excuse:
21. Because that, when they knew God, they glorified him not as God, neither were thankful; but became vain in their imaginations, and their foolish heart was darkened.
22. Professing themselves to be wise, they became fools,
23. And changed the glory of the uncorruptible God into an image made like to corruptible man, and to birds, and fourfooted beasts, and creeping things.
24. Wherefore God also gave them up to uncleanness through the lusts of their own hearts, to dishonour their own bodies between themselves:
25. Who changed the truth of God into a lie, and worshipped and served the creature more than the Creator, who is blessed for ever. Amen.
26. For this cause God gave them up unto vile affections: for even their women did change the natural use into that which is against nature:
27. And likewise also the men, leaving the natural use of the woman, burned in their lust one toward another; men with men working that which is unseemly, and receiving in themselves that recompence of their error which was meet.
28. And even as they did not like to retain God in their knowledge, God gave them over to a reprobate mind, to do those things which are not convenient;
29. Being filled with all unrighteousness, fornication, wickedness, covetousness, maliciousness; full of envy, murder, debate, deceit, malignity; whisperers,
30. Backbiters, haters of God, despiteful, proud, boasters, inventors of evil things, disobedient to parents,

> **31. Without understanding, covenantbreakers, without natural affection, implacable, unmerciful:**
> **32. Who knowing the judgment of God, that they which commit such things are worthy of death, not only do the same, but have pleasure in them that do them.**

Paul did not sugar coat anything in this passage. He was right to the point. The wrath of God is revealed against all ungodliness and unrighteousness of men—men who maintain unrighteousness is truth itself—because the things that may be known of God are manifest in them already. God himself has already revealed it to them. The things we can't see that have existed since the begining of creation can be clearly understood by the things we do see, providing we actually understand what we see. Mankind is therefore without any excuse at all.

When men knew God, they neither glorified him as God nor were thankful to him for anything. Their imaginations became empty, useless, wicked, idolatrous foolishness that darkened their hearts. They professed themselves to be wise and, in so doing, became fools.

They changed the glory of the God who cannot be corrupted ever into images of corruptible men, of birds, of four footed beasts, and of creeping things. God allowed them to be consumed by the uncleaness of their own hearts through their own lusts and desires to dishonor their own bodies between themselves.

Mankind changed the truth of God into a lie. Mankind worshipped and served the creature more than the Creator of all things, who himself is blessed for ever. Because mankind did these things, God allowed mankind to be consumed by vile and repulsive desires. Even the women changed the natural use of their bodies into things that are against natural use. Likewise, the men turned away from the natural use of women and were overcome by uncontrollable desire for one another, working things among themselves that are shameful and indecent. They call this action love, yet the love described in the previous chapter does not act this way at all—ever. As a result, they receive the payment of their error which is due for such actions.

Since they had no desire to retain God in their knowledge at all, God allowed them to develop a reprobate mind (intellect) that is incapable of making sound judgment at all. This allows them to justify doing things among themselves that are not fit to do. Such men are constantly filled with all unrighteousness, fornication, wickedness, covetousness, maliciousness; filled with envy, murder, debate, deceit, malignity; whisperers, backbiters, haters of God, despiteful, proud, boasters, inventors of evil things, disobedient to parents, without understanding, covenantbreakers, without natural affection, implacable, and unmerciful. People who do these things as a way of life know that the judgment of God is that those who do these things are worthy of death, yet they not only do these things anyway, but also they have pleasure in those who do the same things as well. They also encourage others to join them—truly a sign of an intellect that is totally incapable of making sound judgment.

Church, these are terrible things to consider, yet, I will show you something worse still. Many of you will say that homosexuals and lesbians get what they deserve from God. Many of you will say such people are abominations and unnatural. Many of you will say such people are mentally sick and detestable. You know what? You are absolutely right. Now, I show you a worse thing. This passage is a list of consistent behaviors that are ALL a sign of an intellect that is incapable of making sound judgment, yet many of you will either apply these behaviors to homosexuals and lesbians only, or simply ignore the rest of the list as not applying to any of you.

Either you do not realize or you do not care to realize that any of these behaviors practiced consistently is a sign of a defiled intellect. By behaving in this manner, you have openly declared yourself to be an iniquitous and adulterous generation. You must realize that our natural self is defiled in the very center of our intellect and if we are ever going to be able to judge rightly (be righteous), we must learn how to overcome and change the very nature of our own intellect first.

Romans 11

25. For I would not, brethren, that ye should be ignorant of this mystery, lest ye should be wise in your own conceits; that blindness in part is happened to Israel, until the fullness of the Gentiles be come in.
26. And so all Israel shall be saved: as it is written, There shall come out of Sion the Deliverer, and shall turn away ungodliness from Jacob:
27. For this is my covenant unto them, when I shall take away their sins.
28. As concerning the gospel, they are enemies for your sakes: but as touching the election, they are beloved for the fathers' sakes.
29. For the gifts and calling of God are without repentance.
30. For as ye in times past have not believed God, yet have now obtained mercy through their unbelief:
31. Even so have these also now not believed, that through your mercy they also may obtain mercy.
32. For God hath concluded them all in unbelief, that he might have mercy upon all.
33. O the depth of the riches both of the wisdom and knowledge of God! how unsearchable are his judgments, and his ways past finding out!
34. For who hath known the mind of the Lord? or who hath been his counseller?
35. Or who hath f irst given to him, and it shall be recompensed unto him again?
36. For of him, and through him, and to him, are all things: to whom be glory for ever. Amen.

Paul begins this passage declaring that he would not have the church to be ignorant of the great mystery God is working in their very presence. Otherwise their own conceits will cause them to think themselves wise. They will stop listening to God and develop their own foolish wisdom.

God has not disinherited the children of Israel at all. They have only been partially blinded so the gentiles themselves can receive the word of God and act on it until they develop themselves to the fullness of the stature of Christ himself.

Church listen to this: ALL Israel shall be saved. God made a covenant with Israel. Out of Sion shall come the deliverer and he shall turn away ungodliness from Jacob. God did not say he was going to make a new Israel and throw the old one away. Do not think for a minute that you are a new "spiritual" Israel and are entitled to all the promises God made to the children of Israel. Do not try to disinherit Israel from the promises of God. If you do, you are an abomination to God. Do not claim to be the glorious bride prepared for the King of Israel. Do not claim to be the very elect. If you do, you are piling abominations upon abominations.

Concerning the gospel of the death and resurrection of Christ, they are enemies for your sakes so you could receive the salvation of God. However, concerning the election of God, they are beloved for the fathers' sakes because of the covenants God made with their fathers. The gifts and callings are without repentance. He will not take away a gift nor will he abandon a calling.

Church, before the death and resurrection of Christ, you didn't know God, didn't care about God, and didn't believe God. It is only through the refusal of the children of Israel to accept the death and resurrection of Christ that you have even received God's mercy. It is through your mercy, not your offerings, not your sacrifice, that these same children of Israel will obtain God's mercy. God has concluded them all in unbelief so he can have mercy upon all.

Church, the depths and riches of the wisdom and the knowledge of God are absolutely staggering—they are completely beyond description. His judgments are completely unsearchable. His ways are past finding out. Yet in all this, the things we do know already reveal to us that there is more than we could ever know at once. We won't accept what we already do, or at least should, know.

Church, who among you has at any time known the intellect of God? Don't be shy. Step forward and reveal yourselves. Where are you? Which one of you has ever been his counsellor concerning anything at all? Which one of you has ever done anything for God at all that He should have to pay you for doing it? Surely among all these divisions among you there are quite a few that have contributed something to God that He would owe you special honor for. You are filled with great swelling words of pride. You are the most pleasing to God. Where are you? You wicked and adulterous generation of vipers.

You have perverted God's word. You seek the glory of men and not God. The only time any of you "have to give God the glory" is when you are showing false humility so men can praise you for being a true man or woman of God.

You have forgotten, or don't care to know, that of God, and through God, and to God, do all things exist. To God be the glory always and forever.

Romans 12

1. **I beseech you therefore, brethren, by the mercies of God, that ye present your bodies a living sacrifice, holy, acceptable unto God, which is your reasonable service.**
2. **And be not conformed to this world: but be ye transformed by the renewing of your mind, that ye may prove what is that good, and acceptable, and perfect, will of God.**

Church, I beg each one of you individually, by the mercies of God, that you present your bodies a living sacrifice, holy, acceptable unto God, which is your reasonable service. Do not allow yourselves to be conformed to the ways of this world. Instead be transformed by the renewing of your intellect that each of you yourselves may know what is that good, and acceptable, and perfect, will of God. Consider this, you would not have been told to renew your intellect if it were not possible for you to do it.

The power of God in you is the power you have and need to make this change. This is not an impossible task, but it does depend on you.

Romans 14

1. **Him that is weak in the faith receive ye, but not to doubtful disputations.**
2. **For one believeth that he may eat all things: another, who is weak, eateth herbs.**
3. **Let not him that eateth despise him that eateth not; and let not him which eateth not judge him that eateth: for God hath received him.**
4. **Who art thou that judgest another man's servant? to his own master he standeth or falleth. Yea, he shall be holden up: for God is able to make him stand.**
5. **One man esteemeth one day above another: another esteemeth every day alike. Let every man be fully persuaded in his own mind.**

Receive those among you that are weak in the faith, but not to argue with or to cause doubtful disputations with them. One believes he may eat all things. Another, who is weak because of incomplete understanding, will only eat herbs. Do not allow the one who eats all things despise the one who doesn't eat all things. Do not allow the one who doesn't eat all things judge the one who does eat all things. What special appointment does any one of you have to judge another man's servant? A servant stands or falls to his own master, not to you. The servant shall be held up. God himself is able to make him stand, not you.

One man gives honor to one day above another. Another man honors each and every day alike. Let each one of you be fully persuaded in the center of his own intellect. This is the same intellect that we are told to change by renewing it. We must be fully persuaded that the power God himself has given us will reveal to us that perfect recognition of the things around us in spite of our naturally flawed intellect. We must also be fully persuaded that with this power comes the necessary knowledge, wisdom, patience, and understanding in ourselves as needed to accomplish this. If we will not accept this, and be fully persuaded in the very center of our intellect, then our intellect remains defiled no matter how we try to represent it to others.

1 Corinthians 1

10. Now I beseech you, brethren, by the name of our Lord Jesus Christ, that ye all speak the same thing, and that there be no divisions among you; but that ye be perfectly joined together in the same mind and in the same judgment.

Brothers, Paul begged you by the name of our Lord Jesus Christ to all speak the same thing. He begged you to have no divisions of any kind among you for any reason at all—ever. Instead, Paul instructed you to be joined together in the very same intellect and in the very same judgment.

Church, you stand today as a living global monument to your own disobedience to God. There are over 50,000 different "divisions" among you that are officially recognized as respectable denominations. There are untold more that the 'respectable' among you call cults and sects. Your pride, hatreds, and jealousies run rampant among you for the whole world to witness. Yet there are those who go to your assemblies who understand what Paul said and they suffer and grieve for you. They don't dare speak out to you because you would cast them away and tell them to go find another church if they didn't like the one they were in.

Whether you do these things in ignorance or deliberately, you do them. Each group has its own creeds, doctrines, regulations, by-laws, traditions and such that are more important to you than the word of God itself. I do not grieve for you—I grieve for those under your instruction. In order for you to change what has been done over generations, you must become perfectly joined together in the very same intellect and in the very same judgment. To accomplish this, each and every one of you must be fully persuaded in the center of your own intellect.

1 Corinthians 2

9. But as it is written, Eye hath not seen, nor ear heard, neither have entered into the heart of man, the things which God hath prepared for them that love him.
10. But God hath revealed them unto us by his Spirit: for the Spirit searcheth all things, yea, the deep things of God.
11. For what man knoweth the things of a man, save the spirit of man which is in him? even so the things of God knoweth no man, but the Spirit of God.
12. Now we have received, not the spirit of the world, but the spirit which is of God; that we might know the things that are freely given to us of God.
13. Which things also we speak, not in the words which man's wisdom teacheth, but which the Holy Ghost teacheth; comparing spiritual things with spiritual.
14. But the natural man receiveth not the things of the Spirit of God: for they are foolishness unto him: neither can he know them, because they are spiritually discerned.
15. But he that is spiritual judgeth all things, yet he himself is judged of no man.
16. For who hath known the mind of the Lord, that he may instruct him? But we have the mind of Christ.

The scriptures tell us that there is no way for us to know or even imagine the things that God has prepared for those that love him. Yet the spirit of God himself has revealed those things to us because his spirit searches all things—even the deep things of God himself.

What man knoweth the things of a man save the spirit of man that is in him? Does that say that man has a spirit of his own, or does it say that man has a spirit in him? Do all men have a spirit in them? There are some that deny spirit exists at all. They only accept the things they can physically prove exist. They are living proof that man is not nor has ever been a spiritual creature in a physical body. But, what about this spirit that is in a man? The scriptures say that there are two categories of spirit. The spirit of this world—this physical arrangement—that tends it and preserves it—is one spirit or power. The spirit or power of God is the other. Man has neither, yet man can allow either one to enter him. One is that power that knows the things of man. Yet the only thing that knows things of God is the spirit of God himself.

We, as Christians, have not received the spirit of the world. Rather, we have received the spirit of God by which we may know the thingsGod himself has freely given us. When we speak of these things, we do not speak in words that man's wisdom teaches. Rather, we speak things that the holy spirit reveals and teaches to us. We compare spiritual things with spiritual things.

The natural man—both the one who denies the existence of spirit at all and the man who has another spirit in him—cannot receive the things of the spirit of God because to him they are foolishness. Neither can the natural man know these things because they are spiritually discerned only by the spirit of God himself.

He that is spiritual—he that has the spirit of God—judges all things by the revelation of the spirit of God in him, yet he himself is judged of no man. This is because through the operation of the spirit of God in us, we have the intellect of Jesus Christ himself. Not we will have it when we are more perfect; rather we have the intellect of Jesus Christ himself right now—this very second. It's time to start using what we have been given instead of relying on what we have always had before.

The only way we can be perfectly joined together in one intellect and in one judgment is through sharing the intellect of Jesus Christ with one another. As long as we have divisions among us, we are not doing what God expects us to do. We are rather deceiving ourselves and others about what God has given us.

Ephesians 4

17. This I say therefore, and testify in the Lord, that ye henceforth walk not as other Gentiles walk, in the vanity of their mind,

18. Having the understanding darkened, being alienated from the life of God through the ignorance that is in them, because of the blindness of their heart:
19. Who being past feeling have given themselves over unto lasciviousness, to work all uncleanness with greediness.
20. But ye have not so learned Christ;
21. If so be that ye have heard him, and have been taught by him, as the truth is in Jesus:
22. That ye put off concerning the former conversation the old man, which is corrupt according to the deceitful lusts;
23. And be renewed in the spirit of your mind;
24. And that ye put on the new man, which after God is created in righteousness and true holiness.
25. Wherefore putting away lying, speak every man truth with his neighbour: for we are members one of another.
26. Be ye angry, and sin not: let not the sun go down upon your wrath:
27. Neither give place to the devil.
28. Let him that stole steal no more: but rather let him labour, working with his hands the thing which is good, that he may have to give to him that needeth.
29. Let no corrupt communication proceed out of your mouth, but that which is good to the use of edifying, that it may minister grace unto the hearers.
30. And grieve not the holy Spirit of God, whereby ye are sealed unto the day of redemption.
31. Let all bitterness, and wrath, and anger, and clamour, and evil speaking, be put away from you, with all malice:
32. And be ye kind one to another, tenderhearted, forgiving one another, even as God for Christ's sake hath forgiven you.

Church, do not walk as the gentiles walk in the vanity of their own intellect. Their understanding has been darkened and they are completely alienated from the Eternal Life of God through their own ignorance because they have been blinded by their own hearts. They are past feeling and given themselves over to uncontrollable desires in order to work all forms of uncleanness with all greediness.

Church, you have not learned to act that way from Christ, that is if you have truly heard his words, and have been taught by his words, as the truth is in Jesus himself. Turn completely away from the conduct of your old nature which is corrupt according to your own deceitful desires. Allow the spirit of God to guide your intellect instead of the spirit of this world with its insatiable desires and uncontrollable greediness.

Instead of your old nature, embrace the new nature you have been given which, after the likeness of God is created in righteousness and true holiness. Quit lying. Instead, speak truth each one of you to your neighbor. Do not; however, use this as a pretext to hurt one another. We are each members in particular of the very same body of Christ. As such, we are also members one of another.

If you become angry for any reason, do not use this as an occasion to justify sin. Do not let the sun go down on the anger you harbor. Neither give place to the devil in this matter. Do not even consider retribution or progressively destructive retaliation at all. These are ungodly things and you dishonor yourself and the mercy God himself has already shown you.

If, in the past, you have stolen as a way of living, stop stealing altogether. Instead, work for a living and be productive. That way you will have enough to give to others who may be in need from time to time. Remember, a gift is freely given. Any expectations attached to a gift makes it a contract for service, not a gift. Be careful what you give and how you give it. That is entirely your responsibility.

Think very carefully about what you say to others. Do not utter any form of corrupt communication at all. Instead, see that the things you utter build, strengthen, and encourage others, or be silent. That way the things you utter from your own mouth may minister grace to those who hear you. Pay attention. This isn't just ugly or dirty words here. Corrupt communication is any form of communication that does not build, strengthen, or encourage the hearer period.

Church, you were sealed by the very spirit of God himself that will instruct you until the day of redemption itself when the possession purchased by the life-blood of Jesus Christ himself will be restored to the perfect condition that Adam himself was before he sinned. Do not do anything to grieve that spirit. Don't think for a minute that you can combine the "best of both worlds" or that you can have a better idea.

Each one of you personally turn completely away from all bitterness, wrath, anger, clamor, evil speaking, and all malice. Instead, be kind one to another, tenderhearted, forgive one another, even as God for the sake of his only begotten son, Jesus Christ, has already forgiven you.

Church, this is that straight gate that you enter in and the narrow way you travel to have Eternal Life. This is how you remove the log from your eye in order to see how to help your brother remove the speck you see in his eye. This is a hard thing for any of us to do. That's why we are sealed with the holy spirit of God unto the very day of redemption itself.

I am not saying these things to judge you. I am merely revealing these things to you for you to see what I have learned about myself. These words come from my heart to you, inspired by the spirit of God that is in me. In order for each of you to accomplish this, you must be fully persuaded in the very center of your own intellect. It is a battle well worth fighting, because the end is Eternal Life itself.

Colossians 2

8. **Beware lest any man spoil you through philosophy and vain deceit, after the tradition of men, after the rudiments of the world, and not after Christ.**
9. **For in him dwelleth all the fullness of the Godhead bodily.**
10. **And ye are complete in him, which is the head of all principality and power:**
11. **In whom also ye are circumcised with the circumcision made without hands, in putting off the body of the sins of the flesh by the circumcision of Christ:**

12. Buried with him in baptism, wherein also ye are risen with him through the faith of the operation of God, who hath raised him from the dead.
13. And you, being dead in your sins and the uncircumcision of your flesh, hath he quickened together with him, having forgiven you all trespasses;
14. Blotting out the handwriting of ordinances that was against us, which was contrary to us, and took it out of the way, nailing it to his cross;
15. And having spoiled principalities and powers, he made a shew of them openly, triumphing over them in it.
16. Let no man therefore judge you in meat, or in drink, or in respect of an holyday, or of the new moon, or of the sabbath days:
17. Which are a shadow of things to come; but the body is of Christ.
18. Let no man beguile you of your reward in a voluntary humility and worshipping of angels, intruding into those things which he hath not seen, vainly puffed up by his fleshly mind,
19. And not holding the Head, from which all the body by joints and bands having nourishment ministered, and knit together, increaseth with the increase of God.
20. Wherefore if ye be dead with Christ from the rudiments of the world, why, as though living in the world, are ye subject to ordinances,
21. (Touch not; taste not; handle not;
22. Which all are to perish with the using;) after the commandments and doctrines of men?
23. Which things have indeed a shew of wisdom in will worship, and humility, and neglecting of the body; not in any honour to the satisfying of the flesh.

Church, beware to keep any man from spoiling you through philosophy and vain deceit, after the traditions of men, or after the principles of the world, and not after the words of Christ. In Christ dwells the fulness of the Godhead bodily. You are, not someday will be—already are—, complete in Christ whom God himself has chosen as the head of all principalities and power.

You are also circumcised in Christ with the circumcision made without hands, in putting away the body of the sins of the flesh by the circumcision of Christ himself. You were buried with Christ in baptism. You are risen with Christ through the faith of the operation of God himself, who raised Christ from the dead.

And you, being dead in your own sins and in the uncircumcision of your own flesh, has God himself quickened with Christ, having forgiven you all trespasses. He blotted out the handwriting of the law that was against us, which was contrary to us because we could not obey it, and took it completely out of the way, nailing it to the cross of Christ. God spoiled principalities and powers, openly showing them for what they were, triumphing over them in it by raising Christ from the dead.

Since this is the case, let no man judge you by what foods you eat or don't eat, or by what you drink or don't drink, or in respect to any holyday, or of the new moon, or to sabbaths. These things are merely a shadow of what is yet to come, but the body is of Christ.

Let no man trick you out of your reward in a voluntary humility and worshipping of angels. He is intruding into things he has not seen. He is puffed up by the vanity of his own intellect. He is not holding Christ as the head, from which all the body by joints and bands having nourishment ministered, and knit together, increases with the increase of God.

Now, if you be dead with Christ from the principles of this world, why do you subject yourself to laws, such as touch, taste, or handle not, which cause death to those who use them. These laws are the doctrines and commandments of men. These things do have an outward show of wisdom in will worship, and humility, and neglecting the body, and in not giving honor to the satisfying of fleshly desires. These things show a form of righteousness before others, yet doing these things is contrary to what God wants us to do.

By setting up laws to be righteous before other men and before God, you are openly declaring the that death and resurrection of Christ have absolutely no meaning whatsoever. His righteousness was not good enough for your salvation, so you have to obey laws to make yourself righteousness. Such practices are an abomination to God and men as well. Men see the hypocrisy and don't want any part of it.

Such things are the result of a defiled intellect just like the intellect Paul revealed in Romans 1:18-32. We cannot allow ourselves to be robbed of the mercy God has given us.

2 Thessalonians 2

1. **Now we beseech you, brethren, by the coming of our Lord Jesus Christ, and by our gathering together unto him,**
2. **That ye be not soon shaken in mind, or be troubled, neither by spirit, nor by word, nor by letter as from us, as that the day of Christ is at hand.**
3. **Let no man deceive you by any means: for that day shall not come, except there come a falling away first, and that man of sin be revealed, the son of perdition;**
4. **Who opposeth and exalteth himself above all that is called God, or that is worshipped; so that he as God sitteth in the temple of God, shewing himself that he is God.**

Church, we beg you by the coming of Jesus Christ himself and by our gathering together unto him, that each one of you not soon be shaken in the center of your intellect. Neither be troubled by spirit (power), nor by word spoken as though it were the very oracle of God himself, nor by letter of instruction, that the day of Christ is near at hand. Do not be deceived by any means.

There are several steps involved that lead to the day of Christ. First, there has to be a falling away in the church itself. This doesn't mean false teachings. This means a complete turning away from the truth. This event has not happened yet and can not happen so long as anyone in the body has the love of the truth in his heart. That love will overcome any obstacle and inspire those who have it to continually search the word of God for the truth that is there, regardless of what is being taught in any church. Until those people are gone completely, the church can not turn completely from the truth.

Once the church has turned completely away from the truth, the man of sin—the very son of destruction itself—can be revealed. However, so long as even one person exists who has the love of the truth in his heart, this man of sin cannot be revealed because he would be immediately exposed for exactly what he is—the very son of destruction himself. This man's greatest weapon is deceit and he can not afford to be exposed before he has assumed all power.

He will oppose and magnify himself above everything that is called God. He will himself sit in the temple of God and declare himself to be God almighty in the flesh. The church that has turned completely from the truth will declare him to be so. It will worship him and forcefully cause others to worship him as God also.

There are other events that must occur as well—very terrible things—before the day of Christ can occur. I will touch on some of these things in a later chapter. Just for now, remember to not be shaken in the center of your intellect by any means. You must be totally persuaded in the center of your own intellect.

Titus 1

15. Unto the pure all things are pure: but unto them that are defiled and unbelieving is nothing pure; but even their mind and conscience is defiled.
16. They profess that they know God; but in works they deny him, being abominable, and disobedient, and unto every good work reprobate.

Christ said that the pure in heart shall see God. Paul said that to the pure, all things are pure. Paul said that to the defiled and unbelieving is nothing pure. They shall not see God because even their intellect and conscience is defiled. They claim to know God, yet the things they do themselves deny the very God they claim to know and worship. They are an abomination. They are disobedient and incapable of good work. Church, these people are all around you in your congregations. Mark those that are this way and get away from them. Their words and actions will grieve the spirit in you, and may even lead some of you away from the truth. Do not be deceived.

The next function of the mind that the scriptures describe is the function of perception. It is with this function we define and reason in the center of our intellect.

2 Corinthians 3

12. Seeing then that we have such hope, we use great plainness of speech:
13. And not as Moses, which put a vail over his face, that the children of Israel could not stedfastly look to the end of that which is abolished:
14. But their minds were blinded: for until this day remaineth the same vail untaken away in the reading of the old testament; which vail is done away in Christ.
15. But even unto this day, when Moses is read, the vail is upon their heart.
16. Nevertheless when it shall turn to the Lord, the vail shall be taken away.

Paul is comparing the words he spoke to the words Moses spoke to the people. Paul said they used great plainness of speech. When Moses read the law to the children of Israel, he had to put a vail over his face because he shone with a radiance the people could not look at. Because of this, the children of Israel could not steadfastly look at the completion of the law which was fulfilled in the death and resurrection of Christ himself.

They were blinded in their perception and understanding of the purpose of the law. Even today, the same vail remains untaken away in reading the old testament. This is the vail that is done away with in

Christ. Even now, whenever Moses is read, the same vail is upon their heart. Nevertheless, when the children of Israel shall turn to the Lord, the vail shall be taken away and their understanding shall be fuller.

This vail is caused by legalistic definitions without understanding the intent and purpose of the law itself. Once the Children of Israel realize that all the law is fulfilled in the death and resurrection of Christ, they will have a very rich understanding of the word of God.

2 Corinthians 4

1. **Therefore seeing we have this ministry, as we have received mercy, we faint not;**
2. **But have renounced the hidden things of dishonesty, not walking in craftiness, nor handling the word of God deceitfully; but by manifestation of the truth commending ourselves to every man's conscience in the sight of God.**
3. **But if our gospel be hid, it is hid to them that are lost:**
4. **In whom the god of this world hath blinded the minds of them which believe not, lest the light of the glorious gospel of Christ, who is the image of God, should shine unto them.**

Since we have this ministry because we have received mercy, we remain strong and do not grow weary of well doing. Instead, we have renounced the hidden things of dishonesty with its subtilties. We walk not in craftiness, nor do we deceitfully handle the word of God, if indeed we have received and accepted the word of God for what it is—truth itself. We clearly demonstrate the truth commending ourselves to every man's conscience in the sight of God. We are to become an open book for anyone and everyone to read and understand.

If our gospel is hidden, it is hidden only to those that are lost, in whom the god of this world has blinded the perceptions and reasonings of those who do not believe the truth. He has done this to keep the light of the glorious gospel of Christ, himself the perfect human representation of God for everyone to see, from shining unto them and they themselves then want to be like him.

1 Corinthians 1

20. Where is the wise? where is the scribe? where is the disputer of this world? hath not God made foolish the wisdom of this world?
21. For after that in the wisdom of God the world by wisdom knew not God, it pleased God by the foolishness of preaching to save them that believe.
22. For the Jews require a sign, and the Greeks seek after wisdom:
23. But we preach Christ crucified, unto the Jews a stumblingblock, and unto the Greeks foolishness;
24. But unto them which are called, both Jews and Greeks, Christ the power of God, and the wisdom of God.

Where is the wise man among you? Where is the writer among you? Where is the great debater among you? Hasn't God himself reduced the wisdom of this world to utter foolishness? God's wisdom is this: since the world by wisdom did not know God, it has pleased God by the utter foolishness of something so simple as preaching to save the ones who themselves believe the truth when they hear it.

The Jews require a sign to believe what is said. The Greeks seek after deep wisdom and great mysteries. Instead, we preach the death and resurrection of Christ.

The Jews stumble over this looking for a specific sign. To the Greeks, resurrection from the dead is complete foolishness.

However to those who are called of God, both Jews and Greeks, Christ's death and resurrection is both the power and the wisdom of God.

2 Corinthians 11

> 3. But I fear, lest by any means, as the serpent beguiled Eve through his subtilty, so your minds should be corrupted from the simplicity that is in Christ.
> 4. For if he that cometh preacheth another Jesus, whom we have not preached, or if ye receive another spirit, which ye have not received, or another gospel, which ye have not accepted, ye might well bear with him.

Paul's concern for the church of Corinth was that due to the divisions they already had, their perceptions and reasonings might be corrupted by the subtilely of others. This is still a great concern today, church, with all your divisions. Anyone could come in and preach another Jesus from the one the scriptures reveal. Another spirit which you have not received could just as easily enter in. Another gospel could be preached that you haven't received. With your divisions, it would be hard to spot, especially if it was well crafted. With the confusion already prevalent, not only would you tolerate such things, but also, you could be carried away by these very things.

Since the functions of reasoning and perception interact with the intellect, one can and does corrupt the other. To be fully persuaded in your own intellect, you must make sure that your reasonings and perceptions are sound and are not removed from the simplicity that is in Christ.

Titus 1

> 15. Unto the pure all things are pure: but unto them that are defiled and unbelieving is nothing pure; but even their mind and conscience is defiled.
> 16. They profess that they know God; but in works they deny him, being abominable, and disobedient, and unto every good work reprobate.

Jesus said that the pure in heart shall see God. Paul said that to the pure all things are pure—even their hearts—they shall see God! However, to the defiled and unbelieving is nothing pure—not even their hearts. Their perceptions and reasonings and even their conscience is defiled. Church, Paul was writing to a pastor about the condition of his congregation. He was instructing Titus to set things in order.

With all the divisions among the body today, we have the same problems that must be set in order. There are those among us who would give us laws for righteousness as if the death and resurrection of Christ had no meaning at all. There are those among us who explain away the scriptures as being part of philosophies that existed before the children of Israel. These people are being tolerated and followed as great men of God with a vision to help us be better people.

There are those among you who openly declare that they know God personally, yet their works are an abomination to God. They are disobedient and totally incapable of doing good works. The more you tolerate these things, the more corrupt you will become. It's time to return to the simplicity that is in Christ before your hearts are seared beyond the point of repentance.

The next function of the mind the scriptures deal with are your actual thoughts themselves. Thoughts are produced by the interaction of the perceptions and reasonings with the intellect. Thoughts can also be produced by outside influences that bypass the perceptions and intellect altogether. There are a great many motivational books, marketing books, self-help books, and such like that deal heavily with bypassing the thinking process or with limiting the thinking process. Sometimes thoughts just randomly occur in our mind. The scriptures deal with the thinking process and how to recognise anything that disrupts it.

Romans 8

> **3. For what the law could not do, in that it was weak through the flesh, God sending his own Son in the likeness of sinful flesh, and for sin, condemned sin in the flesh:**

> 4. That the righteousness of the law might be fulfilled in us, who walk not after the flesh, but after the Spirit.
> 5. For they that are after the flesh do mind the things of the flesh; but they that are after the Spirit the things of the Spirit.
> 6. For to be carnally minded is death; but to be spiritually minded is life and peace.
> 7. Because the carnal mind is enmity against God: for it is not subject to the law of God, neither indeed can be.
> 8. So then they that are in the flesh cannot please God.

Church, listen carefully. Even though the law defined righteousness, it was weak because the selfish nature of man could not and would not obey it. God sent his only begotten son in the likeness of sinful flesh itself. Even though Christ himself was flesh—he was perfect flesh—just as Adam himself was perfect before he sinned and became imperfect and selfish. Christ was subject to the same temptations and desires as all of us are, yet never once did he yield to any one of them. He maintained himself as perfect flesh. He died for the sin of men, and in so doing, made it possible for God himself to condemn sin in the flesh.

It is not hopeless. It is possible for those of us who are of the body of Christ to fulfill the righteousness of the law as long as we do not follow our own selfish nature, but, instead, follow the inspiration of the spirit God gives us when we accept the death and resurrection of Christ himself.

Those that are after the flesh think about satisfying selfish desires. Those who are after the spirit think about fulfilling the things the spirit of God inspires in them. To think carnally to the satisfying of selfish desires results in death. Thinking spiritually brings Eternal Life and peace. The carnally selfish thoughts are enmity against God. Such thoughts are not subject to the law of God, nor can they ever be. Therefore, those that are in the flesh with their thoughts cannot please God.

Church, this was written to you. It is instruction. There are those who walk among you who are still carnal in their thoughts. Whether it is because they have not been fully instructed or whether they would rather be that way by choice does not matter. They are still carnal. It is up to each one of us to recognise these things and to correct them in ourselves.

Romans 8

> 26. Likewise the Spirit also helpeth our infirmities: for we know not what we should pray for as we ought: but the Spirit itself maketh intercession for us with groanings which cannot be uttered.
> 27. And he that searcheth the hearts knoweth what is the mind of the Spirit, because he maketh intercession for the saints according to the will of God.
> 28. And we know that all things work together for good to them that love God, to them who are the called according to his purpose.
> 29. For whom he did foreknow, he also did predestinate to be conformed to the image of his Son, that he might be the firstborn among many brethren.
> 30. Moreover whom he did predestinate, them he also called: and whom he called, them he also justified: and whom he justified, them he also glorified.

The spirit in us also helps us with our weaknesses. We don't always know what we should pray for or even how to pray for what we need. The power in us makes intercession to God for us with groanings that we can't even utter. God knows the thoughts the spirit reveals to him and the same spirit reveals the thoughts of God to us. This is God's way of communicating directly with each one of us.

We know that all things work together for good to them that love God, those who are called according to his purpose. Those God foreknew, he predestinated to be conformed to the image of his only begotten son, that his son might be the firstborn among many brethren. Those God predestinated to be conformed to the image of his son,

God called. Those God called, he justified. Those God justified, he also glorified.

Church these things described are in the past. They are already completed works of God. These are not promises to be fulfilled one day when we are righteous enough, good enough, or obedient enough.

These things were completed by God when we accepted the death and resurrection of Christ.

The only thing for each of us to do is accept these things and use the power God has given us to change our thoughts, reasonings and perceptions, and our intellect to become a new man created in righteousness by God himself. Will we ever be perfect? Not as long as we live on this earth. We are still flawed by nature and can never be perfect. We must accept that as well. However, the power of God can perfect us from within so that each one of us can reflect the image of the risen son of God in our lives in spite of our imperfections.

Romans 12

16. **Be of the same mind one toward another. Mind not high things, but condescend to men of low estate. Be not wise in your own conceits.**
17. **Recompense to no man evil for evil. Provide things honest in the sight of all men.**
18. **If it be possible, as much as lieth in you, live peaceably with all men.**
19. **Dearly beloved, avenge not yourselves, but rather give place unto wrath: for it is written, Vengeance is mine; I will repay, saith the Lord.**
20. **Therefore if thine enemy hunger, feed him; if he thirst, give him drink: for in so doing thou shalt heap coals of fire on his head.**
21. **Be not overcome of evil, but overcome evil with good.**

Church, since each of us are members one of another, think the same things one toward another. Do not think about high and vain things.

Instead condescend to men of low estate. Do not allow your own conceits to make you think you are wiser than others. Do not repay evil for evil. Do all things honest in the sight of all men. As much as you possible can, live peaceably with all men.

Do not seek personal revenge for wrongs done to you. Instead, get rid of the anger and wrath in you for these things. It is written, Vengeance is mine: I will repay, saith the Lord. If your enemy is hungry, feed him. If he is thirsty, give him something to drink. By doing these things you shall heap coals of fire on his head. Do not allow evil an occasion to overcome you, rather overcome evil with good.

2 Corinthians 10

3. For though we walk in the flesh, we do not war after the flesh:
4. (For the weapons of our warfare are not carnal, but mighty through God to the pulling down of strong holds;)
5. Casting down imaginations, and every high thing that exalteth itself against the knowledge of God, and bringing into captivity every thought to the obedience of Christ;
6. And having in a readiness to revenge all disobedience, when your obedience is fulfilled.

Even though we live in this world and walk after the flesh, we do not war after the manner of the flesh. Our weapons of warfare are not fleshly weapons, rather they are mighty through God to the pulling down of strongholds. These weapons cast down vain imaginations, and every high thing that exalts itself against the knowledge of God. These weapons allow us to bring into captivity every thought to the obedience of Christ. Notice this says the obedience of Christ and not to Christ. We are to have the same obedience to God that Christ himself had—even to death—if it is required. We can be ready to revenge all disobedience only when our own obedience is fulfilled and no sooner.

2 Corinthians 13

10. Therefore I write these things being absent, lest being present I should use sharpness, according to the power which the Lord hath given me to edification, and not to destruction.
11. Finally, brethren, farewell. Be perfect, be of good comfort, be of one mind, live in peace; and the God of love and peace shall be with you.

Church, Paul wrote these things in a letter because he was somewhere else when he heard of the problems developing in the congregations. Had he been present, he would have been much sharper towards them but only to build and strengthen them and not to destroy them. The same thing applies today. The spirit in us reacts sharply toward selfishness and selfishness reacts sharply toward spiritual thoughts because they are totally contrary to one another.

Worldly sharpness seeks to destroy anything but its own. Spiritual sharpness is tempered with the grace and mercy of God himself. It seeks rather to build, strengthen, and comfort its hearers. Be perfect in that you are perfecting yourselves from within. Will you ever be totally without flaw? No, but each of you can recognise your own faults and overcome them with the power of God that is in you. Be of good comfort—know that God is working in you both to will and do of his good pleasure. Be unified in your thoughts. Live in peace, and the God of love and peace shall be with you.

Galatians 5

1. Stand fast therefore in the liberty wherewith Christ hath made us free, and be not entangled again with the yoke of bondage.
2. Behold, I Paul say unto you, that if ye be circumcised, Christ shall profit you nothing.

3. For I testify again to every man that is circumcised, that he is a debtor to do the whole law.
4. Christ is become of no effect unto you, whosoever of you are justified by the law; ye are fallen from grace.
5. For we through the Spirit wait for the hope of righteousness by faith.
6. For in Jesus Christ neither circumcision availeth any thing, nor uncircumcision; but faith which worketh by love.
7. Ye did run well; who did hinder you that ye should not obey the truth?
8. This persuasion cometh not of him that calleth you.
9. A little leaven leaveneth the whole lump.
10. I have confidence in you through the Lord, that ye will be none otherwise minded: but he that troubleth you shall bear his judgment, whosoever he be.

Church, stand fast and immovable in the liberty wherewith the death and resurrection has made us free from any law unto righteousness. Do not at any time allow yourself to again be put under the bondage of any law unto righteousness for any reason whatsoever. If you agree to to keep any part of the law unto righteousness, then the death and resurrection of Christ is of no benefit to you at all.

Anyone who agrees to keep any part of the law unto righteousness agrees to keep every single part of that law. Christ's death and resurrection have absolutely no meaning for you at all because you seek to be justified before God by keeping his law. You are then under the whole law to do it and not under the grace of God. We through the spirit in us wait for the hope of righteousness by the working of faith and not by the works of the law.

In Christ Jesus neither agreeing to keep the law is good for us, nor not agreeing to keep the law is good for us. What is good for us is faith which works by the love that God himself has given us. Church, you started out well. Who have you allowed among you that you can not and will not accept the truth that is in the death and resurrection of

Jesus Christ? Who has taught you that Christ died for all your sins up to the point you accepted him, but after that you must obey the law to be righteous before God? Beware, such thoughts do not come from God who called you in the first place.

A little leaven will leaven the whole lump. You will become self righteous, judgmental, jealous of others, despiteful, boasters, implacable, without natural affection, unmerciful, and worse if you replace the death and resurrection of Jesus Christ with any other doctrine. There is an assurance in Christ that, once you understand what God accomplished by the death and resurrection of his only begotten son, none of you would ever think any other way at all. Remember this, whoever troubles you about this will bear his own judgment because he is rebelling against God himself.

Philippians 2

1. If there be therefore any consolation in Christ, if any comfort of love, if any fellowship of the Spirit, if any bowels and mercies,
2. Fulfil ye my joy, that ye be likeminded, having the same love, being of one accord, of one mind.
3. Let nothing be done through strife or vainglory; but in lowliness of mind let each esteem other better than themselves.
4. Look not every man on his own things, but every man also on the things of others.
5. Let this mind be in you, which was also in Christ Jesus:
6. Who, being in the form of God, thought it not robbery to be equal with God:
7. But made himself of no reputation, and took upon him the form of a servant, and was made in the likeness of men:
8. And being found in fashion as a man, he humbled himself, and became obedient unto death, even the death of the cross.
9. Wherefore God also hath highly exalted him, and given him a name which is above every name:

> 10. That at the name of Jesus every knee should bow, of things in heaven, and things in earth, and things under the earth;
> 11. And that every tongue should confess that Jesus Christ is Lord, to the glory of God the Father.
> 12. Wherefore, my beloved, as ye have always obeyed, not as in my presence only, but now much more in my absence, work out your own salvation with fear and trembling.
> 13. For it is God which worketh in you both to will and to do of his good pleasure.
> 14. Do all things without murmurings and disputings:
> 15. That ye may be blameless and harmless, the sons of God, without rebuke, in the midst of a crooked and perverse nation, among whom ye shine as lights in the world;
> 16. Holding forth the word of life; that I may rejoice in the day of Christ, that I have not run in vain, neither laboured in vain.

Church, if there be any consolation in Christ, any comfort of the love God has given us, any fellowship of the spirit in us, any bowels and mercies in us at all, fulfil my joy, that you share the same thoughts, that you have the same love one toward another, being in complete agreement, having one overall thought toward accomplishing the goal set before each one of us.

Do not do anything through strife or through commotions. Do not seek glory among yourselves or great reputations. In true humility of thought, let each one of you honor others above the honor you give yourself or expect others to give to you. Do not look only at your own accomplishments, but each one of you look also at the accomplishments of others as well. You are each part of one body that has only one head—Jesus Christ himself.

Allow this thought to be in you which was also in Christ Jesus himself: who, being the perfect physical image of God, did not think it robbery to be equal with God in judgment and authority. Instead of lording his authority over others, he sought no reputation at all among men. He became a servant to those he taught. He was physically a man, and being so, he humbled himself and was obedient to God completely—even to death on the cross.

As a result, God has given him the very highest of honors and has given him a name that is above every name. At the name of Jesus every knee should bow, whether in heaven, on the earth, or under the earth. Also every tongue should confess that Jesus Christ is lord, to the glory of God himself, the father of Jesus Christ.

It is up to each one of us to work out our own salvation with fear and trembling, but how can we do that? We can't do this by setting up laws, ordinances, rules of behavior, codes of conduct, or such things. We, through the power God himself has given us, are to allow the thoughts Christ has to become our thoughts. We are to allow the reasonings Christ has to become our reasonings. We are to allow the intellect Christ has to become our intellect.

It is God that works in each one of us through the power he has given us both to will and do his good pleasure. It is his good pleasure that we conform ourselves to the image of his only begotten son so Christ can be the firstborn among many brethren.

Since this is the case, do all things without murmurings and disputings among yourselves. That way, you may be blameless and harmless, sons of God without rebuke, in the midst of a crooked and perverse nation. You will shine among them as lights in the world as you hold forth the word of Eternal Life itself. Then the dedication and efforts of men like Paul, Peter, James, John, and others that have come before us will not be reduced to utter meaninglessness.

Philippians 3

13. Brethren, I count not myself to have apprehended: but this one thing I do, forgetting those things which are behind, and reaching forth unto those things which are before,

14. I press toward the mark for the prize of the high calling of God in Christ Jesus.
15. Let us therefore, as many as be perfect, be thus minded: and if in any thing ye be otherwise minded, God shall reveal even this unto you.
16. Nevertheless, whereto we have already attained, let us walk by the same rule, let us mind the same thing.
17. Brethren, be followers together of me, and mark them which walk so as ye have us for an ensample.
18. (For many walk, of whom I have told you often, and now tell you even weeping, that they are the enemies of the cross of Christ:
19. Whose end is destruction, whose God is their belly, and whose glory is in their shame, who mind earthly things.)
20. For our conversation is in heaven; from whence also we look for the Saviour, the Lord Jesus Christ:
21. Who shall change our vile body, that it may be fashioned like unto his glorious body, according to the working whereby he is able even to subdue all things unto himself.

Church, Paul did not consider himself to have achieved perfection, but rather have accomplished things that were part of a growing process. He did not glory in his past accomplishments, nor did he wallow in the misery of his past failures. Instead he continually looked forward to the things that were ahead that would help him reach the goal set before him by the high calling of God in Christ Jesus. Church, every calling of God is a high calling in Christ Jesus because God wants each one of us to conform ourselves to the image of Christ himself regardless of how we serve one another.

Let any of us who would be perfect, not as without any flaws, but rather as perfected, think the same way. If you think any other way, God will reveal it to you. Concerning the things we have already accomplished, let us follow the same rule and think the same thing.

Paul wanted us to follow his example and note those who were following his example. He did this because many were claiming to follow, but were actually enemies of the cross of Christ. These people are headed for destruction. Their God is their belly. They are self serving and self gratifying. They glory in their shame and they think continually about earthly things.

Our residence is in heaven, from where we look for the savior, Jesus Christ himself. He shall change our vile body so it can be fashioned to be like his glorious body, according to the working of the power whereby he is able to subdue all things to himself.

Church, this concludes the mind. The mind is an amazing thing. Its overlapping functions make each one of us individually who we are. These functions work in us whether we believe in God or not. This is a process that separates us from animals altogether.

Now for the surprise I promised. The bible talks a great deal about the mind all through it. However, the scriptures call it by another term. These overlapping functions together make what the scriptures refer to over and over as the heart. From Genesis to Revelations, the scriptures speak of the heart—its thoughts, desires, intentions—its joy, its love, etc.—with a depth and richness that you should read and appreciate in its fulness. By doing so, you will come to a far greater understanding and assurance as you continue to grow more fully into the image of Christ himself.

CHAPTER 9

Church, after having defined and explained Eternal Life, the love of God, and the mind, this book is going to turn darker. There are things that are yet to happen that are tremendously powerful—terrible things to be sure—but powerful things nevertheless. Before going into these things, I will call to your remembrance some of the things we have already discussed. If this seems foolish to you, please bear with my folly.

2 Corinthians 3

1. **Do we begin again to commend ourselves? or need we, as some others, epistles of commendation to you, or letters of commendation from you?**
2. **Ye are our epistle written in our hearts, known and read of all men:**
3. **Forasmuch as ye are manifestly declared to be the epistle of Christ ministered by us, written not with ink, but with the Spirit of the living God; not in tables of stone, but in fleshy tables of the heart.**

Church, do you think this book is an effort to show you how great we are? Do we need letters of recommendation written to you from others to listen to what we say? Do we need letters of recommendation from you so others will listen to what we say? Those of you who have the love of the truth are our letters written in our hearts known and read of all men.

Those who have the love of the truth in your hearts by your nature are manifestly declared to be the epistle of Christ ministered by us.

This epistle is not written in ink. It is instead written by the spirit of the living God, not engraved in stone tables, but in the fleshly tables of your own heart. Remember when I discussed the mind I told you that all three of the functions of the mind working together is referred to by the scriptures as the heart? Your heart makes you what you are.

Church, Jesus himself said that man is not defiled by what enters his mouth because those things pass through the body and what is not used is passed out as waste. However, man is defiled by the things that come out from his mouth because out of the mouth flow the issues of the heart. Proverbs states that as he thinks in his heart, so is he. It is crucial that you understand the functions of your mind and bring each function under control to the obedience of Christ himself.

2 Corinthians 5

17. Therefore if any man be in Christ, he is a new creature: old things are passed away; behold, all things are become new.

Church, if any man truly is in Christ, he is a new creature. Literally he is a totally new creation that is growing and learning to reflect the very image of Christ himself. Old things and ways of thinking are passed away. Mortify them. Treat them as though they were dead. They have no place in the new man you are. This is a constant battle in the mind of each of you. With the power of God that is in you, you can accomplish this goal.

Colossians 1

12. Giving thanks unto the Father, which hath made us meet to be partakers of the inheritance of the saints in light:
13. Who hath delivered us from the power of darkness, and hath translated us into the kingdom of his dear Son:

> **14. In whom we have redemption through his blood, even the forgiveness of sins:**
> **15. Who is the image of the invisible God, the firstborn of every creature:**

We should give thanks to the Father, who himself made it fitting for us to be equal sharers of the inheritance of the saints in light. He has delivered us from the power of darkness and has moved us into the kingdom of his dear son. We have redemption through the blood of the son of God, even the forgiveness of sins. Jesus is the image—the physical representation of the invisible God. He is the firstborn of literally every creation. Notice that these things are written from the standpoint that God himself has already done these things. He doesn't withhold these things until we are righteous enough, nor does he take them away if we are not righteous enough.

1 Timothy 3

> **15. But if I tarry long, that thou mayest know how thou oughtest to behave thyself in the house of God, which is the church of the living God, the pillar and ground of the truth.**
> **16. And without controversy great is the mystery of godliness: God was manifest in the flesh, justified in the Spirit, seen of angels, preached unto the Gentiles, believed on in the world, received up into glory.**

Church, each of you should already know how to behave yourself in the house of God. The church of the living God is the pillar and ground of the truth itself. The mystery of godliness itself cannot be disputed at all. God was clearly demonstrated to men in the flesh by the only begotten son of God himself. The angels witnessed this from his birth all the way through his resurrection and subsequent ascension. The death and resurrection of Jesus Christ was preached to the Gentiles starting with Peter going to Caesarea. Jesus was received up into glory with his apostles witnessing the event.

Hebrews 1

1. **God, who at sundry times and in divers manners spake in time past unto the fathers by the prophets,**
2. **Hath in these last days spoken unto us by his Son, whom he hath appointed heir of all things, by whom also he made the worlds;**
3. **Who being the brightness of his glory, and the express image of his person, and upholding all things by the word of his power, when he had by himself purged our sins, sat down on the right hand of the Majesty on high;**

Church, God has in the past spoken to the fathers at different times and in different ways by the ones of them he called to be his prophets. He has spoken to us in these times by his only begotten son. He appointed his son to be heir of all things. It was for his son that he made the ages. The only begotten son of God is the very brightness of the glory of his Father. He is the exact physical copy of God himself. He upheld all things by the word of his power. When Jesus Christ himself purged our sins by shedding his own blood, he sat down on the right hand of the Majesty on high. His work was perfectly completed.

2 Peter 1

20. **Knowing this first, that no prophecy of the scripture is of any private interpretation.**
21. **For the prophecy came not in old time by the will of man: but holy men of God spake as they were moved by the Holy Ghost.**

Church, know this before you try to know anything else. Make this a living part of your mind and keep it there always. No prophecy of the scripture, whether foretelling or forthtelling, is of any individual interpretation. These guys didn't just write or say things that sounded good to them at the time. These men spoke and wrote the things they saw and heard as they were inspired by the spirit of God himself. When Jesus spoke, he said that the things he saw and heard from his Father were the things he said and did. When the apostles were brought before the temple priests, they said they could not help but to speak of the things they had seen and heard themselves.

2 Peter 2

1. **But there were false prophets also among the people, even as there shall be false teachers among you, who privily shall bring in damnable heresies, even denying the Lord that bought them, and bring upon themselves swift destruction.**
2. **And many shall follow their pernicious ways; by reason of whom the way of truth shall be evil spoken of.**
3. **And through covetousness shall they with feigned words make merchandise of you: whose judgment now of a long time lingereth not, and their damnation slumbereth not.**
4. **For if God spared not the angels that sinned, but cast them down to hell, and delivered them into chains of darkness, to be reserved unto judgment;**
5. **And spared not the old world, but saved Noah the eighth person, a preacher of righteousness, bringing in the flood upon the world of the ungodly;**
6. **And turning the cities of Sodom and Gomorrha into ashes condemned them with an overthrow, making them an ensample unto those that after should live ungodly;**
7. **And delivered just Lot, vexed with the f ilthy conversation of the wicked:**
8. **(For that righteous man dwelling among them, in seeing and hearing, vexed his righteous soul from day to day with their unlawful deeds;)**
9. **The Lord knoweth how to deliver the godly out of temptations, and to reserve the unjust unto the day of judgment to be punished:**

Eternal Life

10. But chiefly them that walk after the flesh in the lust of uncleanness, and despise government. Presumptuous are they, selfwilled, they are not afraid to speak evil of dignities.
11. Whereas angels, which are greater in power and might, bring not railing accusation against them before the Lord.
12. But these, as natural brute beasts, made to be taken and destroyed, speak evil of the things that they understand not; and shall utterly perish in their own corruption;
13. And shall receive the reward of unrighteousness, as they that count it pleasure to riot in the day time. Spots they are and blemishes, sporting themselves with their own deceivings while they feast with you;
14. Having eyes full of adultery, and that cannot cease from sin; beguiling unstable souls: an heart they have exercised with covetous practices; cursed children:
15. Which have forsaken the right way, and are gone astray, following the way of Balaam the son of Bosor, who loved the wages of unrighteousness;
16. But was rebuked for his iniquity: the dumb ass speaking with man's voice forbad the madness of the prophet.
17. These are wells without water, clouds that are carried with a tempest; to whom the mist of darkness is reserved for ever.
18. For when they speak great swelling words of vanity, they allure through the lusts of the flesh, through much wantonness, those that were clean escaped from them who live in error.
19. While they promise them liberty, they themselves are the servants of corruption: for of whom a man is overcome, of the same is he brought in bondage.
20. For if after they have escaped the pollutions of the world through the knowledge of the Lord and Saviour Jesus Christ, they are again entangled therein, and overcome, the latter end is worse with them than the beginning.

> **21. For it had been better for them not to have known the way of righteousness, than, after they have known it, to turn from the holy commandment delivered unto them.**
>
> **22. But it is happened unto them according to the true proverb, the dog is turned to his own vomit again; and the sow that was washed to her wallowing in the mire.**

Church, just as there were false prophets in Israel, there also will come in among you false teachers, who will deceitfully bring in damnable heresies, and even deny the lord that paid for them with his own life. They will bring upon themselves swift destruction. Many of you shall follow their pernicious ways. This will cause others to speak evil of the way of truth.

Through a desire for self gain they shall with false words make merchandise of you, thinking no more of you than a piece of property—just one more trophy on their wall. Their judgment of a long time now doesn't linger and their damnation doesn't slumber even though God is longsuffering with all of us—their judgment is already upon them, being spoken from their own mouths.

If God didn't spare the angels that sinned, and delivered them into chains of darkness, to reserve them until judgment; and spared not the old world, but spared Noah, a preacher of righteousness, bringing in the flood upon the world of the ungodly; and turning the cities of Sodom and Gomorrha into ashes condemned them with an overthrow as an example to the ungodly who came after them; and delivered just Lot, vexed with the filthy conduct of the wicked (who, by living among them was vexed daily by seeing and hearing their unlawful deeds).

The Lord knows how to deliver the godly out of temptation, and, at the same time, to reserve the unjust unto the day of judgment to be punished: but chiefly those who walk after the flesh in the lust of uncleanness, and despise government. Such people are presumptious, self willed, and not afraid to speak evil of dignities. Angels, on the other hand, who are far greater in power and might, do not bring any railing accusation of them before the Lord.

Yet these people, as natural brute beasts, are made by their own actions to be taken and destroyed. They speak evil of things they do not understand. They shall utterly perish in their own corruption and receive the reward of unrighteousness because they derive pleasure from living in self indulgence in the daytime not even trying to keep it secret. They are spots and blemishes, sporting themselves with their own deceivings, while they feast with you in your own assemblies.

They have eyes full of adultery that cannot cease from sin. They beguile unstable souls. They have exercised their hearts with covetous practices. They are cursed children who have forsaken the right way and gone astray, following the same way as Balaam son of Bosor who loved the wages of unrighteousness. He was rebuked by a dumb ass speaking with a man's voice, withstanding and preventing the prophet's madness.

Such people are wells without water. They are clouds carried with a storm. The mist of darkness is reserved for them forever. They speak great swelling words of vanity. They allure through the lusts of the flesh, through much wantonness, those who were clean escaped those who live in error.

They promise liberty, yet they themselves are servants of corruption: for of whom a man is overcome, of the same is he brought into bondage. If after they have escaped the pollutions of the world through the knowledge of the lord and savior Jesus Christ, they become entangled again and overcome by the same pollutions, their latter end is worse than it was for them in the beginning. It would have been better for them not to have known the ways of righteousness at all, than after having known it, to turn away from the holy commandment that was delivered to them. What has happened is according to the true proverb, the dog has turned to his own vomit again; and the sow that was washed to wallowing in the mire.

Church, these people are not outside your assemblies trying to lead you away. These people are inside your assemblies at most every level trying to lead you away from the truth. They walk among you and represent you to those outside. It is by their words and actions that the truth is evil spoken of. You must become very aware of the things going on around you—your very Life is at stake.

1 Peter 4

17. For the time is come that judgment must begin at the house of God: and if it first begin at us, what shall the end be of them that obey not the gospel of God?

Church, judgment must begin at the house of God and the time is now. Why is this important to know? The church is the pillar and ground of the truth itself. It follows then that judgment must begin with us. If it begins first at us, what shall be the end of those who obey not the gospel of God? This is not talking about those who are outside. It is talking to those of us who are inside the church. We are the ones who are supposed to know and teach the gospel of God. This judgment will be witnessed by the whole world.

1 John 4

1. Beloved, believe not every spirit, but try the spirits whether they are of God: because many false prophets are gone out into the world.
2. Hereby know ye the Spirit of God: Every spirit that confesseth that Jesus Christ is come in the flesh is of God:
3. And every spirit that confesseth not that Jesus Christ is come in the flesh is not of God: and this is that spirit of antichrist, whereof ye have heard that it should come; and even now already is it in the world.

Church, here is the judgment that stands before us. John said not to believe every spirit. Rather, we are to test the spirits to see whether they are of God or not because there are many false prophets gone out into the world—and there are many that have come into the church as well. This is how we can tell which spirit is of God. Every spirit that confesses that Jesus Christ is come in the flesh is of God. This is where we must be very careful. What does in the flesh mean exactly? Does it mean part flesh and part spirit? Does it mean spirit that took the form of flesh so people could see him? Does it mean part human and part God?

The expression "in the flesh" means exactly what it says—100% totally absolutely completely flesh period. In the gospel of John, Jesus himself said that God is a spirit and those that worship him must worship him in spirit and in truth. In the gospel of Luke, this same Jesus appeared to his apostles after he was resurrected and said " I am not a spirit as you suppose, for a spirit does not have flesh and bones as you see me have.". If he had been any part spirit at all he could not have said that to his apostles without lying to them—it's that simple church. He did not tell them that he just assumed a fleshly body so they could see him. He denied being spirit of any kind at all.

The letter to the Colossians states that Jesus Christ was the physical representation of the invisible God. The letter to the Hebrews states the Jesus Christ was the exact physical copy of God. None of these references—either what Jesus said himself or what the writers of each book said about this same Jesus—contradict one another at all. Each one of them meets the standard of John's definition of the spirit that is of God.

Every spirit that does not confess that Jesus Christ is come in the flesh is not of God at all. This is the spirit of antichrist which was told would come and is already here working all manner of deception and, in the end, destruction. Any doctrine that says that Jesus Christ was part man and part God, or that he was really God himself who took on a human form so people could see him, or any such other thing is not of God at all. John defines such things as the spirit of antichrist which is already at work even when John wrote this message.

2 Timothy 4

1. **I charge thee therefore before God, and the Lord Jesus Christ, who shall judge the quick and the dead at his appearing and his kingdom;**
2. **Preach the word; be instant in season, out of season; reprove, rebuke, exhort with all longsuffering and doctrine.**

> 3. For the time will come when they will not endure sound doctrine; but after their own lusts shall they heap to themselves teachers, having itching ears;
> 4. And they shall turn away their ears from the truth, and shall be turned unto fables.

Pastors, Paul gave a solemn charge to you before God himself, and Jesus Christ, who shall judge the quick and the dead (remember who Jesus considered dead?) at his appearing and his kingdom. You are to preach the word; be instant in season, out of season; reprove, rebuke, exhort with all longsuffering and doctrine. Don't lose heart.

The time will come when those you instruct will not endure sound doctrine. They will heap to themselves teachers that will satisfy their own selfish desires, having itching ears that are not satisfied with hearing the truth. They shall turn away from the truth and turn instead to fables to satisfy themselves.

2 Peter 3

> 3. Knowing this first, that there shall come in the last days scoffers, walking after their own lusts,
> 4. And saying, Where is the promise of his coming? for since the fathers fell asleep, all things continue as they were from the beginning of the creation.

This passage plays havoc among the churches. People are looking at the conditions around us and getting nervous. They are pointing to those outside who are scoffing and saying it is a sign of the end times. This passage refers to those scoffers who arise inside the church—not outside.

Every day scoffers came to mock Noah as he built the ark. They all died. Scoffers mocked Lot in Sodom. Their city was destroyed and they all died. Pharaoh mocked Moses and Aaron and his nation was destroyed. There were scoffers when Moses went up the mountain to talk to God. They died. Scoffers refused to believe the report of the spies who said the promised land was ripe for taking. An entire generation died as a result. The king of Jerico mocked Joshua and his city was destroyed. The scoffers died. All these examples have to do with those who are outside of God.

The scoffers Peter is referring to come from within the church itself. These are driven by their own selfish desires for gain and they willingly turn from the truth. They see no promised return of Christ. They magnify themselves above everything else. They consider things to be as they always have been.

As the scriptures state, judgment will begin first in the house of God. The whole world will witness the event and it will be a warning to them that judgment is coming to them as well. The question occurs as to exactly what will the world witness happen to the church? While the scriptures do not specifically say, they do tell of a process that, in itself, would be a dramatic enough event to catch the attention of the whole world at once.

The church overall has its eyes focused on world events to try to determine when Christ himself will return. The only real object existing today that hinders the rise of antichrist and the subsequent return of Christ to the earth is the church of God. Regardless of the tensions in the world, as long as the church of God exists there is still hope. In order for antichrist to be revealed as the only hope for the world, there must be no discernible hope left at all. For conditions to get that bad, the church of God itself must no longer exist on the earth.

This is a particularly unique period in the history of mankind. On the one hand, man has the capacity at his fingertips to destroy every living thing on the face of the earth. On the other hand, the church has at its fingertips, the capacity to literally change the way every man, woman, and child thinks on the face of the earth. Yet, neither man nor the church can accomplish their goals. Both are frustrated. Both seem to be incapable of carrying out their desires and goals. Never before have we been in such a position.

There is a parable Christ told about the end of the age that does not prophecy about the church, but the process described is similar to the process the church is about to go through. The world will witness this and be stunned by the events as they unfold. Church, it's time to stop watching world events and start watching events in the house of God. Powerful things are about to happen and we need to be awake when these things occur.

Matthew 13

24. Another parable put he forth unto them, saying, The kingdom of heaven is likened unto a man which sowed good seed in his field:
25. But while men slept, his enemy came and sowed tares among the wheat, and went his way.
26. But when the blade was sprung up, and brought forth fruit, then appeared the tares also.
27. So the servants of the householder came and said unto him, Sir, didst not thou sow good seed in thy field? from whence then hath it tares?
28. He said unto them, An enemy hath done this. The servants said unto him, Wilt thou then that we go and gather them up?
29. But he said, Nay; lest while ye gather up the tares, ye root up also the wheat with them.
30. Let both grow together until the harvest: and in the time of harvest I will say to the reapers, Gather ye together first the tares, and bind them in bundles to burn them: but gather the wheat into my barn.

While this parable is not about the church, the process described is very similar to what is about to happen inside the church during the time judgment occurs in the church. Though the process may not necessarily be violent, it will be dramatic enough for the whole world to notice and consider what is yet to come when they themselves face the judgment of God. Thus we see that the judgment of God is still tempered with his mercy. In the end, God's final judgment will not be tempered with mercy because man's atrocities will be so great that they can no longer be forgiven.

Eternal Life

If we look at the church as a good field especially prepared to produce a bountiful crop, we can see how the process can apply. The owner of the field, in this case, God himself plants good seed (his own word) and would naturally expect a good and bountiful crop to result. However, while his workers slept, an enemy came into the field and sowed tares among the wheat seeds and went his way. If we look at the people in the congregations as plants developing from seeds (different spoken and written words) in the same ground side by side, we see how the process develops.

When the blades sprang up (the people responded to what they were being taught) the servants of the landowner saw that there were other plants in the field. They went to the landowner and asked him why there were other plants there and should they remove them. The landowner said an enemy had planted tares among the good seed, but allow them to grow together side by side in the very same field until harvest to avoid pulling out the good wheat while they were pulling out the tares because they resembled each other too much to see a clear difference at that stage.

Here, we need to understand the tares. The word translated tares is the word darnel. Darnel isn't just some weed. Darnel looks so much like wheat that it is mistaken for wheat. If you take grains of wheat, grind them, and make bread, you have food that, when eaten, sustains life. However, if you take grains of darnel, grind them, and make bread, you have poison that, when eaten, causes death.

What we have in the church is two different crops growing side by side at the same time in the same place. People who don't know God can't look at them and see a clear difference. One group is inspired by the word of truth itself. The other group is inspired by self motivated desires. On the surface, they look and sound almost alike. For a person making a life and death choice, this is a difficult position to be in, not knowing which choice to make. In order for such a choice to be made, a clear difference between the two must be demonstrated. This is why judgment begins first in the house of God—the pillar and ground of truth itself—the good field that should have produced a good and bountiful harvest from the beginning. Even during the time of Peter, James, John, and Paul, there were false teachers coming in and bringing false teachings with them. Today, after 1900 years of traditions and doctrines that men have added, the time has come to separate truth from error completely so those outside of God can see the choice that they are about to make.

It is now that the separation in the church is about to be made. Those who have the love of the truth in their hearts will see the truth as it is and will commit to it will be bound to and by the truth. They will be gathered together and put into the landowner's barn and no longer be in the field (the church) at all. Those who are driven by their own desires and selfish natures will be bound to and by their desires and left in the field (the church) to be burned. Their will be no turning from either side once each has made his choice and committed to it. The world will be stunned because nothing like this has happened on this scale before.

The separation and gathering process has been the subject of much speculation and argument for years. I will not even attempt to debate that. However, the process will happen and it will be final. In the end, the church that is left will not have one single person involved with it that has the love of the truth in his heart. The only thing left in the church will be those who are led by their own uncontrollable selfish desires. They will be bound to and by their own desires and will not turn from them no matter what. They will completely deny the very God they claim to worship.

Church, pay close attention. This process will set off a series of events so devastating that, as they progress, will cause the earth itself to reel as a drunkard. All the things you are looking at to try to determine the coming of Christ are diverting your attention away from what is about to happen to you. Like it or not, you are the key to what is about to happen to the whole world. It is time for you to decide in your own hearts who you serve—God or yourself. Wake up. Be aware. Search your hearts. The judgment of God is about to begin.

This warning to the church is also a warning to the world. The judgment of the church is a sign of the coming judgment of God against the whole world. While God will temper his judgment with mercy toward those who seek him during this time, there will come a final point when the judgment of God against man will be poured out unmingled with mercy at all. World, as you witness the process going on in the church, know and understand that God's judgment against you follows quickly behind—and it's a terrible thing to go through.

CHAPTER 10

2 Thessalonians 2

1. Now we beseech you, brethren, by the coming of our Lord Jesus Christ, and by our gathering together unto him,
2. That ye be not soon shaken in mind, or be troubled, neither by spirit, nor by word, nor by letter as from us, as that the day of Christ is at hand.
3. Let no man deceive you by any means: for that day shall not come, except there come a falling away first, and that man of sin be revealed, the son of perdition;
4. Who opposeth and exalteth himself above all that is called God, or that is worshipped; so that he as God sitteth in the temple of God, shewing himself that he is God.
5. Remember ye not, that, when I was yet with you, I told you these things?
6. And now ye know what withholdeth that he might be revealed in his time.
7. For the mystery of iniquity doth already work: only he who now letteth will let, until he be taken out of the way.
8. And then shall that Wicked be revealed, whom the Lord shall consume with the spirit of his mouth, and shall destroy with the brightness of his coming:
9. Even him, whose coming is after the working of Satan with all power and signs and lying wonders,
10. And with all deceivableness of unrighteousness in them that perish; because they received not the love of the truth, that they might be saved.

> 11. And for this cause God shall send them strong delusion, that they should believe a lie:
> 12. That they all might be damned who believed not the truth, but had pleasure in unrighteousness.

Church, this part gets really dark, but it's written as a warning to all. Paul is begging you to listen by the coming of Christ himself and by our gathering together unto him. That's a strong sense of urgency. You are warned not to be soon shaken in the center of your intellect by anything to the point that you can no longer see what is going on around you and recognise these things for what they are. Neither are you to be frightened by any events you witness. Do not allow spirit (working of power), nor word spoken, thoughts, or reasonings of any kind, nor letters written as though they were prophecies or instruction convince you that the day of Christ is at hand.

The day of Christ was foretold in the old testament and was one of the reasons his own people turned against him. The day of Christ was promised to the apostles on the mount of Olives after Christ had ascended while they were watching. Just to make sure you understand what day this is, we are going to look at these references.

Acts 1

> 4. And, being assembled together with them, commanded them that they should not depart from Jerusalem, but wait for the promise of the Father, which, saith he, ye have heard of me.
> 5. For John truly baptized with water; but ye shall be baptized with the Holy Ghost not many days hence.
> 6. When they therefore were come together, they asked of him, saying, Lord, wilt thou at this time restore again the kingdom to Israel?
> 7. And he said unto them, It is not for you to know the times or the seasons, which the Father hath put in his own power.

8. But ye shall receive power, after that the Holy Ghost is come upon you: and ye shall be witnesses unto me both in Jerusalem, and in all Judaea, and in Samaria, and unto the uttermost part of the earth.
9. And when he had spoken these things, while they beheld, he was taken up; and a cloud received him out of their sight.
10. And while they looked stedfastly toward heaven as he went up, behold, two men stood by them in white apparel;
11. Which also said, Ye men of Galilee, why stand ye gazing up into heaven? this same Jesus, which is taken up from you into heaven, shall so come in like manner as ye have seen him go into heaven.
12. Then returned they unto Jerusalem from the mount called Olivet, which is from Jerusalem a sabbath day's journey.

Luke records that Christ was assembled together with his apostles and commanded them to stay in Jerusalem until they had received the promise of the Father Christ had told them about. He said John truly baptized with water, but they were going to be baptized with holy ghost (holy spirit—power from on high) not too many days from then. They then asked if he was going to restore the kingdom to Israel at that time. He told them it was not for them to know the times or seasons that God himself had put in his own power.

Instead, they were to receive power from God and be witnesses of Christ in Jerusalem, all Judea, Samaria, and to the uttermost parts of the earth. After he had said these things, while the apostles were watching intently, Christ was taken up and a cloud received him out of their sight.

While they were were steadfastly watching as he ascended, two men in white apparel stood beside them and promised them that the very same Christ they saw ascend would return to exactly the same place in exactly the same manner. That will be the day of Christ and that day will not occur until Christ himself returns exactly the same way he left.

The men returned to Jerusalem from the mount of Olives where they had watched Christ himself ascend.

When they asked Christ about restoring the kingdom to Israel, the apostles were referring to a prophecy in the old testament. We are going to look at it next and see greater detail than what the angels said on the mount of Olives.

Zechariah 14

1. Behold, the day of the Lord cometh, and thy spoil shall be divided in the midst of thee.
2. For I will gather all nations against Jerusalem to battle; and the city shall be taken, and the houses rifled, and the women ravished; and half of the city shall go forth into captivity, and the residue of the people shall not be cut off from the city.
3. Then shall the Lord go forth, and fight against those nations, as when he fought in the day of battle.
4. And his feet shall stand in that day upon the mount of Olives, which is before Jerusalem on the east, and the mount of Olives shall cleave in the midst thereof toward the east and toward the west, and there shall be a very great valley; and half of the mountain shall remove toward the north, and half of it toward the south.
5. And ye shall flee to the valley of the mountains; for the valley of the mountains shall reach unto Azal: yea, ye shall flee, like as ye fled from before the earthquake in the days of Uzziah king of Judah: and the Lord my God shall come, and all the saints with thee.
6. And it shall come to pass in that day, that the light shall not be clear, nor dark:
7. But it shall be one day which shall be known to the Lord, not day, nor night: but it shall come to pass, that at evening time it shall be light.

8. And it shall be in that day, that living waters shall go out from Jerusalem; half of them toward the former sea, and half of them toward the hinder sea: in summer and in winter shall it be.
9. And the Lord shall be king over all the earth: in that day shall there be one Lord, and his name one.
10. All the land shall be turned as a plain from Geba to Rimmon south of Jerusalem: and it shall be lifted up, and inhabited in her place, from Benjamin's gate unto the place of the first gate, unto the corner gate, and from the tower of Hananeel unto the king's winepresses.
11. And men shall dwell in it, and there shall be no more utter destruction; but Jerusalem shall be safely inhabited.
12. And this shall be the plague wherewith the Lord will smite all the people that have fought against Jerusalem; Their flesh shall consume away while they stand upon their feet, and their eyes shall consume away in their holes, and their tongue shall consume away in their mouth.
13. And it shall come to pass in that day, that a great tumult from the Lord shall be among them; and they shall lay hold every one on the hand of his neighbour, and his hand shall rise up against the hand of his neighbour.
14. And Judah also shall fight at Jerusalem; and the wealth of all the heathen round about shall be gathered together, gold, and silver, and apparel, in great abundance.
15. And so shall be the plague of the horse, of the mule, of the camel, and of the ass, and of all the beasts that shall be in these tents, as this plague.

This is a prophecy to Jerusalem that has not yet occurred, and it will not occur until a series of terrible events happen first. All nations shall be gathered against Jerusalem to battle. The city shall be taken. The houses shall be plundered. The women shall be violated. Half the city shall go into captivity, yet the residue shall not be cut off from the city.

It is after these events that the Lord shall go forth and fight against those nations as he did in the day of battle—and not before then will he do it. Revelations describes the seven last judgments of God that pour out his wrath unmixed with mercy. The very last judgment is the personal return of Christ himself to exactly the same spot on the mount of Olives he ascended from.

Once Christ himself stands on the mount of Olives, it will split right down the middle from east to west. Half the mountain will shift to the north and half the mountain will shift to the south. This action will cause a huge valley to form. The residue left in Jerusalem are told to flee to the valley of the mountains because the valley of the mountains shall reach to Azal. They are told to flee as their fathers had done before the earthquake in the days of Uzziah king of Judah. They are told that the Lord shall come and all the saints with them through the valley.

The day this occurs, the light shall not be clear nor shall it be dark. It is a day that Christ himself told his apostles that is known only to the Father and is under his power. It shall be neither day nor night, but it shall come to pass at evening time while it is still light before nightfall. That day, fresh waters shall go out from Jerusalem itself. Half the waters shall flow toward the eastern sea and half the waters shall flow toward the western sea. These waters shall flow year round and not just be a seasonal occurrence. Since it will be at evening before nightfall, this will occur at the beginning of a new day, a truly fitting time for the king of Israel to return to claim his throne.

Not only will he be the king of Israel, but also king over all the earth. He will be lord over all the earth with one name everywhere. All the land shall become as a wasteland from Geba to Rimmon south of Jerusalem. Jerusalem itself, however, shall be lifted up and inhabited from Benjamin's gate unto the place of the first gate, unto the corner gate, and from the tower of Hananeel unto the king's winepresses. Men shall dwell in it and there shall be no more utter destruction. Jerusalem shall be safely inhabited.

The lord shall strike all the people that have fought against Jerusalem with a terrible plague. Their flesh shall consume away while they are standing on their feet, their eyes shall consume away in their sockets, and their tongues shall consume away in their mouths. Also, on that very day, there shall be a tumult among them from the Lord so that every one shall lay hand on his neighbor and rise up against him.

Judah will also fight at Jerusalem, and the wealth of all the heathen round about shall be gathered together. Gold, silver, and fine clothing shall be in great abundance. The same plague on those fighting against Jerusalem shall also be on their horses, their camels, their mules, their asses, and upon all the beasts they have with them. In the end, every living thing that fights against Jerusalem that day, whether man or beast shall die.

Church, this day has not occurred yet, nor can it occur until many other specific things happen first. The day of Christ is the day he personally returns to rule the whole earth from Jerusalem. Do not allow yourselves to be deceived by any means at all. The day of Christ shall not come until there is a complete turning away from God first. Just as was explained by studying the parable of the wheat and the darnel, the separation of the church will be complete and final. Not one person will change his commitment once he has made it. For a complete turning away to occur, there must not be one single person in the church at all that has the love of the truth in his heart. The only ones left are the ones who make up the false church. That event has not occurred yet, either. People debate how this will happen. The bottom line is that it must happen for the false church to appear in its fulness.

Only when the church has become the false church can the man of sin, the son of perdition be revealed. This man will oppose all that is called God and will exalt himself above all that is called God to the point that he himself will be seated in the temple of God and declare himself to be God almighty in the flesh. Paul had told the Thessalonians earlier about this very thing.

We all know now that both the true church and the false church must grow side by side until they are separated and the true church removed before the man of sin (whom John calls antichrist) can be revealed. The mystery of iniquity already works in the church because there are already false teachings there. They were even there in the time of the apostles. Look at the letters to the churches and the things that were discussed in those letters. The things discussed were actually happening inside the church, just like they are today.

Once the true church and the false church are separated and the true church removed, then and only then can the man of sin be revealed. This is the man that Christ shall consume with the spirit (power) of his mouth and destroy with the brightness of his coming. This man will come after the working of Satan himself with all power. He will be able to work all miracles, and signs, and lying wonders. He will work all manner of deceivableness of unrighteousness in them that perish because they, by their own choice, received not the love of the truth, that they might be saved, starting with the false church.

Because of this, God shall allow them to be strongly deluded to the point that they shall believe a lie—the lie of antichrist himself—in order for them to be judged who would not accept the truth but would rather find pleasure in unrighteousness—starting with the false church. Church, this is serious. Those of you who will not accept the truth of the word of God will follow the Antichrist himself. You will worship him and declare him to be God almighty in the flesh. You will do worse than that, though.

Once those in the world witness the separation in the church and the removal of the true church, there will be many who really desire to know the truth, but haven't heard the truth that is in Christ. If they have heard anything at all, what they have heard is a lie and they will not accept it. Church, those of you left will hunt these people down and kill them if they do not accept Antichrist as you declare him to be—God almighty himself in the flesh. Not only that, but also you will find pleasure in serving the god you worship and will not repent at all of anything you do.

All these things and many more judgments will occur before Christ himself finally returns to the mount of Olives. Do not allow anyone to tell you Christ is here or he is there. Do not follow anything that causes you to doubt the word of God. Keep steadfastly the love of the truth in your hearts, and you shall see Eternal Life. Refuse to have the love of the truth in your hearts, and you are dead already. The choice is yours. You are the greatest witness to the world of the love of God. You are the pillar and ground of truth itself. Judgment must begin first with you, and if you barely survive what chance does the rest of the world have? The only chance they have is your witness, beginning with the separation of the true and false church. Whoever has ears to hear, let him hear.

Much has been said here, but there are other things that need to be understood as well. For instance, the major attack from outside and inside the church is one of the most subtle and hardest to detect. The attack is against the word of God itself and takes many forms. To be aware and prepared for the attacks, you must understand what the word of God says about itself.

Romans 2

1. **Therefore thou art inexcusable, O man, whosoever thou art that judgest: for wherein thou judgest another, thou condemnest thyself; for thou that judgest doest the same things.**
2. **But we are sure that the judgment of God is according to truth against them which commit such things.**
3. **And thinkest thou this, O man, that judgest them which do such things, and doest the same, that thou shalt escape the judgment of God?**

Church, listen carefully. You are inexcusable when you judge another. You only condemn yourself because you do the very same things yourself. Be assured that the judgment of God is according to truth against those who do such things—including you. Do you honestly think that by doing the same thing you judge others for that you shall escape the judgment of God against you?

John 17

17. Sanctify them through thy truth: thy word is truth.

This verse was from a prayer that Christ was praying when he declared the word of God to be truth itself. That means God's judgment will be strictly by his word and his word alone.

Acts 17

**10. And the brethren immediately sent away Paul and Silas by night unto Berea: who coming thither went into the synagogue of the Jews.
11. These were more noble than those in Thessalonica, in that they received the word with all readiness of mind, and searched the scriptures daily, whether those things were so.
12. Therefore many of them believed; also of honourable women which were Greeks, and of men, not a few.
13. But when the Jews of Thessalonica had knowledge that the word of God was preached of Paul at Berea, they came thither also, and stirred up the people.**

There are two things to note here that are important. First, Paul and Silas were sent away from Thessalonica by night to Berea, where they went to the synagogue and began teaching just as before. The Bereans were more noble than those in Thessalonica in that they received the word of God with all readiness of mind and searched the scriptures themselves to see whether what they were being taught was indeed the word of God. As a result, many believed, also honorable Greek women and quite a number of men as well. People with readiness of mind will hear the truth, check it to make sure, and accept it as the truth.

But when the Jews (the leaders) of Thessalonica heard that Paul was in Berea preaching the word of God, they came and stirred up the people. Enemies of the truth will not just leave you alone and let you teach and encourage others to seek the truth. They will come after you and seek to drive you away and corrupt the truth as quickly as possible. In many cases, the ones who come after you are the ones who stand to lose the most because the truth exposes their false teachings.

2 Timothy 3

14. But continue thou in the things which thou hast learned and hast been assured of, knowing of whom thou hast learned them;
15. And that from a child thou hast known the holy scriptures, which are able to make thee wise unto salvation through faith which is in Christ Jesus.
16. All scripture is given by inspiration of God, and is profitable for doctrine, for reproof, for correction, for instruction in righteousness:
17. That the man of God may be perfect, throughly furnished unto all good works.

Church and pastors, you are to continue only in the things you have learned and been assured of. The only way you can be assured of the things you learn is to check what you are taught against what the scriptures themselves say. Augustine said that it is not what one scripture says, but what all the scriptures say together. The Bereans searched the scriptures daily to see if what they were being taught was true. That's the only way you can be assured of what you are being taught.

The scriptures Timothy had learned from childhood made him wise unto salvation through faith which is in Christ Jesus. Others knew the same scriptures, but did not understand what they knew. All scripture is given by inspiration of God himself. As such, all scripture is truth. Scripture is good for learning how to think and live rightly, for showing us how and where we have erred in our understanding, for showing us how to correct our errors, all together showing us how to make right judgments in our lives. This enables the man of God to be perfected from within so he is completely prepared to do all good works.

2 Timothy 2

> 14. Of these things put them in remembrance, charging them before the Lord that they strive not about words to no profit, but to the subverting of the hearers.
> 15. Study to shew thyself approved unto God, a workman that needeth not to be ashamed, rightly dividing the word of truth.
> 16. But shun profane and vain babblings: for they will increase unto more ungodliness.

Pastors and congregations, do not strive about words or meanings of words that serve no purpose other than the subverting of the hearers and, in the end, corrupting them. Instead, each one of you study to show yourself approved unto God, a workman that doesn't need to be ashamed, rightly dividing the word of truth itself. Be like the Bereans were. Search out the scriptures yourself to see if what is being taught is true. Remember, it's not what one scripture says, it's what all the scriptures say together. Do not become involved at all in common and useless babblings because such things only increase to more ungodliness.

2 Peter 1

> 20. Knowing this first, that no prophecy of the scripture is of any private interpretation.
> 21. For the prophecy came not in old time by the will of man: but holy men of God spake as they were moved by the Holy Ghost.

Church, each one of you burn this into every level of your mind. No prophecy of the scripture, whether forthtelling or foretelling, is of any individual interpretation at all. The prophets did not just sit down and write things that sounded good to them, or that would make good stories to tell children. Rather, holy men of God spoke as they were inspired by the spirit of God himself. Paul said all scripture is given by the inspiration of God. Peter just said the same thing here. For anyone to pick a scripture or several scriptures and turn around and say what it means to him dishonors the man who wrote it and God himself who inspired it to be written.

Psalms 138

2. I will worship toward thy holy temple, and praise thy name for thy lovingkindness and for thy truth: for thou hast magnified thy word above all thy name.

The psalmist here is declaring to God that he will worship towards God's holy temple and praise his name for his lovingkindness and for his truth because God has made his word greater to himself than all that his name represents. This is the same word of God that Christ declared was truth itself. Therefore, God has made truth more important to himself than all that his name is. We are to develop the love of the truth in our own hearts to the point that truth itself is more important to us than all that is represented by the name of God. When we are able to do this, we will be able to think thoughts that are the thoughts of God and not thoughts of Men.

Amos 4

13. For, lo, he that formeth the mountains, and createth the wind, and declareth unto man what is his thought, that maketh the morning darkness, and treadeth upon the high places of the earth, the Lord, The God of hosts, is his name.

The name of the God that formed the mountains, creates the wind, declares to man what is his thought, makes the morning darkness, and treads upon the high places of the earth is the Lord, the God of hosts.

Amos 5

8. Seek him that maketh the seven stars and Orion, and turneth the shadow of death into the morning, and maketh the day dark with night: that calleth for the waters of the sea, and poureth them out upon the face of the earth: the Lord is his name:

The name of him that makes the seven stars and Orion, that turns the shadow of death into the morning, that makes the day dark with night, that calls for the waters of the sea and pours them out upon the face of the earth is the Lord.

Amos 9

6. It is he that buildeth his stories in the heaven, and hath founded his troop in the earth; he that calleth for the waters of the sea, and poureth them out upon the face of the earth: the Lord is his name.

The name of him that builds his stories in the heaven, and founded his troop in the earth, that calls the waters of the sea and pours them out on the face of the earth is the Lord.

These three passages show that all of creation is tied up in the name of God himself. That means that God values his word—truth itself—above all of creation and everything in it. How can any of us claim to honor and worship God without putting the same value on truth that God himself does? If we try to do anything less, we are dishonoring and denying the very God we claim to worship.

With the word of God being so important to God himself, it is only natural for those who oppose him to attack his word any way they can. Their reasoning is that if you can destroy God's word, you can destroy all that God is. Be prepared church, the attack is always first and foremost against the integrity of God's word itself.

CHAPTER 11

It may seem that the last four chapters wandered away from the topic of Eternal Life, but each chapter has been written in terms of Eternal Life itself. Eternal Life is a promise to us. Whether we accept this or not depends entirely upon the way we each think. The purpose of the last four chapters was to show that to each of you. The rest of the book will deal with learning how (not what) to think. The constant battle we face is to individually decide whether the scriptures are actually true or not. We claim they are true—yet we act and teach as though they were open to debate and can be changed in some way. Our reception of Eternal Life is based totally on our acceptance of the word of God as truth itself. We can reject Eternal Life by rejecting that the word of God is truth itself.

What we face is is a life long battle within ourselves. Our enemy is the same enemy that ultimately controls the way the world thinks. When dealing with those in the world, we must remember that those in the world are being influenced and controlled by the same enemy that is seeking to control us as well. We are to see those in the world the way God sees them, as lost and without hope until we can show it to them. If those in the world cannot see any difference in us, then we are doing something terribly wrong. The purpose of these chapters is to show each of you how to think in terms of the Eternal Life, the same way God himself does. You will be shown how to arm yourself against anything that comes against you, trying to change your thinking to a different pattern. To do this, we are going to take a close look at Ephesians 6:10-17 where Paul reveals the whole armor of God to us.

Ephesians 6

10. Finally, my brethren, be strong in the Lord, and in the power of his might.
11. Put on the whole armour of God, that ye may be able to stand against the wiles of the devil.
12. For we wrestle not against flesh and blood, but against principalities, against powers, against the rulers of the darkness of this world, against spiritual wickedness in high places.
13. Wherefore take unto you the whole armour of God, that ye may be able to withstand in the evil day, and having done all, to stand.
14. Stand therefore , having your loins girt about with truth, and having on the breastplate of righteousness;
15. And your feet shod with the preparation of the gospel of peace;
16. Above all, taking the shield of faith, wherewith ye shall be able to quench all the fiery darts of the wicked.
17. And take the helmet of salvation, and the sword of the Spirit, which is the word of God:

When Paul wrote this, he was in Rome waiting to appear before Caesar to appeal his case. People teach a great many things about Paul being a prisoner, but Paul's circumstances were unique, just like Paul himself was. In spite of repeated warnings, Paul went to Jerusalem for the feast of Pentecost and was taken by a group of Jews who were beating and trying to kill him. Roman soldiers took him because of the disturbance, and when they found out he was Roman by birth, they unbound him because it was against Roman law to bind and imprison a Roman citizen who had not been found guilty of committing a crime.

After uncovering a plot to kill Paul, the Roman troop commander sent Paul by night with a sizeable armed escort to Felix, the governor with a request to hear both sides of the dispute between the Jewish leaders and Paul himself. Paul was treated fairly well by Felix. Paul was given freedom and none of his acquaintances were forbidden to see him, yet he was constantly accompanied by a Roman guard for his own protection. Felix kept Paul in Caesarea for two years, hoping to get money from him in order to release him.

After two years, Porcius Festus came to see Felix and Felix, wishing to please the Jews, made sure Paul was bound. After three days, Festus went to Jerusalem and the high priest wanted him to send Paul back to Jerusalem so he could be killed on the way. Festus decided Paul should stay in Caesarea and any accusations against him would be heard there. After Festus came back with Paul's accusers, he heard the complaints and Paul's answers. When he asked Paul if he would go to Jerusalem, Paul claimed his right as a Roman citizen to be heard before Caesar himself.

After some time, king Agrippa came to Caesarea to see Festus, and finally Festus told king Agrippa about Paul's situation and his appeal to Caesar, and king Agrippa agreed to hear him. After king Agrippa had heard Paul, he concluded, as had both Felix and Festus, that Paul had committed no crime at all. However, since Paul himself had appealed to Caesar, Paul had to be sent to Rome.

Paul was sent to Rome under the watchful eye of a centurion named Julius who was a member of Caesar's personal cohort. He was literally sent to Caesar without any charge of wrongdoing, only that his appeal be heard. The whole idea that Paul was a prisoner of the Roman state and charged with any crime is totally false. When Paul got to Rome, the other prisoners were sent to lockup, but Paul was set in his own dwelling under the company of Caesar's personal guard. He was treated more like a visiting dignitary than like a criminal. He had his own hired house, friends could come and go, just Paul could not leave Rome until he appeared before Caesar himself.

Paul was in bonds, but the bonds were restrictions caused by the utterance from his own mouth. He was not chained or put in a dungeon. He simply was bound to stay in Rome until he could be heard by Caesar. Paul put himself in that situation just as surely as he put himself in Jerusalem when he knew he shouldn't go at the time. Even though he was stuck in Rome for two whole years, Paul continued to teach and preach the kingdom of God to all who would come to him with no one forbidding him at any time.

When Paul wrote this passage about the whole armor of God, he had been up close and personal with combat ready members of the elite Roman guard for about four years. Regardless of the soldier in his presence, all the soldiers were battle ready at all times. Paul became intimately familiar with each piece of the armor he described. We are going to look at each piece and, hopefully, we can reach an intimate understanding of what Paul was illustrating to us by each piece of the whole armor of God and how we can put it to use to improve ourselves to conform ourselves to the image of the son of God himself. Each piece will be examined separately, yet we will never leave the context of Ephesians 6:10-17.

What is the purpose of this armor in the first place? As in any battle, last man standing—wins. The goal of having this armor is then to enable you to stand—no matter what. Your stand should be totally in Christ, therefore, you should learn to conform yourself to the image of Christ himself in order to reflect his image—not yours.

Ephesians 6

> **10. Finally, my brethren, be strong in the Lord, and in the power of his might.**
> **11. Put on the whole armour of God, that ye may be able to stand against the wiles of the devil.**
> **12. For we wrestle not against flesh and blood, but against principalities, against powers, against the rulers of the darkness of this world, against spiritual wickedness in high places.**
> **13. Wherefore take unto you the whole armour of God, that ye may be able to withstand in the evil day, and having done all, to stand.**

Church, your strength should rest entirely in the working of the mighty power of God himself. At no time should you try to use your own. First, you are weak compared to the power of the things you face. Secondly, your flawed judgment makes you incapable of even knowing what you are up against, much less how to deal with it. Church, God has filled each one of you with his own power. You are to wrap (clothe) yourself with this power like personal armor and use it to protect yourself from any attack that will cause you to falter in your stand.

We don't just wrestle against flesh and blood, but against governments, powers of various kinds, against the rulers of the darkness of the world themselves, and against spiritual wickedness in high places. All these things have one common goal—to break us and make us falter in our stand. Take the whole armor of God and use it to withstand in the evil day, and having done all, to stand. Withstand simply means to stand against. Notice it doesn't say fight, conquer, or repel. It simply tells each one of you to stand. Stand means to be firmly established.

Jeremiah 17

> **5. Thus saith the Lord; Cursed be the man that trusteth in man, and maketh flesh his arm, and whose heart departeth from the Lord.**
> **6. For he shall be like the heath in the desert, and shall not see when good cometh; but shall inhabit the parched places in the wilderness, in a salt land and not inhabited.**
> **7. Blessed is the man that trusteth in the Lord, and whose hope the Lord is.**
> **8. For he shall be as a tree planted by the waters, and that spreadeth out her roots by the river, and shall not see when heat cometh, but her leaf shall be green; and shall not be careful in the year of drought, neither shall cease from yielding fruit.**

Jeremiah said that the man who trusts in man, makes flesh his arm of power, and whose heart departs from the lord is cursed. He shall be like heath in the desert, and not see when good comes. He shall inhabit the parched places in the wilderness in a salt land that is not inhabited. However, the man whose trust and hope are in the lord is blessed. He is as a tree planted by waters whose roots are deep and spread out by the river. Such a tree does not suffer from the heat nor from the drought. Instead, it's leaves are green and the tree continually yields fruit. Therefore, to stand means to be firmly established or to be rooted and grounded.

To stand then, we each need to be firmly rooted and grounded in the word of God—the word of truth itself. If we try anything else, we will not be able to stand because we eventually will trust in man and in our own power. The attack against us is to convince us we don't need to rely on the word of God. Our own wisdom and intelligence is enough. Such thoughts turn us from God and inward toward ourselves. We will fall miserably if we allow that to happen to us.

Mark 3

> **13. And he goeth up into a mountain, and calleth unto him whom he would: and they came unto him.**
> **14. And he ordained twelve, that they should be with him, and that he might send them forth to preach,**
> **15. And to have power to heal sicknesses, and to cast out devils:**
> **16. And Simon he surnamed Peter;**
> **17. And James the son of Zebedee, and John the brother of James; and he surnamed them Boanerges, which is, The sons of thunder:**
> **18. And Andrew, and Philip, and Bartholomew, and Matthew, and Thomas, and James the son of Alphaeus, and Thaddaeus, and Simon the Canaanite,**
> **19. And Judas Iscariot, which also betrayed him: and they went into an house.**
> **20. And the multitude cometh together again, so that they could not so much as eat bread.**
> **21. And when his friends heard of it, they went out to lay hold on him: for they said, He is beside himself.**

> 22. And the scribes which came down from Jerusalem said, He hath Beelzebub, and by the prince of the devils casteth he out devils.
> 23. And he called them unto him, and said unto them in parables, How can Satan cast out Satan?
> 24. And if a kingdom be divided against itself, that kingdom cannot stand.
> 25. And if a house be divided against itself, that house cannot stand.
> 26. And if Satan rise up against himself, and be divided, he cannot stand, but hath an end.

Jesus went up into a mountain and called those with him. A group came and, from that group, he chose twelve to be with him, so he could send them out to teach and preach. He gave them power to heal sickness and to cast out devils. They came down and went into a house. When the people heard, so many of them came that these men weren't even able to sit down and eat. When his friends and other close associates heard what Jesus was doing, they went to lay hold of him because they thought he was crazy. Scribes came down from Jerusalem and accused Jesus of being possessed of Beelzebub, and that by the prince of the devils was he casting out devils.

Jesus answered the scribes in parables. How can Satan cast out Satan? If a kingdom is divided against itself, then it cannot be firmly established. And if a house is divided against itself, that house cannot be firmly established. If Satan rises up against himself, he cannot be firmly established either. Rather, Satan has an end. Church, pay attention—a house—any house—even the house of God cannot be firmly established if it is divided against itself. That's why there are to be no divisions among you.

Matthew 18

> 15. Moreover if thy brother shall trespass against thee, go and tell him his fault between thee and him alone: if he shall hear thee, thou hast gained thy brother.

16. But if he will not hear thee, then take with thee one or two more, that in the mouth of two or three witnesses every word may be established.

Jesus instructed us to handle differences in a specific manner. If you have a fault with a brother, go first to him privately and try to resolve the matter. If you are successful, you will have gained a brother. If he refuses to hear you, take one or two others with you and try again to resolve the matter. It doesn't say for you to take some of your friends and confront him and some of his friends. The one or two others should have nothing to gain by going with you. Their purpose is to witness only what is said between you and your brother. It is from their witness that which ever one of you, if either, is being reasonable can be established. The witness of two or more will firmly establish the events and every word spoken.

2 Corinthians 13

1. This is the third time I am coming to you. In the mouth of two or three witnesses shall every word be established.

Paul's instruction to the church of Corinth was the same. In the mouth of two or three witnesses shall every word be established. This is the same word Paul used for stand in his letter to the Ephesians. To stand or be established, you must be in agreement.

Acts 1

1. The former treatise have I made, O Theophilus, of all that Jesus began both to do and teach,
2. Until the day in which he was taken up, after that he through the Holy Ghost had given commandments unto the apostles whom he had chosen:
3. To whom also he shewed himself alive after his passion by many infallible proofs, being seen of them forty days, and speaking of the things pertaining to the kingdom of God:

4. And, being assembled together with them, commanded them that they should not depart from Jerusalem, butwait for the promise of the Father, which, saith he, ye have heard of me.
5. For John truly baptized with water; but ye shall be baptized with the Holy Ghost not many days hence.
6. When they therefore were come together, they asked of him, saying, Lord, wilt thou at this time restore again the kingdom to Israel?
7. And he said unto them, It is not for you to know the times or the seasons, which the Father hath put in his own power.
8. But ye shall receive power, after that the Holy Ghost is come upon you: and ye shall be witnesses unto me both in Jerusalem, and in all Judaea, and in Samaria, and unto the uttermost part of the earth.
9. And when he had spoken these things, while they beheld, he was taken up; and a cloud received him out of their sight.
10. And while they looked stedfastly toward heaven as he went up, behold, two men stood by them in white apparel;
11. Which also said, Ye men of Galilee, why stand ye gazing up into heaven? this same Jesus, which is taken up from you into heaven, shall so come in like manner as ye have seen him go into heaven.
12. Then returned they unto Jerusalem from the mount called Olivet, which is from Jerusalem a sabbath day's journey.
13. And when they were come in, they went up into an upper room, where abode both Peter, and James, and John, and Andrew, Philip, and Thomas, Bartholomew, and Matthew, James the son of Alphaeus, and Simon Zelotes, and Judas the brother of James.
14. These all continued with one accord in prayer and supplication, with the women, and Mary the mother of Jesus, and with his brethren.

From the time of his resurrection until the time of his ascension, Jesus spent 40 days witnessing himself only to those that were his, including the apostles he had chosen himself. However, after the ascension, only the eleven Galilean apostles returned to Jerusalem. They were living in the upper room of a house in Jerusalem. Women were not allowed in men's quarters. Yet, they all continued with one accord in prayer and supplication with the women, with Mary the mother of Jesus, and with his brothers. The only place they could have been together like that was in the temple—the house of God.

Acts 2

1. **And when the day of Pentecost was fully come, they were all with one accord in one place.**
2. **And suddenly there came a sound from heaven as of a rushing mighty wind, and it filled all the house where they were sitting.**
3. **And there appeared unto them cloven tongues like as of fire, and it sat upon each of them.**
4. **And they were all filled with the Holy Ghost, and began to speak with other tongues, as the Spirit gave them utterance.**
5. **And there were dwelling at Jerusalem Jews, devout men, out of every nation under heaven.**
6. **Now when this was noised abroad, the multitude came together, and were confounded, because that every man heard them speak in his own language.**
7. **And they were all amazed and marvelled, saying one to another, Behold, are not all these which speak Galilaeans?**
8. **And how hear we every man in our own tongue, wherein we were born?**
9. **Parthians, and Medes, and Elamites, and the dwellers in Mesopotamia, and in Judaea, and Cappadocia, in Pontus, and Asia,**

> 10. Phrygia, and Pamphylia, in Egypt, and in the parts of Libya about Cyrene, and strangers of Rome, Jews and proselytes,
> 11. Cretes and Arabians, we do hear them speak in our tongues the wonderful works of God.
> 12. And they were all amazed, and were in doubt, saying one to another, What meaneth this?
> 13. Others mocking said, These men are full of new wine.
> 14. But Peter, standing up with the eleven, lifted up his voice, and said unto them, Ye men of Judaea, and all ye that dwell at Jerusalem, be this known unto you, and hearken to my words:
> 15. For these are not drunken, as ye suppose, seeing it is but the third hour of the day.
> 16. But this is that which was spoken by the prophet Joel;
> 17. And it shall come to pass in the last days, saith God, I will pour out of my Spirit upon all flesh: and your sons and your daughters shall prophesy, and your young men shall see visions, and your old men shall dream dreams:
> 18. And on my servants and on my handmaidens I will pour out in those days of my Spirit; and they shall prophesy:

Note two things in this passage. First, they were all in one place at the same time in complete agreement (in one accord) when the day of Pentecost was fully come. Since that was a holy day, they had to be in the temple. Second, all the men involved (12 apostles) were Galilean. Sometime between the time that Christ himself ascended and the day of Pentecost was fully come, it suddenly became necessary to appoint another to Judas' post to fulfill the scriptures. Had Judas not been among the twelve when Christ witnessed to them and to others for forty days, it would have been necessary for him to appoint someone else in order for him to fulfill all the law and the prophets as the scriptures declare he did. We will discuss this more later. For now, just know that these apostles were standing in one place at the same time in one accord when they drew a huge crowd.

Acts 4

7. And when they had set them in the midst, they asked, By what power, or by what name, have ye done this?
8. Then Peter, filled with the Holy Ghost, said unto them, Ye rulers of the people, and elders of Israel,
9. If we this day be examined of the good deed done to the impotent man, by what means he is made whole;
10. Be it known unto you all, and to all the people of Israel, that by the name of Jesus Christ of Nazareth, whom ye crucified, whom God raised from the dead, even by him doth this man stand here before you whole.
11. This is the stone which was set at nought of you builders, which is become the head of the corner.
12. Neither is there salvation in any other: for there is none other name under heaven given among men, whereby we must be saved.
13. Now when they saw the boldness of Peter and John, and perceived that they were unlearned and ignorant men, they marvelled; and they took knowledge of them, that they had been with Jesus.
14. And beholding the man which was healed standing with them, they could say nothing against it.
15. But when they had commanded them to go aside out of the council, they conferred among themselves,
16. Saying, What shall we do to these men? for that indeed a notable miracle hath been done by them is manifest to all them that dwell in Jerusalem; and we cannot deny it.
17. But that it spread no further among the people, let us straitly threaten them, that they speak henceforth to no man in this name.
18. And they called them, and commanded them not to speak at all nor teach in the name of Jesus.
19. But Peter and John answered and said unto them, Whether it be right in the sight of God to hearken unto you more than unto God, judge ye.

20. **For we cannot but speak the things which we have seen and heard.**
21. **So when they had further threatened them, they let them go, finding nothing how they might punish them, because of the people: for all men glorified God for that which was done.**
22. **For the man was above forty years old, on whom this miracle of healing was shewed.**

Church, each one of us individually needs to look closely at this passage. There are whole lodes of gold here, not just nuggets to pick up. As we go through this, the story will unfold with awesome majesty.

Peter and John were brought before the rulers of the temple for healing a lame man at the gate entering the temple. The rulers demanded to know by what power or authority these men had done this thing. Peter, being filled with the spirit and power of God answered these men without hesitation. If these men dared to question how a lame men was made whole, then he would tell them. Peter would make it known to them and all Israel that by the name of Jesus Christ, the one they crucified, the one God himself raised from the dead, was this impotent made restored to complete health he had never had in his entire life and standing there right in front of them.

Peter declared Christ to be the stone that the builders had rejected but God had placed as the chief corner stone of his temple. Peter then declared there was salvation in no other because no other name was given whereby we might be saved. The council marvelled at the boldness of Peter and John because they were basically unlearned and untrained in the scriptures. They made note that these men were among those who had been with Jesus himself. They also saw the healed standing firmly established with Peter and John and they could not speak against what had been done.

The council sent Peter, John, and the healed man outside while they conferred among themselves as to how to handle this situation. They knew they could not deny that the miracle had been done because all of Jerusalem knew the man and knew of the miracle. The best thing they could do was to threaten Peter and John not to speak of the name of Christ any more.

The council then called the men back in and commanded them not to speak or teach at all in the name of Jesus for any reason. Peter and John then answered as to whether it was right in the sight of God to listen to them or to God, they should judge for themselves. However, Peter and John could not help but to speak of they things they saw and heard. This is the same thing Jesus said when he said that the things he saw and heard from his Father were the things he said and did.

Church, here's the key. They only spoke of the things they saw and heard themselves. We do not do this any more. We teach moral lessons, stories for children, and other things and we call this witnessing for God. If we follow the inspiration of the power of God as completely as the apostles did, we would be saying different things. We would only say and do the things we ourselves hear and see by the inspiration of the spirit God has given us. What a dramatic difference it would make in our lives and in the lives of those around us.

The council threatened Peter and John some more and then released them because they had done nothing wrong to be punished for. The people had witnessed the miracle and were glorifying God for it and the council didn't want to be on the wrong side of the people. The man who was healed was over forty years old. That means he was at the gate whenever Jesus came through with his disciples, yet Jesus never acknowledged him or healed him. He never saw or heard from his Father to do so, or he would have. After Jesus ascended, the apostles themselves never noticed the man either until that particular day when Peter and John went to the temple. It was that day that Peter and John saw and heard to heal this man, so they did.

Acts 5

17. Then the high priest rose up, and all they that were with him, (which is the sect of the Sadducees,) and were filled with indignation,

18. And laid their hands on the apostles, and put them in the common prison.
19. But the angel of the Lord by night opened the prison doors, and brought them forth, and said,
20. Go, stand and speak in the temple to the people all the words of this life.
21. And when they heard that, they entered into the temple early in the morning, and taught. But the high priest came, and they that were with him, and called the council together, and all the senate of the children of Israel, and sent to the prison to have them brought.
22. But when the officers came, and found them not in the prison, they returned, and told,
23. Saying, The prison truly found we shut with all safety, and the keepers standing without before the doors: but when we had opened, we found no man within.
24. Now when the high priest and the captain of the temple and the chief priests heard these things, they doubted of them whereunto this would grow.
25. Then came one and told them, saying, Behold, the men whom ye put in prison are standing in the temple, and teaching the people.
26. Then went the captain with the officers, and brought them without violence: for they feared the people, lest they should have been stoned.
27. And when they had brought them, they set them before the council: and the high priest asked them,
28. Saying, Did not we straitly command you that ye should not teach in this name? and, behold, ye have filled Jerusalem with your doctrine, and intend to bring this man's blood upon us.
29. Then Peter and the other apostles answered and said, We ought to obey God rather than men.

The apostles had been in the temple teaching and healing people to the point that large crowds were coming to them. This enraged the high priest and the Sadducees to the point they grabbed the apostles and threw them into the common prison under guard. That same night, the angel of the lord opened the prison doors, brought the apostles forth and told them to go, stand (be firmly established) and speak in the temple to the people all the words of Eternal Life.

Early in the morning, the apostles went to the temple and began teaching in the temple just as they were doing before. When the high priest came and those with him, they called the council together and sent to the prison for the apostles. The temple guards went to the prison, but the apostles weren't there. The guards went to the council and said that they found the prison shut with all safety, the guards standing (firmly planted and established) without the doors, yet when they opened the doors, no one was inside. The high priest and the temple guard commander wondered where this would lead.

Another guard came in and told the council that the men who were imprisoned were standing in the temple and teaching, just as before. The captain took some officers and brought the apostles to the council without violence at all because they feared what the people might do. They set the apostles before the council and the high priest asked them if they remembered that he had commanded them not to teach in Jesus' name. They were filling all Jerusalem with their doctrine and the priests were afraid that they were going to be blamed for the death of Jesus. Peter and the other apostles told the council that they ought to obey God rather than men.

Romans 11

13. For I speak to you Gentiles, inasmuch as I am the apostle of the Gentiles, I magnify mine office:
14. If by any means I may provoke to emulation them which are my flesh, and might save some of them.
15. For if the casting away of them be the reconciling of the world, what shall the receiving of them be, but life from the dead?

16. For if the firstfruit be holy, the lump is also holy: and if the root be holy, so are the branches.
17. And if some of the branches be broken off, and thou, being a wild olive tree, wert graffed in among them, and with them partakest of the root and fatness of the olive tree;
18. Boast not against the branches. But if thou boast, thou bearest not the root, but the root thee.
19. Thou wilt say then, The branches were broken off, that I might be graffed in.
20. Well; because of unbelief they were broken off, and thou standest by faith. Be not highminded, but fear:
21. For if God spared not the natural branches, take heed lest he also spare not thee.
22. Behold therefore the goodness and severity of God: on them which fell, severity; but toward thee, goodness, if thou continue in his goodness: otherwise thou also shalt be cut off.
23. And they also, if they abide not still in unbelief, shall be graffed in: for God is able to graff them in again.
24. For if thou wert cut out of the olive tree which is wild by nature, and wert graffed contrary to nature into a good olive tree: how much more shall these, which be the natural branches, be graffed into their own olive tree?
25. For I would not, brethren, that ye should be ignorant of this mystery, lest ye should be wise in your own conceits; that blindness in part is happened to Israel, until the fulness of the Gentiles be come in.
26. And so all Israel shall be saved: as it is written, There shall come out of Sion the Deliverer, and shall turn away ungodliness from Jacob:
27. For this is my covenant unto them, when I shall take away their sins.

Paul was writing a letter to the Gentile church at Rome. He was hoping by making his office as apostle to the Gentiles more important, some of his fellow Judeans would copy him and receive the salvation he was preaching in Christ. If casting them away meant reconciling the world, then receiving them would be no less than Eternal Life from the dead.

If the firstfruit is holy, then the lump is holy. If the root is holy, so are the branches. If some of the branches were broken off, and you, being a wild olive tree were grafted in among the other branches and, with them, enjoy the root and fatness of the olive tree; don't boast against those that were cut off. The root bears you—you don't bear the root. Don't say they were cut off for you to be grafted in. They were cut off because they refused to accept the death and resurrection of Jesus as the way to salvation because they held the keeping of the law to be their salvation. You are firmly established by faith, not in keeping of the law for righteousness. Faith will be explained by itself later.

Don't be highminded and consider yourselves to be superior to them. Instead, show reverence and respect to God. If God made no exception for the natural branches that knew his righteousness through the law and the prophets, do not even think for a minute he will make an exception for you—the grafted in branches. Take a really close look at the goodness and severity of God: on those that were cut off, severity; but towards you, who were before time enemies of God and all that he is, goodness, so long as you continue in his goodness: otherwise, you shall be cut off as well.

If those who were cut off change and accept the death and resurrection of Jesus as the way to salvation, they shall be grafted in again because God can graft them back in again. If the Gentiles were branches of a wild olive tree that were cut off and grafted into a good olive tree, how much more than those that were the natural branches be grafted into the good olive tree?

Do not be ignorant of this mystery, or you will become wise in your own conceits and think yourself superior. God has not turned his back and rejected Israel. He has not given her inheritance and promises to another in Israel's place. Blindness has come in part to Israel so salvation could come to the Gentiles. When their time is full, God will again turn to Israel. All Israel shall be saved. It is written, "There shall come out of Sion the Deliverer, and shall turn away ungodliness from Jacob: for this is my covenant unto them, when I shall take away their sins.".

Church, you are not the new Israel. You are not the true Israel. You are not the "spiritual Israel". Quit teaching these things that come from your own egos and read the word of God. Israel is chosen of God himself. Do not try to claim her inheritance. Accept what God has given you, and leave what God has given Israel to Israel herself. Your own greed and vanity will make you an enemy of God if you don't stop doing these things.

Romans 14

1. **Him that is weak in the faith receive ye, but not to doubtful disputations.**
2. **For one believeth that he may eat all things: another, who is weak, eateth herbs.**
3. **Let not him that eateth despise him that eateth not; and let not him which eateth not judge him that eateth: for God hath received him.**
4. **Who art thou that judgest another man's servant? to his own master he standeth or falleth. Yea, he shall be holden up: for God is able to make him stand.**
5. **One man esteemeth one day above another: another esteemeth every day alike. Let every man be fully persuaded in his own mind.**

Church, there are some among you at any given time that may not be as fully instructed as you are. Receive such, but do not cause disputations that would make either them or you doubt. One may believe he can eat all things. Another may hold to eating only certain meats. Yet another will not eat meat at all—only herbs.

If you eat meat, do not despise anyone who doesn't eat meat. If you don't eat meat, don't judge anyone who does eat meat. God has received each of you and not one of you has he received any better than the other. Who are you to think you can judge another man's servant? A servant is established or falls to his own master—not you. The servant shall be held up because God is able to establish him—again not you.

One man may honor one day above another. Another gives honor to every day. Don't argue over which day to honor or how to honor such a day. Such things are petty and do dishonor the God who called you in the first place. Let each one of you be fully persuaded in his own mind at whatever level of instruction you have. Always be open to further instruction. God is able to establish you through the truth that is his word.

1 Corinthians 10

12. Wherefore let him that thinketh he standeth take heed lest he fall.

13. There hath no temptation taken you but such as is common to man: but God is faithful, who will not suffer you to be tempted above that ye are able; but will with the temptation also make a way to escape, that ye may be able to bear it.

If any of you think that you are a strong standing believer firmly established in God's word, beware, you could fall flat very quickly. You are taken in nothing more than the temptations common to any other man. There aren't special temptations reserved just for strong standing believers. Remember this. God is faithful to his word whether you are or not. God will not allow you to be tempted above what you can handle. With temptation, God provides a way to escape so you can handle the temptation. You may not like the way God has provided, but the way is there for you to escape the temptation and still be able to stand without falling.

1 Corinthians 15

1. Moreover, brethren, I declare unto you the gospel which I preached unto you, which also ye have received, and wherein ye stand;

2. By which also ye are saved, if ye keep in memory what I preached unto you, unless ye have believed in vain.
3. For I delivered unto you first of all that which I also received, how that Christ died for our sins according to the scriptures;
4. And that he was buried, and that he rose again the third day according to the scriptures:
5. And that he was seen of Cephas, then of the twelve:
6. After that, he was seen of above five hundred brethren at once; of whom the greater part remain unto this present, but some are fallen asleep.
7. After that, he was seen of James; then of all the apostles.
8. And last of all he was seen of me also, as of one born out of due time.
9. For I am the least of the apostles, that am not meet to be called an apostle, because I persecuted the church of God.
10. But by the grace of God I am what I am: and his grace which was bestowed upon me was not in vain; but I laboured more abundantly than they all: yet not I, but the grace of God which was with me.
11. Therefore whether it were I or they, so we preach, and so ye believed.

Church, Paul is telling about his conversion to Christianity. Pay very close attention to what he says.

I (Paul) declare to you the gospel which I (Paul) preached to you, which also you have received, wherein you stand firmly established both rooted and grounded. By this gospel you are saved, if you keep in memory what I (Paul) preached to you, unless you have believed what I (Paul) delivered to you in vain.

I (Paul) delivered to you first of all that which I (Paul) received, how that Christ died for our sins according to the scriptures; that he was buried, and that he rose again the third day according to the scriptures: and that he was seen of Cephas, then of the twelve. After that he was seen of above five hundred brethren at once; of whom the greater part remain still in this present time, but some are fallen asleep. After that, he was seen of James, then all of the apostles.

Church, we need to stop for a few minutes here and look at what Paul said. Paul was a Pharisee. He showed the things he stated about Christ's death and resurrection in synagogue after synagogue until the Jewish leaders refused to hear him any more before he ever went to the Gentiles specifically. He had to use the scriptures to prove what he said in the synagogues. Therefore, Paul knew that the death and resurrection were according to the scriptures and he reminded the Corinthian congregation of that very thing. He then went on to mention some of the appearances of Christ. He mentions Christ's appearance to the apostles two different times. The first time Christ appeared to Cephas, then to the twelve. The next mention is he appeared to James, then to all the apostles.

Tradition teaches that Judas went out and hanged himself before Christ was ever crucified. Church, some of you teach that there were only eleven apostles left when Christ was resurrected, but were there eleven, or were there twelve? Paul said he appeared to all twelve apostles, which would include Judas. Did Paul make a mistake as some of you teach? Does it really matter? Christ declared the word of God to be truth itself. It matters to Christ. It matters to God, because God is going to judge by the truth itself—the same word of truth he magnified above his own name. It matters to anyone who has the love of the truth in his heart. It should matter to you because you are the pillar and ground of the truth. Let's have a look at the scriptures that have to be ignored to teach that there were only eleven apostles left and each one of you decide for yourself.

Acts 1

1. **The former treatise have I made, O Theophilus, of all that Jesus began both to do and teach,**
2. **Until the day in which he was taken up, after that he through the Holy Ghost had given commandments unto the apostles whom he had chosen:**

> **3. To whom also he shewed himself alive after his passion by many infallible proofs, being seen of them forty days, and speaking of the things pertaining to the kingdom of God:**

Luke wrote this book and referred to an earlier work where he told of all that Jesus began both to do and teach until the day he was taken up (he ascended). This last event took place after Jesus himself through the power of the Holy Spirit had given commandments to the apostles whom he himself had personally chosen. He showed himself alive to the very same apostles after his passion by many infallible proofs, being seen of the apostles he had personally chosen himself forty days, and speaking of the things pertaining to the kingdom of God.

From this, we can see that Luke is saying the same thing Paul said. Christ appeared to all twelve apostles. How can we be sure though? After all the tradition of Judas's death has been handed down for so long, no one can say exactly when it was started. It has been taught for so long, who would dare question it? Let's continue and see whether there were twelve or eleven.

> **Mark 16**
>
> **13. And they went and told it unto the residue: neither believed they them.**
> **14. Afterward he appeared unto the eleven as they sat at meat, and upbraided them with their unbelief and hardness of heart, because they believed not them which had seen him after he was risen.**

When you begin at the first of chapter 16, you see that it is a record of several appearances on the first day of the week. The last recorded event occurred as the eleven were sitting down to eat the evening meal. Christ appeared to eleven specific apostles, yet not one of them is named in this passage only that the eleven were there.

Luke 24

33. And they rose up the same hour, and returned to Jerusalem, and found the eleven gathered together, and them that were with them,
34. Saying, The Lord is risen indeed, and hath appeared to Simon.
35. And they told what things were done in the way, and how he was known of them in breaking of bread.
36. And as they thus spake, Jesus himself stood in the midst of them, and saith unto them, Peace be unto you.
37. But they were terrified and affrighted, and supposed that they had seen a spirit.
38. And he said unto them, Why are ye troubled? and why do thoughts arise in your hearts?
39. Behold my hands and my feet, that it is I myself: handle me, and see; for a spirit hath not flesh and bones, as ye see me have.
40. And when he had thus spoken, he shewed them his hands and his feet.
41. And while they yet believed not for joy, and wondered, he said unto them, Have ye here any meat?
42. And they gave him a piece of a broiled fish, and of an honeycomb.
43. And he took it, and did eat before them.
44. And he said unto them, These are the words which I spake unto you, while I was yet with you, that all things must be fulfilled, which were written in the law of Moses, and in the prophets, and in the psalms, concerning me.
45. Then opened he their understanding, that they might understand the scriptures,
46. And said unto them, Thus it is written, and thus it behoved Christ to suffer, and to rise from the dead the third day:

> 47. And that repentance and remission of sins should be preached in his name among all nations, beginning at Jerusalem.
> 48. And ye are witnesses of these things.

As before, if you look at the beginning of the chapter, Luke, like Mark, is recording several appearances Jesus made on the first day of the week. Again, this is the last recorded appearance of the first day and it is at the time of the evening meal. In this account, the eleven are there along with some others who were not apostles. Therefore, the eleven refers specifically to the number of apostles at that meal as opposed to the others who were there as well. The only apostle named is Peter because they were discussing an appearance Jesus had made to Peter earlier that same day.

John 20

> 19. Then the same day at evening, being the first day of the week, when the doors were shut where the disciples were assembled for fear of the Jews, came Jesus and stood in the midst, and saith unto them, Peace be unto you.
> 20. And when he had so said, he shewed unto them his hands and his side. Then were the disciples glad, when they saw the Lord.
> 21. Then said Jesus to them again, Peace be unto you: as my Father hath sent me, even so send I you.
> 22. And when he had said this, he breathed on them, and saith unto them, Receive ye the Holy Ghost:
> 23. Whose soever sins ye remit, they are remitted unto them; and whose soever sins ye retain, they are retained.
> 24. But Thomas, one of the twelve, called Didymus, was not with them when Jesus came.

John specifically states that this appearance occurs on the first day of the week at evening. John uses the word disciples to include everyone there. All the apostles were disciples, but not all the disciples were apostles. John does not say how many apostles were there. He only said that Thomas, one of the twelve was not with them when Jesus came. Therefore, Thomas was specifically singled out by name as an apostle. Since both Mark and Luke specifically state that there were eleven apostles there and other disciples were there as well, and John stated that the specific apostle not present was Thomas, the only way for there to be eleven apostles in the group was for Judas to still be alive and still with the apostles.

Church, the scriptures show that Judas saw the resurrected Christ. The scriptures say the Christ fulfilled all the law and the prophets. There is one more thing to look at.

Acts 1

> **15. And in those days Peter stood up in the midst of the disciples, and said, (the number of names together were about an hundred and twenty,)**
> **16. Men and brethren, this scripture must needs have been fulfilled, which the Holy Ghost by the mouth of David spake before concerning Judas, which was guide to them that took Jesus.**
> **17. For he was numbered with us, and had obtained part of this ministry.**
> **18. Now this man purchased a field with the reward of iniquity; and falling headlong, he burst asunder in the midst, and all his bowels gushed out.**
> **19. And it was known unto all the dwellers at Jerusalem; insomuch as that field is called in their proper tongue, Aceldama, that is to say, The field of blood.**
> **20. For it is written in the book of Psalms, Let his habitation be desolate, and let no man dwell therein: and his bishoprick let another take.**
> **21. Wherefore of these men which have companied with us all the time that the Lord Jesus went in and out among us,**

22. Beginning from the baptism of John, unto that same day that he was taken up from us, must one be ordained to be a witness with us of his resurrection.

Peter was addressing a group of about 120 disciples when he described the death of Judas. He then referred to a place in Psalms and applied the passage to Judas. He then declared there must be one appointed to take the place of Judas to be ordained to be a witness of the resurrection of Jesus himself. Since Peter referred to something written in the scriptures and said another must be appointed, Christ himself would have had to do that himself during the forty days he witnessed to his apostles and disciples or he would not have fulfilled all the law and prophets. Therefore Judas was alive during the forty days Christ witnessed to his apostles. His death occurred after Christ ascended and before the day of Pentecost was fully come. Judas never returned from the mount of Olives with the other apostles to Jerusalem after Christ ascended.

Church, the scriptures themselves have shown you something that tradition denies. Each of you now must decide whether the scriptures are true or whether the traditions handed down by men are true. Read and reread these passages until you are sure. We have been taught many things that are not true. I am not accusing our teachers of being terrible—they teach what they have been taught. These things have been going on for many generations, but now, we have to choose. We will continue now with Paul.

Last of all, he was seen of me (Paul) also, as one born out of due time. Paul never came across Jesus before Jesus was crucified. He didn't have the pleasure of walking with Jesus and listening to him teach. Yet, Christ appeared to Paul and Paul actually saw and spoke to him. Paul said he did not deserve to be called an apostle because he persecuted the church of God. Paul declared that he was an apostle strictly by the grace of God himself. God's grace to Paul was not in vain because Paul labored more abundantly than all the other apostles, yet it wasn't Paul, it was the grace of God that was with him. Whether Paul or the other apostles, so they preached and so you believed.

1 Corinthians 16

10. Now if Timotheus come, see that he may be with you without fear: for he worketh the work of the Lord, as I also do.
11. Let no man therefore despise him: but conduct him forth in peace, that he may come unto me: for I look for him with the brethren.
12. As touching our brother Apollos, I greatly desired him to come unto you with the brethren: but his will was not at all to come at this time; but he will come when he shall have convenient time.
13. Watch ye, stand fast in the faith, quit you like men, be strong.

Paul wrote the church in Corinth not to give Timothy any trouble if he happened to come to them because Timothy was doing the work of the lord, just like Paul. No one was to despise him. Rather they were to conduct him forth in peace so he could go to Paul because Paul was expecting him. When Paul wrote Timothy, he was a pastor of a church and Paul told him not to let the elders despise his youth. This is the same warning he gave to the elders and congregation in the Church of Corinth.

Paul also told them that Apollos did not want to come to them at that time, but he would come to them at a more convenient time for him. He then gave them instruction in what we call the imperative tense today. It is polite, but it is a command, not a suggestion. He told them to watch, to stand fast (be firmly established) in the faith, behave yourselves like men, and to be strong.

2 Corinthians 1

18. But as God is true, our word toward you was not yea and nay.
19. For the Son of God, Jesus Christ, who was preached among you by us, even by me and Silvanus and Timotheus, was not yea and nay, but in him was yea.

> 20. For all the promises of God in him are yea, and in him Amen, unto the glory of God by us.
> 21. Now he which stablisheth us with you in Christ, and hath anointed us, is God;
> 22. Who hath also sealed us, and given the earnest of the Spirit in our hearts.
> 23. Moreover I call God for a record upon my soul, that to spare you I came not as yet unto Corinth.
> 24. Not for that we have dominion over your faith, but are helpers of your joy: for by faith ye stand.

Church, pay attention to what Paul said to the Corinthians here. We should be this way with one another.

As God himself is true, our (Paul and others) word toward you was not yea and nay. The son of God, Jesus Christ, who was preached among you by us (Paul, Timothy, and Silvanus), was not yea and nay, but in him (Christ) was yea. All the promises of God in him (Christ) are yea, and in him (Christ) so be it, unto the glory of God by us.

Now he which establishes us with you in Christ, and hath anointed us (all of us), is God; who hath sealed us (all of us), and given the earnest of the spirit (God's own spirit) in our (all of our) hearts. Paul does not separate himself as an apostle, or Timothy and Silvanus as pastors from the others in the congregation. Instead, he includes all of them as being joined together in Christ. Why then, church, do you separate yourselves into clergy, laity, elders etc. as though these are better than common worshippers? We may have different functions to perform in our service to the body as a whole, but God himself has joined each one of us and established each one of us in Christ. We are not nor should we ever be a hierarchy where some are more important than others. We are all one in Christ. God himself anointed us all. God himself sealed us all. God himself gave each one of us the earnest of his very own spirit. If God has made us one body, why are there those among you who seek to divide it?

Moreover, I (Paul) call God for a record upon my soul, that to spare you, I (Paul) came not to Corinth yet. Not that we are rulers over your faith, but are helpers (coworkers) of your joy: for by faith you stand (are firmly established both rooted and grounded). Church, Paul here stated that he was just like any other member of the Corinthian congregation. He was not, and would not be, superior to any of them. He was not there to lord his "special calling from God" over them. Nor was he there to rule over them by claiming any authority to do so. They were coworkers and fellow laborers in life. Why have you departed from this way of thinking? It only causes more divisions among you. We will look at faith in greater detail in another section and some of these questions will answer themselves.

Ephesians 2

> **8. For by grace are ye saved through faith; and that not of yourselves: it is the gift of God:**
> **9. Not of works, lest any man should boast.**
> **10. For we are his workmanship, created in Christ Jesus unto good works, which God hath before ordained that we should walk in them.**

Church, let's see just how much gold we have missed in these three verses for the longest time. By the grace of God himself you are saved through faith you don't even have because the faith that saves you is the gift of God himself to you. If you had this faith Paul is talking about, God would not have to give it to you, would He?

Neither salvation nor faith are based on works of any kind. That keeps us from being proud of our personal accomplishments and from comparing ourselves with one another. It stops us from judging one another. Church, we are the workmanship of God himself, created in Christ Jesus to be able to do the good works which God has before ordained for us to do. The good works we do are the result of using the faith God has given us, not the method we use to receive the faith God gives us with salvation. The works we do through this faith God gives us are part of our being firmly established with God in Christ. A huge deposit of gold is here. It is not seen because we spend too much time looking for nuggets.

Philippians 1

27. Only let your conversation be as it becometh the gospel of Christ: that whether I come and see you, or else be absent, I may hear of your affairs, that ye stand fast in one spirit, with one mind striving together for the faith of the gospel;

28. And in nothing terrified by your adversaries: which is to them an evident token of perdition, but to you of salvation, and that of God.

Church, let your conduct be worthy of the gospel of Christ. Whether anyone comes to see you or not, let your conduct reflect that you stand firmly established and immovable in one spirit, unified laboring together for the faith spoken of in the gospel. Do not let those who oppose you terrify you by any means. To them it is an evident token of perdition, but to you of salvation, each according to the judgment of God Himself.

2 Thessalonians 2

1. Now we beseech you, brethren, by the coming of our Lord Jesus Christ, and by our gathering together unto him,

2. That ye be not soon shaken in mind, or be troubled, neither by spirit, nor by word, nor by letter as from us, as that the day of Christ is at hand.

3. Let no man deceive you by any means: for that day shall not come, except there come a falling away first, and that man of sin be revealed, the son of perdition;

4. Who opposeth and exalteth himself above all that is called God, or that is worshipped; so that he as God sitteth in the temple of God, shewing himself that he is God.

5. Remember ye not, that, when I was yet with you, I told you these things?

Paul is begging you by the coming of Christ himself and by our gathering together unto him that you not be soon shaken in mind, or be troubled. Your stand is one that is to be firmly established, rooted and grounded in the word of truth—the word of God—itself. Let no one deceive you by any means, neither by spirit (power), nor by word (as prophecy), nor by letter as from an apostle, that the day of Christ is at hand. First there shall come a falling away, so the man of sin can be revealed, the son of perdition himself who opposes and exalts himself above all that is called God or is worshipped. He shall sit as God in the temple, showing that he himself is God.

Just exactly what is this "falling away"? Is it false teaching? If you read the scriptures at all, you will quickly see that Paul, James, John, and Peter were dealing with false teachings that were already in the congregations. This "falling away" is much more and far worse than just false teaching. In order for the man of sin to be revealed and sit as God himself in the temple of God, there can not be one single Christian left on this earth with the love of the truth in his heart. That means that the church that is here will be a completely false church that may still call itself Christian. This has not happened yet.

For us to stand firmly established, rooted and grounded in the word of God itself, we need to compare every tradition with the word of God to determine the truth of the traditions that have been handed down to us. It doesn't mean we oppose the word of God, it means we are determining the truth of the traditions we have been taught. This simple action will cause a separation in the church itself—one group seeking the truth and the other accepting whatever is taught without question. This event hasn't happened yet, but the time for it to happen is approaching.

Acts 17

10. And the brethren immediately sent away Paul and Silas by night unto Berea: who coming thither went into the synagogue of the Jews.

> 11. These were more noble than those in Thessalonica, in that they received the word with all readiness of mind, and searched the scriptures daily, whether those things were so.
> 12. Therefore many of them believed; also of honourable women which were Greeks, and of men, not a few.
> 13. But when the Jews of Thessalonica had knowledge that the word of God was preached of Paul at Berea, they came thither also, and stirred up the people.

Paul and Silas went to Berea in the middle of the night because people were trying to kill them in Thessalonica. They went into the synagogue in Berea and began teaching the same thing that they taught in Thessalonica. Those in Berea heard with all readiness of mind as we should and searched the scriptures daily to see if what they were being taught was true as we should. As a result, many believed Paul and Silas. Also honorable women who were Greeks (gentile) and many men believed them as well. However, as soon as the leaders in Thessalonica heard what was happening in Berea, they came and stirred up the people. When you start questioning the truth of what you are being taught by comparing it to the word of God, beware. There will come those among you to stir you up against your teachers, against one another, or whatever it takes to stop you from seeking the truth.

2 Timothy 2

> 15. Study to shew thyself approved unto God, a workman that needeth not to be ashamed, rightly dividing the word of truth.

You must study to show yourself approved unto God. How else can you know what, when, where, or how to do what God wants, if you don't know what he says in his own word? Study God's word as a workman working a trade not as a hobby or as an occasional social event. That way there will be no need for you to ever be ashamed of the work you are doing. Make sure that when you do study, you rightly divide the word of truth. When it is rightly divided, the word of truth is truth itself. However, if it is wrongly divided, you no longer have the truth. What you have then is a lie that may or may not sound good. Rightly divided is an exact term that means an absolutely true cutting. Anything other than a true cutting is false, no matter how good it sounds.

1 Thessalonians 4

13. **But I would not have you to be ignorant, brethren, concerning them which are asleep, that ye sorrow not, even as others which have no hope.**
14. **For if we believe that Jesus died and rose again, even so them also which sleep in Jesus will God bring with him.**
15. **For this we say unto you by the word of the Lord, that we which are alive and remain unto the coming of the Lord shall not prevent them which are asleep.**
16. **For the Lord himself shall descend from heaven with a shout, with the voice of the archangel, and with the trump of God: and the dead in Christ shall rise first:**
17. **Then we which are alive and remain shall be caught up together with them in the clouds, to meet the Lord in the air: and so shall we ever be with the Lord.**
18. **Wherefore comfort one another with these words.**

In this passage, Paul is dealing with Christian concerns over the death of their brethren. He considered them to be asleep, rather than permanently dead, and told the brethren not to sorrow like the others that have no hope. He told them that if we believe that Jesus died and rose again, even so them also which sleep in Jesus will God bring with him. Paul said by the word of the lord that those of us who are alive when this happens will not prevent (that is precede) them which are asleep in Jesus.

The lord himself shall descend from heaven with a shout, with the voice of the archangel, and with the trump of God. The dead in Christ (those asleep in Christ) shall rise first. Then, after that, we which are alive and remain shall be caught up together with them (those who were just raised) in the clouds, to meet the lord in the air. Then we shall be ever with the lord. We are to comfort one another with these words.

This says a lot—and there is a lot it doesn't say. For instance, nowhere does it say Christ returns to the same spot that he ascended from on the mount of Olives. It says he is in the air. Nowhere does it say he will come with a great number of saints. It says he himself shall descend. Nowhere does it say he will fight any enemies. The only people mentioned are Christ and those that are his. To understand the importance of this, we need to look at John for a minute.

John 14

1. **Let not your heart be troubled: ye believe in God, believe also in me.**
2. **In my Father's house are many mansions: if it were not so, I would have told you. I go to prepare a place for you.**
3. **And if I go and prepare a place for you, I will come again, and receive you unto myself; that where I am, there ye may be also.**

Jesus promised his apostles that he was going to prepare a place for them, and that he would return and receive them unto himself so they could be where he is. At no time did he say they would be with him when they died and he would bring them back to get their bodies later.

Paul just described how Christ will keep the promise he himself made to his apostles and to anyone who believed their word. Once Christ has received both the dead in Christ and the living unto himself, God will them bring them with him to the place Christ has prepared for those that are his. Regardless what traditions teach, that is what the scriptures say.

The next thing to understand is that the only people who will know about this are those that belong to Christ because until he comes to the mount of Olives, if he appears at all, it will be only to those who are his. This is what he did for forty days after he was resurrected, and finally with Paul.

2 Timothy 2

7. Consider what I say; and the Lord give thee understanding in all things.
8. Remember that Jesus Christ of the seed of David was raised from the dead according to my gospel:
9. Wherein I suffer trouble, as an evil doer, even unto bonds; but the word of God is not bound.
10. Therefore I endure all things for the elect's sakes, that they may also obtain the salvation which is in Christ Jesus with eternal glory.
11. It is a faithful saying: For if we be dead with him, we shall also live with him:
12. If we suffer, we shall also reign with him: if we deny him, he also will deny us:
13. If we believe not, yet he abideth faithful: he cannot deny himself.
14. Of these things put them in remembrance, charging them before the Lord that they strive not about words to no profit, but to the subverting of the hearers.
15. Study to shew thyself approved unto God, a workman that needeth not to be ashamed, rightly dividing the word of truth.
16. But shun profane and vain babblings: for they will increase unto more ungodliness.
17. And their word will eat as doth a canker: of whom is Hymenaeus and Philetus;
18. Who concerning the truth have erred, saying that the resurrection is past already; and overthrow the faith of some.

19. Nevertheless the foundation of God standeth sure, having this seal, The Lord knoweth them that are his. And, Let every one that nameth the name of Christ depart from iniquity.

Paul is writing to Timothy, a young pastor at a church that resisted him because of his youth. He reminded Timothy of the gospel he preached and how it had caused him all kinds of problems for preaching the death and resurrection of Christ. Paul was willing to suffer the consequences for the sake of the elect (the children of Israel), that they too may obtain the salvation which is in Christ Jesus with eternal glory.

This is a faithful saying: if we be dead with him, we shall also live (have eternal life) with him. If we suffer with him, we shall also reign with him. If we deny him, he will also deny us. Even if we don't believe him, he is still faithful because he can not deny himself. Put your congregations in remembrance of these things. Charge them before the lord himself that they strive not about words that serve no purpose other than the subverting of the hearers. Encourage study of the word of God as a workman, not as a hobby.

Turn away from and avoid vain and profane babblings, for they will lead to more ungodliness. Their word will eat away like gangrene: of whom is Hymenaeus and Philetus; who concerning the truth have erred, saying the resurrection is past already; and overthrow the faith of some. Nevertheless the foundation of God stands sure, having this seal, the lord knows those that are his.

Let everyone that names the name of Christ completely depart from iniquity. Iniquity comes from a root word that means to twist or to bend. If you desire to twist or in some way change the word of God to your benefit, then you do not have the love of the truth in your heart. If you do not have the love of the truth in your heart, you are not Christ's and he will not return for you. You will become part of the false church that completely denies the God they claim to worship—even if they still name the name of Christ.

James 2

1. My brethren, have not the faith of our Lord Jesus Christ, the Lord of glory, with respect of persons.
2. For if there come unto your assembly a man with a gold ring, in goodly apparel, and there come in also a poor man in vile raiment;
3. And ye have respect to him that weareth the gay clothing, and say unto him, Sit thou here in a good place; and say to the poor, Stand thou there, or sit here under my footstool:
4. Are ye not then partial in yourselves, and are become judges of evil thoughts?

Do not have the faith of our lord Jesus Christ, the Lord of glory, with respect of persons. If a man enters your assembly with a gold ring and nice clothes, and also a poor man in disgusting clothes, and you tell the well dressed man to sit in a place of honor, yet you tell the poor man to stand in the back, or sit some place where you won't be noticed: are you not partial in yourselves? You have literally become judges who have evil thoughts. Yet you do these things and call it "Christian". You seek honor and dignities. You let appearances determine a person's status with God. The wealthier person must be doing the things God wants because he is wealthy. The poor man must be terribly rebellious because you don't see a material blessing from God. How twisted and evil such thoughts are, yet you teach those very things from your pulpits. Wake up! You are not obeying God yourselves according to James.

James 5

7. Be patient therefore, brethren, unto the coming of the Lord. Behold, the husbandman waiteth for the precious fruit of the earth, and hath long patience for it, until he receive the early and latter rain.

> 8. Be ye also patient; stablish your hearts: for the coming of the Lord draweth nigh.
> 9. Grudge not one against another, brethren, lest ye be condemned: behold, the judge standeth before the door.
> 10. Take, my brethren, the prophets, who have spoken in the name of the Lord, for an example of suffering affliction, and of patience.

Be anxious for nothing, be patient unto the coming of the lord. Observe the husbandman who waits for his crop. He has long patience for it and waits for both the early and latter rain before he begins his harvest. Be patient the same way. Strengthen and establish your hearts firmly in the word of God. The coming of the lord draws near, but the time is not yet. Don't hold grudges against one another. The judge himself stands before the door. Learn from the prophets who have spoken in the name of the Lord. Heed their example of suffering affliction and their patience.

And having done all—stand.

CHAPTER 12

Ephesians 6

17. And take the helmet of salvation, and the sword of the Spirit, which is the word of God:

Paul used the helmet of the Roman soldier to illustrate salvation because the helmet protects you from blows to the head. The head is associated with the mind. A head injury can be totally crippling or deadly. It is very important therefore to understand salvation and it's benefit to you. Salvation is used three different ways in the New Testament. It means defense or defender. It means to deliver, protect, or make whole as a singular event or occurrence. It means an act that is an ongoing process. We will cover each meaning and the scriptures will explain themselves when we understand what each one means by "salvation".

Luke 2

21. And when eight days were accomplished for the circumcising of the child, his name was called Jesus, which was so named of the angel before he was conceived in the womb.
22. And when the days of her purification according to the law of Moses were accomplished, they brought him to Jerusalem, to present him to the Lord;
23. (As it is written in the law of the Lord, Every male that openeth the womb shall be called holy to the Lord;)

24. And to offer a sacrifice according to that which is said in the law of the Lord, A pair of turtledoves, or two young pigeons.
25. And, behold, there was a man in Jerusalem, whose name was Simeon; and the same man was just and devout, waiting for the consolation of Israel: and the Holy Ghost was upon him.
26. And it was revealed unto him by the Holy Ghost, that he should not see death, before he had seen the Lord's Christ.
27. And he came by the Spirit into the temple: and when the parents brought in the child Jesus, to do for him after the custom of the law,
28. Then took he him up in his arms, and blessed God, and said,
29. Lord, now lettest thou thy servant depart in peace, according to thy word:
30. For mine eyes have seen thy salvation,
31. Which thou hast prepared before the face of all people;
32. A light to lighten the Gentiles, and the glory of thy people Israel.
33. And Joseph and his mother marvelled at those things which were spoken of him.
34. And Simeon blessed them, and said unto Mary his mother, Behold, this child is set for the fall and rising again of many in Israel; and for a sign which shall be spoken against;
35. (Yea, a sword shall pierce through thy own soul also,) that the thoughts of many hearts may be revealed.
36. And there was one Anna, a prophetess, the daughter of Phanuel, of the tribe of Aser: she was of a great age, and had lived with an husband seven years from her virginity;
37. And she was a widow of about fourscore and four years, which departed not from the temple, but served God with fastings and prayers night and day.

> 38. And she coming in that instant gave thanks likewise unto the Lord, and spake of him to all them that looked for redemption in Jerusalem.
> 39. And when they had performed all things according to the law of the Lord, they returned into Galilee, to their own city Nazareth.

This passage begins at the circumcising of a male child eight days after his birth. His mother named him Jesus, because the angel named the child that before he was ever conceived by his mother. This child was born in Bethlehem, which was just outside Jerusalem. His parents were in Bethlehem at the time of birth and remained there for a little while.

When the days of her purification were completed, they came from Bethlehem to present the child because the law of the Lord said that every male child that opens the womb shall be called holy to the Lord. They also came to offer a purification sacrifice as was required by the law of the Lord, a pair of turtledoves or two young pigeons.

A just and devout man named Simeon lived in Jerusalem. He was waiting for the consolation of Israel and the spirit of God was upon him. The spirit of God revealed to him that he would not see death until he had seen the Lord's Christ—the Messiah promised to Israel. Simeon was filled with the power of the spirit of God when he came to the temple looking for this Messiah. He didn't know who he was looking for, only that he would recognise him when he saw him.

Imagine a busy place like the temple was, people coming and going, worshipping, giving offerings, offering sacrifices, etc. and Simeon was looking for just one person in that huge crowd of people. It would have been like looking for a needle in a big haystack.

The scriptures don't say how long Simeon was in the temple, only that the parents brought the child Jesus into the temple to offer the required sacrifice for him and for his mother's purification. As soon as Simeon saw them, he took the child Jesus in his arms and blessed God. He then said let thy servant depart in peace according to thy word: for my eyes have seen your salvation, which you have prepared before the face of all people, a light to lighten the Gentiles, and the glory of your people Israel.

Simeon then blessed them, and said to the child's mother, Mary, Behold, this child is set for the fall and rising again of many; and for a sign which shall be spoken against; that the thoughts of many hearts shall be revealed. Mary and Joseph marvelled at the things that Simeon spoke of.

There was also a prohetess named Anna, the daughter of Phanuel, of the tribe of Aser. She was very old and had lived with a husband for seven years from her virginity. She was a widow of about eighty-four who did not depart from the temple, but served God with fastings and prayers continuously night and day.

She came in at the instant Simeon was talking and she herself began to give thanks to the Lord, and spoke of him to all who looked for redemption in Jerusalem. When Joseph and Mary had done all the things according to the law of the Lord they had come to do, they returned into Galilee, to their own city Nazareth. Note they did not return to Bethlehem after this, they went instead to Nazareth.

In this instance, the word salvation refers to a specific person—Jesus, the child of Mary and Joseph.

Luke 3

1. **Now in the fifteenth year of the reign of Tiberius Caesar, Pontius Pilate being governor of Judaea, and Herod being tetrarch of Galilee, and his brother Philip tetrarch of Ituraea and of the region of Trachonitis, and Lysanias the tetrarch of Abilene,**
2. **Annas and Caiaphas being the high priests, the word of God came unto John the son of Zacharias in the wilderness.**
3. **And he came into all the country about Jordan, preaching the baptism of repentance for the remission of sins;**
4. **As it is written in the book of the words of Esaias the prophet, saying, The voice of one crying in the wilderness, Prepare ye the way of the Lord, make his paths straight.**

5. Every valley shall be filled, and every mountain and hill shall be brought low; and the crooked shall be made straight, and the rough ways shall be made smooth;
6. And all flesh shall see the salvation of God.

During the fifteenth year of the reign of Tiberius Caesar, Pontius Pilate was the governor of Judea. Herod was the tetrarch of Galilee, his brother Philip tetrarch of Ituraea and Trachonitis, and Lysanias was the tetrarch of Abilene. Annas and Caiaphas were sharing the office of high priest in Jerusalem. It was at this time the word of God came to John, the son of Zacharias, in the wilderness and he came into all the country about Jordan, preaching the baptism for repentance and the remission of sins. The prophet Isaiah foretold this when he wrote, saying, the voice of one crying in the wilderness, prepare ye the way of the Lord, make his paths straight. Every valley shall be filled, and every mountain and hill shall be made low; the crooked shall be made straight, and the rough ways shall be made smooth; and all flesh shall see the salvation of God. Here salvation refers specifically to a person, yet neither Isaiah nor John named the person.

Acts 28

28. Be it known therefore unto you, that the salvation of God is sent unto the Gentiles, and that they will hear it.
29. And when he had said these words, the Jews departed, and had great reasoning among themselves.
30. And Paul dwelt two whole years in his own hired house, and received all that came in unto him,
31. Preaching the kingdom of God, and teaching those things which concern the Lord Jesus Christ, with all confidence, no man forbidding him.

Paul was in Rome waiting to see Caesar. He told the Jews who were meeting with him that the salvation of God is sent to the Gentiles, and they will hear it. The Jews departed and reasoned greatly among themselves. Paul spent two whole years in his own rented house. He received all that came into him, preaching the kingdom of God, and teaching the things which concern Jesus Christ with all confidence, no man forbidding him.

Paul identif ied Jesus Christ as the person of God's salvation specifically. Simeon held this same Jesus in his arms as a baby and acknowledged him in the temple. Annah acknowledged the same baby Jesus in the temple. Isaiah and John spoke of the same person, yet neither of them named him specifically.

Titus 2

> **9. Exhort servants to be obedient unto their own masters, and to please them well in all things; not answering again;**
> **10. Not purloining, but shewing all good fidelity; that they may adorn the doctrine of God our Saviour in all things.**
> **11. For the grace of God that bringeth salvation hath appeared to all men,**
> **12. Teaching us that, denying ungodliness and worldly lusts, we should live soberly, righteously, and godly, in this present world;**
> **13. Looking for that blessed hope, and the glorious appearing of the great God and our Saviour Jesus Christ;**
> **14. Who gave himself for us, that he might redeem us from all iniquity, and purify unto himself a peculiar people, zealous of good works.**
> **15. These things speak, and exhort, and rebuke with all authority. Let no man despise thee.**

Paul was writing to Titus, who was responsible for straightening things out in the assemblies in Crete. He told Titus to exhort servants to obey their own masters, to be obedient to them, to be well pleasing in their service to them, not to talk back to their masters, be respectful, not stealing, instead to show trustworthiness and loyalty. By doing these things, the servants themselves adorn the doctrine of God our savior in all things. While we no longer have masters and servants as a way of life these days, the way Paul talked about behavior still applies to each one of us today.

Paul said the grace of God that brings salvation has appeared to all men, teaching us, that denying ungodliness and worldly lusts (selfish desires), we should live soberly (with a clear mind), righteously, and godly in this present world. We are to look for the blessed hope and the glorious appearing of the great God. We are also to look for the appearing of our Saviour Jesus Christ who gave himself for us to redeem us from all iniquity, and purify unto himself a peculiar people (purchased people) who are themselves zealous of good works. These are the things Paul told Titus, and every pastor since, to speak, exhort, and rebuke with all authority. Let no man despise you when you do this.

Again Paul mentions salvation in terms of a person. Paul identifies the person as Jesus Christ. These four passages are the only ones that refer to salvation as being a person. All four of them refer to the very same person—Jesus Christ himself.

The next reference to salvation refers to a singular event or occurrence that only occurs once. It is this particular event that allows each of us to establish a direct relationship with God because of the accomplishments of the person of salvation—Jesus Christ himself.

Acts 2

21. **And it shall come to pass, that whosoever shall call on the name of the Lord shall be saved.**
22. **Ye men of Israel, hear these words; Jesus of Nazareth, a man approved of God among you by miracles and wonders and signs, which God did by him in the midst of you, as ye yourselves also know:**
37. **Now when they heard this, they were pricked in their heart, and said unto Peter and to the rest of the apostles, Men and brethren, what shall we do?**

38. Then Peter said unto them, Repent, and be baptized every one of you in the name of Jesus Christ for the remission of sins, and ye shall receive the gift of the Holy Ghost.
39. For the promise is unto you, and to your children, and to all that are afar off, even as many as the Lord our God shall call.
40. And with many other words did he testify and exhort, saying, Save yourselves from this untoward generation.
41. Then they that gladly received his word were baptized: and the same day there were added unto them about three thousand souls.
42. And they continued stedfastly in the apostles' doctrine and fellowship, and in breaking of bread, and in prayers.
43. And fear came upon every soul: and many wonders and signs were done by the apostles.
44. And all that believed were together, and had all things common;
45. And sold their possessions and goods, and parted them to all men, as every man had need.
46. And they, continuing daily with one accord in the temple, and breaking bread from house to house, did eat their meat with gladness and singleness of heart,
47. Praising God, and having favour with all the people. And the Lord added to the church daily such as should be saved.

The day of Pentecost was fully come and Peter was telling the people in the temple about the death and resurrection of Christ. Peter said that it shall come to pass that whosoever shall call on the name of the Lord shall be saved. Here he is talking about being delivered, protected, and made whole as in restored to completeness. This is a singular event. He went on to identify Jesus Christ as a man approved of God by signs and wonders God performed by him in the midst of these same people. They couldn't deny Christ or the miracles because they saw for themselves the things he did.

Peter went on to tell them how they had deliberately delivered Jesus up to be crucified, how God had raised him from the dead and made him the very Messiah they had looked for so long. The people were cut to their hearts when they realized this, and they immediately asked Peter what they should do. Peter told them to repent (turn from their ways) and be baptized in the name of Jesus Christ (not God the Father, God the Son, and God the Holy Ghost) for the remission of sins and you shall receive the gift of God (holy spirit—power from on high) just like the apostles did as these people had witnessed before Peter had begun to speak to them.

This promise was from God to them, their children, those afar off, and to as many as God shall call whenever and wherever he calls them. He spoke many more things to them testifying and exhorting them to save themselves from the untoward generation they were in. Those that gladly received his words were baptized, and that day about three thousand souls were added to their number. These people continued steadfastly in the apostles doctrine, and in fellowship, and in the breaking of bread together.

Great respect and awe came upon them, and the apostles worked many signs and wonders among them. All those that believed were together and had all things in common. Those who had excess sold their goods and property, and gave to all men as they had need. They continued daily with one accord in the temple. They broke bread from house to house and ate their food with gladness and singleness of heart. In today's instant society, we don't have time for such things, unless we decide to make time for such things. However, such things might be an invasion of our own "personal time". Our whole lives would change if we did the things these people did with our "personal time". These people were praising God and found favor with all the people. Church, do we? The Lord added daily to the church such as should be saved.

Acts 4

9. If we this day be examined of the good deed done to the impotent man, by what means he is made whole;
10. Be it known unto you all, and to all the people of Israel, that by the name of Jesus Christ of Nazareth, whom ye crucified, whom God raised from the dead, even by him doth this man stand here before you whole.
11. This is the stone which was set at nought of you builders, which is become the head of the corner.
12. Neither is there salvation in any other: for there is none other name under heaven given among men, whereby we must be saved.
13. Now when they saw the boldness of Peter and John, and perceived that they were unlearned and ignorant men, they marvelled; and they took knowledge of them, that they had been with Jesus.
14. And beholding the man which was healed standing with them, they could say nothing against it.

Peter and John had healed a man lame from birth and the next day they were taken before the temple rulers to explain themselves. Peter said that if they were to be questioned about the good deed they had done by making this man whole, then the leaders and everybody else should know that by the name of Jesus Christ of Nazareth, whom you crucified, whom God has raised from the dead, even by him does this man stand before you whole.

Peter said Jesus Christ was the stone that was worthless to the builders (leaders of the temple), which has become the chief corner stone. Peter said there was not salvation (deliverance, protection, wholeness) in any other. That is why Jesus Christ has become the chief corner stone. There is no other name under heaven given among men whereby we must be saved (not Buddha, not Hare Krishna, not Mohammed, not God the Father, God the Son, God the Holy Ghost, not any other name of any kind at all).

When the leaders saw the boldness of Peter and John, two ignorant and untrained fishermen, they marvelled. They then took knowledge of Peter and John, that they had been with Jesus. And seeing the healed man standing with Peter and John, the leaders could say nothing at all.

Acts 15

> **1. And certain men which came down from Judaea taught the brethren, and said, Except ye be circumcised after the manner of Moses, ye cannot be saved.**
> **7. And when there had been much disputing, Peter rose up, and said unto them, Men and brethren, ye know how that a good while ago God made choice among us, that the Gentiles by my mouth should hear the word of the gospel, and believe.**
> **8. And God, which knoweth the hearts, bare them witness, giving them the Holy Ghost, even as he did unto us;**
> **9. And put no difference between us and them, purifying their hearts by faith.**
> **10. Now therefore why tempt ye God, to put a yoke upon the neck of the disciples, which neither our fathers nor we were able to bear?**
> **11. But we believe that through the grace of the Lord Jesus Christ we shall be saved, even as they.**

Certain men came down from Judea and began teaching that, unless you were circumcised after the manner of Moses, you cannot be saved (delivered, made whole). This caused quite a stir among the people, and there were a great many disputes because of this teaching. Finally,

Peter stood up and reminded them that some time before, God had chosen him to go preach the gospel to the Gentiles so they too could be saved.

Peter said that God, who knows the hearts of men, bore witness of the Gentiles, and gave them the same holy spirit he had given the apostles. God put no difference between Jew and Gentile, purifying their hearts by faith. Why would you tempt God by putting a yoke upon the neck of the disciples that neither you nor our fathers could bear? Why would want them to keep all the law or any part of the law to be righteous enough for God to offer them salvation? Instead we believe that through the grace of Jesus Christ himself we shall be delivered and made whole. At least, that is what we are supposed to believe, according to Peter.

Acts 16

> **28. But Paul cried with a loud voice, saying, Do thyself no harm: for we are all here.**
> **29. Then he called for a light, and sprang in, and came trembling, and fell down before Paul and Silas,**
> **30. And brought them out, and said, Sirs, what must I do to be saved?**
> **31. And they said, Believe on the Lord Jesus Christ, and thou shalt be saved, and thy house.**
> **32. And they spake unto him the word of the Lord, and to all that were in his house.**

This passage is near the end of a story. Paul and Silas were in Thyatira and managed to get themselves beaten and thrown into prison. They were put in stocks and chained. During the night, there was an earthquake that broke all the chains, loosened the bindings, and opened all the doors in the prison. The jailor was about to kill himself because he was afraid the prisoners had escaped. It is here that the passage picks up the story.

Paul called to the jailor and told him not to harm himself because all the prisoners were still there—not even one had escaped. The jailor called for someone to bring him a light. He went in himself to see that everyone was there. He fell down before Paul and Silas and asked them what he must do to be delivered and restored. They told him to believe on the lord Jesus Christ and he would be saved, and his house. He brought them out into his own house and they spoke the word of the Lord to him and those of his house.

Romans 5

8. But God commendeth his love toward us, in that, while we were yet sinners, Christ died for us.
9. Much more then, being now justified by his blood, we shall be saved from wrath through him.
10. For if, when we were enemies, we were reconciled to God by the death of his Son, much more, being reconciled, we shall be saved by his life.

God demonstrates his love toward us, in that, while we were still sinners—still disobedient—still rebellious—still self ish—Christ died for us. Even more, being justified by his blood, we shall yet be saved from wrath through him. If, when we were enemies of God and everything he stands for, God reconciled us to himself by the death of his only begotten son, much more, being reconciled, we shall be restored and made whole by his life. This life is the life that is in Christ himself right now—Eternal Life. Since Eternal Life can never grow old or die under any circumstances, our wholeness and restoration are guaranteed to us.

Romans 10

9. That if thou shalt confess with thy mouth the Lord Jesus, and shalt believe in thine heart that God hath raised him from the dead, thou shalt be saved.
10. For with the heart man believeth unto righteousness; and with the mouth confession is made unto salvation.
11. For the scripture saith, Whosoever believeth on him shall not be ashamed.
12. For there is no difference between the Jew and the Greek: for the same Lord over all is rich unto all that call upon him.
13. For whosoever shall call upon the name of the Lord shall be saved.

This passage is taught commonly among many churches, yet it is terribly misunderstood. Let's take a very close look at this passage to see what it says and what it doesn't say.

If you confess with your mouth the lord Jesus—not that you are a worthless sinner and go about to name every sin you have ever committed from the day you were born, including the times when you were a baby and did selfish things just to be held—and believe in your heart—the very essence of who you are—that God himself raised Jesus Christ from the dead—not that Christ somehow raised himself—you shall be delivered, restored, and made whole.

Man believes unto righteousness with the heart—not by scrupulously keeping any laws. With his mouth, man confesses the lord Jesus unto salvation—deliverance, restoration, wholeness. To God, there is no difference between the Jew who has the law of God to begin with that defined righteousness itself and the Greek (Gentile) who does not have the law, does not know God, and is without God and without hope in this world.

The scriptures say whosoever believes on him shall not be ashamed. There is no difference between the Jew and the Greek (Gentile) to God because he is the same Lord over all and is rich unto all who call upon him. Whosoever calls upon the name of the Lord shall be saved—delivered, restored, made whole.

These passages refer to a singular event initiated by confessing the lord Jesus who died for our disobedience and believing that God himself raised Jesus from the dead. This singular event begins a process that continues the rest of our lives. There is no instant salvation—just add water. It is a growing and learning process that helps each of us to overcome our shortcomings. We will discuss the process later in another section of this study.

1 Corinthians 1

18. For the preaching of the cross is to them that perish foolishness; but unto us which are saved it is the power of God.

> 19. For it is written, I will destroy the wisdom of the wise, and will bring to nothing the understanding of the prudent.
> 20. Where is the wise? where is the scribe? where is the disputer of this world? hath not God made foolish the wisdom of this world?
> 21. For after that in the wisdom of God the world by wisdom knew not God, it pleased God by the foolishness of preaching to save them that believe.
> 22. For the Jews require a sign, and the Greeks seek after wisdom:
> 23. But we preach Christ crucified, unto the Jews a stumblingblock, and unto the Greeks foolishness;
> 24. But unto them which are called, both Jews and Greeks, Christ the power of God, and the wisdom of God.

The preaching of the cross and the resulting death and resurrection of Christ is utter foolishness to them that perish; however, it is the power of God to those of us who are delivered, restored, and made whole. It is written, I will destroy the wisdom of the wise and will bring to nothing the understanding of the prudent. Where is the wise person among you? Where is the scribe among you? Who among you will stand as the disputer of this world? Has not God reduced the wisdom of this world to utter foolishness?

The world in its greatest wisdom knew not and still does not know God. It therefore pleases God to save those who believe through the foolishness of preaching the death and resurrection of Christ. The Jews require a sign that would constitute that Christ is indeed the foretold Messiah. The Greeks (Gentiles) seek great wisdom and philosophical understanding.

However, both are totally confounded by the death and resurrection of Christ. The Jews were looking for the conquering Messiah who would restore their kingdom to them and rule them. They were not looking for a man to come and die, especially on a cross. The Jews themselves were divided over resurrection from the dead. The Greeks (Gentiles), however, considered a bodily resurrection to be utter foolishness. They believed that the body was a place where their immortal spirit was housed until it was freed by death—never to be entrapped again in a body. Surprisingly these two beliefs are still maintained by large numbers of people today who look at Christians as ignorant, deluded followers of myths and fairy tales.

However, to those that answer God's call, the death and resurrection of Christ is both the power and the wisdom of God.

1 Corinthians 15

1. Moreover, brethren, I declare unto you the gospel which I preached unto you, which also ye have received, and wherein ye stand;
2. By which also ye are saved, if ye keep in memory what I preached unto you, unless ye have believed in vain.
3. For I delivered unto you first of all that which I also received, how that Christ died for our sins according to the scriptures;
4. And that he was buried, and that he rose again the third day according to the scriptures:
5. And that he was seen of Cephas, then of the twelve:
6. After that, he was seen of above five hundred brethren at once; of whom the greater part remain unto this present, but some are fallen asleep.
7. After that, he was seen of James; then of all the apostles.
8. And last of all he was seen of me also, as of one born out of due time.
9. For I am the least of the apostles, that am not meet to be called an apostle, because I persecuted the church of God.
10. But by the grace of God I am what I am: and his grace which was bestowed upon me was not in vain; but I laboured more abundantly than they all: yet not I, but the grace of God which was with me.
11. Therefore whether it were I or they, so we preach, and so ye believed.

Paul was recounting the things he himself had learned and reminding the church at Corinth of the things they had been originally taught. These were the things they had received directly from him, and the things they believed, and were standing in. The things he taught them would deliver them, restore them, and make them whole if they continued in them. Otherwise, they had believed in vain—for no purpose at all.

Paul reminded them that Christ himself died for our sins according to the scriptures. Christ was buried and rose again on the third day according to the scriptures. Christ was seen of Cephas (Peter), then of the twelve—all twelve. Later, he was seen of over 500 brethren at once. Some were already dead by the time Paul came to Corinth, but most were still alive. Later, he was seen of James, then all of the apostles. Finally, years later, Paul himself saw Christ while he was going to Damascus to bring the Christians there back to Jerusalem in chains.

Paul considered himself to be the least among the apostles and did not consider himself worthy to even be an apostle because he had persecuted the church of God. Yet he considered himself to be an apostle by the grace of God himself. God's grace was not given to Paul in vain because Paul labored more than any of the other apostles. Yet it wasn't Paul himself, rather the grace of God which was with him that strengthened and inspired him. As far as Paul was concerned, whether he taught them or any of the other apostles taught them, they believed what they were taught.

Ephesians 2

4. But God, who is rich in mercy, for his great love wherewith he loved us,

5. Even when we were dead in sins, hath quickened us together with Christ, (by grace ye are saved;)

6. And hath raised us up together, and made us sit together in heavenly places in Christ Jesus:

7. That in the ages to come he might shew the exceeding riches of his grace in his kindness toward us through Christ Jesus.

8. For by grace are ye saved through faith; and that not of yourselves: it is the gift of God:
9. Not of works, lest any man should boast.

God, who himself is rich in mercy, loves us so much that, while we were dead to him in sins and rebelliousness, has made us alive together with Christ (by God's grace and his mercy are you delivered, restored, and made whole), and has raised us up together, and has made us to sit together in heavenly places in Christ Jesus. Notice that all these things are in the past tense. These things have already been accomplished. They were accomplished when God himself raised Christ from the dead. This is the way God sees these things.

We are here and now and we have difficulties allowing ourselves to see things the way God does. We operate under the mistaken conception that because we are unrighteous by nature, we cannot see things the way God does. We think that we have to do things ourselves to be righteous enough before God for him to finally accept us and allow us to be in his presence. We ignore the scriptures. Paul just told us that all these things were accomplished in Christ while we were still rebellious against God. That means there is absolutely nothing we can do of ourselves that will ever allow God to accept us in his presence. Without accepting the accomplishments of the death and resurrection of Christ in its completeness, we will never be able to see things the way God does.

God did all this at once to show through all ages the exceeding riches of his grace in his kindness toward us through Christ. The very rebellious nature we have is the thing that fights so hard to keep us from accepting what God has done through Christ. It tells us we don't deserve it—and we don't. It tells us we are unrighteous before God—and we are. It then tells us that we can do righteous things and God will accept that instead of the death and resurrection of Christ or along with the death and resurrection of Christ—and that is not true. There is nothing we can do in and of ourselves to be righteous before God.

It is by the grace of God himself that you are delivered, restored, and made whole. This is accomplished through faith—something we don't have at all. The faith Paul talks about here is a gift to us from God himself. If we had this faith at all, God would not have to give it to us. It is not through any kind of work we do in and of ourselves. That way, we will not compare ourselves to one another and try to make ourselves more or less important by bragging or judging others.

2 Thessalonians 2

7. For the mystery of iniquity doth already work: only he who now letteth will let, until he be taken out of the way.
8. And then shall that Wicked be revealed, whom the Lord shall consume with the spirit of his mouth, and shall destroy with the brightness of his coming:
9. Even him, whose coming is after the working of Satan with all power and signs and lying wonders,
10. And with all deceivableness of unrighteousness in them that perish; because they received not the love of the truth, that they might be saved.
11. And for this cause God shall send them strong delusion, that they should believe a lie:
12. That they all might be damned who believed not the truth, but had pleasure in unrighteousness.

Church, listen carefully. The mystery of iniquity—of twisting, of changing, of turning—is already at work. It has been working steadily since the beginning as the scriptures plainly show. However, those that are holding onto the truth will continue to hold on until they be taken out of the way. Church, Paul is talking about two groups of people in the church itself—those who twist the truth and those who hold to the truth. Both will exist in the church until those who hold to the truth are taken out of the way. Then the only ones left in the church will be those who twist the truth.

It is then that the Wicked one himself shall be revealed, the one whom the lord shall consume with the power of his mouth, and shall destroy with the brightness of his coming. This is the one whose coming is after Satan with all power and signs and lying wonders. He will come with all deceivableness of unrighteousness in them that perish, because they did not receive the love of the truth that they might be delivered, restored, and made whole.

For this iniquity, God will send those who do this strong delusion that they should believe a lie—the lie the wicked one tells—without question. Because of this, they shall all be judged because they would not accept or believe the truth, but rather found pleasure in unrighteousness. Church, don't look at the world. This is to the church itself. This will happen to the church and the whole world will witness it happen.

1 Timothy 1

15. This is a faithful saying, and worthy of all acceptation, that Christ Jesus came into the world to save sinners; of whom I am chief.

When Paul wrote Timothy, he told Timothy that Christ came into the world to deliver, restore, and make whole sinners, of whom Paul considered himself the chief. He himself persecuted the church of God. In his eyes, that made him worse than any other person. If he could be forgiven, so could anyone else.

1 Timothy 4

16. Take heed unto thyself, and unto the doctrine; continue in them: for in doing this thou shalt both save thyself, and them that hear thee.

Paul's instruction to Timothy is good for all of us. Pay attention to yourself—the things you say and do—and to the doctrine. Paul explained the doctrine in 1Cor 15:1-11. If you do this, you shall deliver, restore, and make whole both yourself and those who hear you.

James 1

> 19. Wherefore, my beloved brethren, let every man be swift to hear, slow to speak, slow to wrath:
> 20. For the wrath of man worketh not the righteousness of God.
> 21. Wherefore lay apart all filthiness and superfluity of naughtiness, and receive with meekness the engrafted word, which is able to save your souls.
> 22. But be ye doers of the word, and not hearers only, deceiving your own selves.
> 23. For if any be a hearer of the word, and not a doer, he is like unto a man beholding his natural face in a glass:
> 24. For he beholdeth himself, and goeth his way, and straightway forgetteth what manner of man he was.

Let every man be swift to hear, slow to speak, and slow to wrath: for the wrath of man does not work the righteousness of God. This is instruction in righteousness—not a suggestion. Lay apart all filthiness and overabundance of naughtiness. Receive with all humility the engrafted word, which is able to deliver, restore, make whole your souls.

Be ye doers of the word and not hearers only, deceiving your own selves. This is not so you can be righteous enough for God to accept you. These are the works you do after God has accepted you. These works are inspired by the spirit of God that is in you. If any is a hearer of the word and not a doer, he is like someone looking in a mirror. He sees himself in the reflection, and goes on about his business, and immediately forgets what manner of man he was.

The first section explained the person of salvation. The second section explained the singular event of salvation. The third section will explain the ongoing process of salvation that is initiated by the singular event.

Romans 1

14. I am debtor both to the Greeks, and to the Barbarians; both to the wise, and to the unwise.
15. So, as much as in me is, I am ready to preach the gospel to you that are at Rome also.
16. For I am not ashamed of the gospel of Christ: for it is the power of God unto salvation to every one that believeth; to the Jew first, and also to the Greek.

Paul considered himself a debtor to the Greeks and to the Barbarians, both to the wise and the unwise because he learned as much from the people as he taught them about God. He was ready to preach the gospel of the death and resurrection of Christ to those in Rome as well. He wasn't ashamed of the gospel of Christ regardless of what men accused him of. The gospel of Christ is the power of God of complete deliverance, restoration, and wholeness to everyone that believes it; to the Jew first, and also to the Greek.

Romans 10

9. That if thou shalt confess with thy mouth the Lord Jesus, and shalt believe in thine heart that God hath raised him from the dead, thou shalt be saved.
10. For with the heart man believeth unto righteousness; and with the mouth confession is made unto salvation.
11. For the scripture saith, Whosoever believeth on him shall not be ashamed.
12. For there is no difference between the Jew and the Greek: for the same Lord over all is rich unto all that call upon him.

Church, pay attention. If you shall confess with your mouth the Lord Jesus, and believe in your heart—in the center of everything you are—that God raised Christ Jesus from the dead, you shall experience the singular event that triggers a lifelong process that shall deliver you from your current state, protect you while you are changing, and when the process is complete, totally restore you to a state of complete wholeness. This process is already complete in Christ right now.

Nowhere does it say to confess you are a sinner and confess every sin that you have ever committed. What did you have to eat on January 13th, three years ago? If you can't remember that, how can you remember every sin you have ever committed? What if you forget one? Will you still be saved? Why do you teach these silly things? You confess the savior from sin. You believe God raised him from the dead. With the heart, you believe unto righteousness by believing God raised Christ from the dead. With the mouth, confession of the savior from sin, initiates a process that, in the end will make you completely whole.

The scripture says, Whosoever believeth on him shall not be ashamed. There is no difference between the Jew and the Greek. The same Lord over all is rich unto all who call upon him.

2 Corinthians 7

> **9. Now I rejoice, not that ye were made sorry, but that ye sorrowed to repentance: for ye were made sorry after a godly manner, that ye might receive damage by us in nothing.**
> **10. For godly sorrow worketh repentance to salvation not to be repented of: but the sorrow of the world worketh death.**

Paul did not rejoice because the Corinthians were sorry for what they had done. Rather, he rejoiced because they were sorrowful enough to turn away from what they were doing. This type of sorrow is godly sorrow and helps each of us to be restored and made whole. However, the sorrow of the world is the one where you are sorry you got caught doing something that was wrong. With that type of sorrow, the only thing you work on is finding a way not to get caught again. You have made no change in yourself, only in the way you present yourself to others. Such thinking is vain, empty, and totally meaningless.

Ephesians 1

12. That we should be to the praise of his glory, who first trusted in Christ.
13. In whom ye also trusted, after that ye heard the word of truth, the gospel of your salvation: in whom also after that ye believed, ye were sealed with that holy Spirit of promise,
14. Which is the earnest of our inheritance until the redemption of the purchased possession, unto the praise of his glory.

Paul explained to the Ephesians that the apostles and the other witnesses were the first to trust in Christ that they should be to the praise of his glory—not their own. This is the same Christ the Ephesians trusted after they heard the word of truth, the gospel of their deliverance and restoration to wholeness. This is the gospel of the death and resurrection of Christ.

After the Ephesians believed the gospel of Christ, they were sealed with the holy spirit of promise. It is the down payment of our inheritance until the redemption of the purchased possession which is the completion of the process of restoration when we will finally be made completely whole. This is all to the praise of the glory of Christ.

1 Thessalonians 5

8. But let us, who are of the day, be sober, putting on the breastplate of faith and love; and for an helmet, the hope of salvation.
9. For God hath not appointed us to wrath, but to obtain salvation by our Lord Jesus Christ,
10. Who died for us, that, whether we wake or sleep, we should live together with him.

Let us who are of the day be sober—clear headed—putting on the breastplate of faith and love; and for a helmet, the hope of deliverance and restoration to complete wholeness. God has not arbitrarily appointed any of us to wrath. Instead, he has appointed us to deliverance, restoration, and wholeness by our lord Jesus Christ, who died for us, that, whether we wake or sleep, we should live together with him. The only way we can live together with him is if we have Eternal Life just like he does. The only way we can receive Eternal Life is to accept the gospel of the death and resurrection of Christ. Otherwise, we will face the wrath of God because we refused to accept what Christ accomplished for us.

2 Thessalonians 2

13. But we are bound to give thanks alway to God for you, brethren beloved of the Lord, because God hath from the beginning chosen you to salvation through sanctification of the Spirit and belief of the truth:
14. Whereunto he called you by our gospel, to the obtaining of the glory of our Lord Jesus Christ.

Church, listen to what the scriptures say. They do not say that God individually chose each person that receives salvation. Godestablished a way for anyone to receive deliverance, restoration, and complete wholeness. The way God chose was through separation of the spirit in you and belief of the truth itself. This way, anyone can receive deliverance and restoration to complete wholeness so long as they choose to accept it. Those who accept the truth of the gospel of the death and resurrection of Christ will obtain the glory of our lord Jesus Christ.

2 Timothy 3

14. But continue thou in the things which thou hast learned and hast been assured of, knowing of whom thou hast learned them;

> **15. And that from a child thou hast known the holy scriptures, which are able to make thee wise unto salvation through faith which is in Christ Jesus.**

Paul's advice to Timothy is to continue in the things he had learned and been assured of, knowing the person he had learned it from. From childhood he had known the holy scriptures. These writings are able to make you wise unto deliverance and restoration to wholeness through faith which is in Christ Jesus. Church, this does not say through faith in Christ Jesus as most of you seem to believe. It says through faith which is in Christ Jesus as in him right now. When we discuss faith in the next chapter, the scriptures themselves will explain that statement.

> **1 Corinthians 15**

> **45. And so it is written, The first man Adam was made a living soul; the last Adam was made a quickening spirit.**
> **46. Howbeit that was not first which is spiritual, but that which is natural; and afterward that which is spiritual.**
> **47. The first man is of the earth, earthy: the second man is the Lord from heaven.**
> **48. As is the earthy, such are they also that are earthy: and as is the heavenly, such are they also that are heavenly.**
> **49. And as we have borne the image of the earthy, we shall also bear the image of the heavenly.**
> **50. Now this I say, brethren, that flesh and blood cannot inherit the kingdom of God; neither doth corruption inherit incorruption.**
> **51. Behold, I shew you a mystery; We shall not all sleep, but we shall all be changed,**
> **52. In a moment, in the twinkling of an eye, at the last trump: for the trumpet shall sound, and the dead shall be raised incorruptible, and we shall be changed.**

53. For this corruptible must put on incorruption, and this mortal must put on immortality.
54. So when this corruptible shall have put on incorruption, and this mortal shall have put on immortality, then shall be brought to pass the saying that is written, Death is swallowed up in victory.

This is a section that has been misunderstood for a long time. Pay very close attention and follow carefully because this is the source of many doctrines that totally disagree with one another.

It is written, the first man Adam was made a living soul; the last Adam was made a quickening spirit. Does it say that the first man was created with an immortal soul? It says the first man Adam was made a living soul. Soul life existed before Adam. The scriptures say that soul life was created in moving creatures that have life or breathing creatures. Nowhere does it say soul life is immortal in the scriptures at all. Does it say that the first Adam had any kind of spirit in him at all or was spirit at all? No.; . . . the last Adam was made a quickening spirit . . . Does that say the last Adam was a spirit? Some people take it that way. Are they right to say so? If the last Adam was made a lifegiving spirit, how was it done? Was he part spirit and part flesh? The last Adam received the spirit of God after John baptized him in the water where John was preaching to the people. Before that, he didn't have any spirit in him at all. The spirit of God stayed in the last Adam until the day he returned it to God just as he died. After he was resurrected, the last Adam denied being or having any spirit at all. He promised his followers that they would soon be filled with the same spirit he had. That occurred at Pentecost and has been going on since. The spirit we each receive from God is a lifegiving spirit—the very same spirit that God filled Jesus with himself the day John baptized him.

The first Adam was not spiritual, but natural. After him came the one that is spiritual. The second Adam obeyed God and followed the inspiration of the spirit God gave him without any flaw—ever. Yet, the second Adam was completely flesh and subject to the very same temptations that any fleshly person is subject to. In all this, he was never disobedient to God.

The first man is of the earth—he is earthy. The second man is the Lord from heaven. Does that say the second man is the Lord of heaven? No. He is the Lord of whom? Since he is the Son of man, he is the Lord of man. The prophets said the king would rule the whole earth from Jerusalem. In the fulness of time, he will.

As is the earthy (the first Adam), so are they who are earthy. As is the heavenly (the last Adam), so are they that are heavenly. As we have borne the image of the earthy, so shall we also bear the image of the heavenly.

Flesh and blood cannot inherit the kingdom of God. Just as certainly, corruption cannot inherit incorruption. Behold, a mystery unfolds. We shall not all sleep in death, but we shall all be changed. The change shall occur in the twinkling of an eye—instantly—at the last trump. The trumpet shall sound and the dead shall be raised incorruptible, and those of us who are not dead shall be changed. The corruptible must put on incorruption (become incorruptible), and this mortal must put on immortality (become immortal).

When this corruption shall have put on incorruption, and this mortal shall have put on immortality, then shall come to pass the saying that is written, Death is swallowed up in victory. Do not be deceived by any tradition, teaching, or doctrine. Only then will this saying come to pass.

Church, there are three accounts where eyewitnesses recorded that they themselves witnessed this new incorruptible body in the very same person. These accounts are misunderstood, mistaught, or just flat out ignored in order to teach established church doctrine. We are going to look at these accounts very closely to see why this has been done for so long.

Luke 24

> **36. And as they thus spake, Jesus himself stood in the midst of them, and saith unto them, Peace be unto you.**
> **37. But they were terrified and affrighted, and supposed that they had seen a spirit.**

> 38. And he said unto them, Why are ye troubled? and why do thoughts arise in your hearts?
> 39. Behold my hands and my feet, that it is I myself: handle me, and see; for a spirit hath not flesh and bones, as ye see me have.
> 40. And when he had thus spoken, he shewed them his hands and his feet.
> 41. And while they yet believed not for joy, and wondered, he said unto them, Have ye here any meat?
> 42. And they gave him a piece of a broiled fish, and of an honeycomb.
> 43. And he took it, and did eat before them.

Actually, the whole chapter is good to read to gather the context of this story; however, for the purpose of explaining what the witnesses saw, I have just skipped down to the reference.

At the end of that first day, the disciples and apostles were discussing the appearances of Jesus. While in the middle of their discussions Jesus himself appeared in their midst. He didn't knock. He didn't call out. He simply appeared in their midst. This terrified them and they supposed they had seen a spirit. He then asked them why they were so troubled and why such thoughts would even arise in their hearts.

He told them to look at his hands and his feet to make sure that it was actually him standing there among them. He told them to handle him and see for themselves because a spirit does not have flesh and bones as they could clearly see he has. Church, we blow past this exchange and don't even look at what it says, or we just ignore this part of the passage because it raises too many questions that conflict with what has become accepted and official doctrine.

Just what exactly happened in this short reference? Christ himself denied being a spirit of any kind at all. Christ denied being part spirit and part anything else at all. He did not even say he had spirit in him at all. Christ denied being flesh and blood. He, instead, told them that his body was flesh and bone, not flesh and blood. Church, if you teach that Jesus Christ is anything other than what he himself declared right here, you are saying that Jesus Christ himself is a liar.

After he showed them his hands and feet, they still had trouble believing what he had just told them and shown them. He then asked them for something to eat. He wasn't hungry. He was simply proving to them that he wasn't a spirit. That which is flesh is flesh. That which is spirit is spirit. We will come back to this a little later.

1 John 1

1. **That which was from the beginning, which we have heard, which we have seen with our eyes, which we have looked upon, and our hands have handled, of the Word of life;**
2. **(For the life was manifested, and we have seen it, and bear witness, and shew unto you that eternal life, which was with the Father, and was manifested unto us;)**
3. **That which we have seen and heard declare we unto you, that ye also may have fellowship with us: and truly our fellowship is with the Father, and with his Son Jesus Christ.**
4. **And these things write we unto you, that your joy may be full.**

Is the apostle John referring to Christ being in the beginning with God to create the heavens and the earth as is recorded in Genesis? No, John is referring to the beginning that they themselves heard, saw with their own eyes, which they gazed intently on, and their hands handled, of the Word of life itself. This refers to a definite event that occurred during their lifetime and not to an event that occurred before even Abraham was born. The life they saw was clearly demonstrated to them. They saw it, and stood as witness to what they saw, and show you that Eternal Life itself, which was with the Father and separate from him, and was clearly demonstrated to them by someone they knew.

The things these men saw and heard, they are openly declaring to you, that you may have fellowship with them. Their fellowship is with the Father and with his son Jesus Christ. He has written these things so your joy may be full.

1 John 4

> **9. In this was manifested the love of God toward us, because that God sent his only begotten Son into the world, that we might live through him.**
> **10. Herein is love, not that we loved God, but that he loved us, and sent his Son to be the propitiation for our sins.**
> **11. Beloved, if God so loved us, we ought also to love one another.**
> **12. No man hath seen God at any time. If we love one another, God dwelleth in us, and his love is perfected in us.**
> **13. Hereby know we that we dwell in him, and he in us, because he hath given us of his Spirit.**
> **14. And we have seen and do testify that the Father sent the Son to be the Saviour of the world.**
> **15. Whosoever shall confess that Jesus is the Son of God, God dwelleth in him, and he in God.**

John declares that God's love was manifested to us after the following manner: God sent his only begotten Son into the world that we might Live—have Eternal Life—through him and his complete obedience to his Father and not through any efforts of our own. Love is not that we loved God or even were capable of loving God, but that God loved us so much that he sent his only begotten son to pay the price for our sin and rebellion. Church, if God loved us that much, we should love one another the very same way. Do we? Then, why are we divided?

John declared that no man has seen God at any time, and he meant that no man has seen God at any time—ever! Church, if we love one another the same way God loved us, God dwells in us and his love is perfected in us. We know that God dwells in us and that we dwell in God because he has given us his very spirit. John's testimony: we have seen and do testify that the Father sent the Son to be the Savior of the world. Whosoever shall confess that Jesus is the Son of God, God dwells in him, and he in God.

Just exactly what did these men see that convinced them so fully that they would make such a public declaration? Luke gives us that information and, for the most part, it has been largely ignored for a very long time.

Luke 24

33. And they rose up the same hour, and returned to Jerusalem, and found the eleven gathered together, and them that were with them,
34. Saying, The Lord is risen indeed, and hath appeared to Simon.
35. And they told what things were done in the way, and how he was known of them in breaking of bread.
36. And as they thus spake, Jesus himself stood in the midst of them, and saith unto them, Peace be unto you.
37. But they were terrified and affrighted, and supposed that they had seen a spirit.
38. And he said unto them, Why are ye troubled? and why do thoughts arise in your hearts?
39. Behold my hands and my feet, that it is I myself: handle me, and see; for a spirit hath not flesh and bones, as ye see me have.
40. And when he had thus spoken, he shewed them his hands and his feet.
41. And while they yet believed not for joy, and wondered, he said unto them, Have ye here any meat?
42. And they gave him a piece of a broiled fish, and of an honeycomb.
43. And he took it, and did eat before them.

This account begins at the end of the time when Jesus had appeared to two men who were traveling to Emmaus. When they finally recognized him, he simply disappeared from their sight. They immediately went back to the apostles in Jerusalem to tell them what had just happened. When they got there, eleven of the apostles were discussing an earlier appearance to Peter. As these two men were relating their account to the apostles, Jesus himself suddenly was standing in their midst. He greeted them by saying "peace be unto you".

These men were terrified and supposed they were looking at a spirit. He immediately asked them why they were troubled and why such thoughts arose in their hearts. He told them to look at his hands and his feet, it was really him standing there. He told them to handle him themselves and see that he was no spirit at all. A spirit does not have flesh and bones as he was clearly demonstrating to them that he himself had. Then he showed them his hands and his feet. While they yet didn't believe what they were seeing to joy, he asked for something to eat. They gave him some broiled fish and a piece of honeycomb, and he ate it in front of them.

The risen Jesus Christ himself declared he was not a spirit of any kind at all. The risen Jesus Christ separated himself from spirit by eating fish and honeycomb in front of his disciples. He totally separated himself from God because God is spirit. That which is spirit is spirit and that which is flesh is flesh. However, the resurrected Jesus Christ was not flesh and blood like his disciples. The resurrected Jesus Christ was flesh and bones. This means that the new resurrected and changed body Paul referred to in 1Corinthians is a flesh and bone body, not a flesh and blood body. Christ's body contained Eternal Life. John said they had closely examined someone who had Eternal Life and had seen this Life clearly demonstrated to them. Paul refers to Christ as the firstborn of a whole new creation. That means that the Life the disciples witnessed had to have been created to come into existence. Eternal Life does not just fill someone as spirit does.

This puts us in a situation where we have to look closely at all the information that has been given us through the scriptures. Paul described a new body to the people in the church of Corinth. Paul said that the corruptible dead would rise and put on incorruption—that is—they would become incorruptible. He then said that the mortal living would put on immortality—that is—become immortal. Paul also wrote that Jesus Christ is the firstborn of a whole new creation and that he would be the firstborn of many brethren. The body Paul described is the same body John said he and the other apostles witnessed the evening of the first day of the week when Christ began making his appearances. This is the same body Luke described in his account of Christ's appearance that first day.

What these men saw was a man that all of them knew and had travelled with. They all knew this man was dead and had been dead for three days and three nights before he appeared to them. From his own mouth, this same man told them that he was not a spirit of any kind at all. He said he was flesh and bone. Therefore the body Paul described is a flesh and bone body. Church, flesh and bone is not the same thing as, or in any way equivalent to mortal, corruptible, flesh and blood. Salvation is already complete in Christ himself. His witness to these men is what it will be in us when he returns for us and our salvation is completed with his return. We will then be like he is—flesh and bone with Eternal Life.

CHAPTER 13

Ephesians 6

16. Above all, taking the shield of faith, wherewith ye shall be able to quench all the fiery darts of the wicked.

Paul used the Roman soldier's shield to paint a picture of faith. This shield was the size of a door and the soldier could stand completely behind it for protection in battle. Paul did not define faith at this point. He implied that the shield of faith could protect it's user the same way the Roman soldier's shield protected him in battle—completely.

What is faith? What makes it so special? Why is it necessary? These are not questions asked in mockery. These are the questions necessary to begin to understand something that God himself has given us to fight the greatest spiritual battle ever fought. Once enjoined, the battle lasts for your entire life. In the end, triumph awaits those who do not give up—those who are in Christ the same way Christ is in God. The reward for victory in this battle is Eternal Life. As this lesson unfolds, the scriptures themselves will answer the questions that have been asked.

One of the problems with understanding faith is that the same word used for faith is also used for believe or belief. One can then assume that faith and belief are basically the same thing. If that is the case, why isn't this word translated as either faith or belief every time it's used? What's the big deal anyway? Eternal Life hangs in the balance—that's the big deal. Every day, we refer to other beliefs as faiths as though belief and faith were actually the same thing. Every day, self improvement gurus make truck loads of money selling books claiming that you can become anything you want through self hypnosis, through recognizing and establishing set points in your life, through goal setting, through hypnotic self control, etc. All these things are based on individual belief.

Napoleon Hill said that whatever the mind of man can conceive and believe, it can achieve. This whole self improvement industry has developed from his ideas and others before him. Do these ideas work? To a point, yes, and for some, these ideas work extremely well. However, for those who desire more from life than surface understanding, these methods can be very disappointing and unsatisfying, even though they may obtain whatever they want. It's hard to imagine, yet, there are deeper things in life that will tug at a person—even one who is in the position of having anything and everything he wants. There are intangible things that we call "purpose" and "fulfillment". There is "happiness", "satisfaction", "joy", "accomplishment", "understanding", and much more—even "love". To give these things a physical, tangible existence as the ultimate goal in our lives only demeans, devalues, and corrupts them to the point that they are merely corruptible shells which contain no substance beneath a surface existence.

In this study, not only do the scriptures explain faith, but they contrast faith and belief. There is no way to contrast two things unless they are different from one another. Church, you know this and yet you teach faith as though it were basically the same thing as belief. The scriptures themselves present faith in a far different way than you teach it. The scriptures themselves show that faith is beyond anything that the human mind can conceive, much less believe, or ever hope to achieve.

Romans 4

3. For what saith the scripture? Abraham believed God, and it was counted unto him for righteousness.

What do the scriptures say about Abraham? They say that Abraham believed God. That simple thing allowed God to consider Abraham to be righteous. Does it say Abraham was perfect or was made perfect? No. Was Abraham perfect? No, not even close. Yet, Abraham continued to believe what God told him and that is why God accounted him to be righteous.

Romans 10

9. That if thou shalt confess with thy mouth the Lord Jesus, and shalt believe in thine heart that God hath raised him from the dead, thou shalt be saved.
10. For with the heart man believeth unto righteousness; and with the mouth confession is made unto salvation.

Church, pay very close attention to these two verses. Do either of them say to confess that you are a sinner? How about confess all your sins? Maybe, confess how unworthy you are to be in God's presence? No? Then, why do you teach these things? Finally, what do these two verses actually say? These two verses talk about two things—confessing and believing. Their instructions to you are to confess what you believe in order for you to then receive the salvation that comes from God himself. That means these verses only apply to those who have not received salvation from God yet.

Let's look at this more closely. The first verse (verse 9), says that, if you confess with your mouth the Lord Jesus . . .—that is a who, not a what. If you shall believe in your heart that God actually has raised him (the Lord Jesus) from the dead, you shall be saved. In other words, you are confessing that, with everything that makes you who you are, you believe that God himself actually raised the Lord Jesus from the dead. You weren't there. You never met him. Yet, from the records made by eyewitnesses, you believe with all your heart that God raised his only begotten son, Jesus Christ himself, from the dead. This is the absolute limit of human belief. This is the way Abraham believed God and why God accounted it to him as righteousness.

The second verse (verse 10) explains that, with the heart, man believes unto righteousness the very same way that Abraham believed God with all his heart. It also explains that, with the mouth, confession of that belief allows God to give you his promised salvation.

Galatians 3

2. This only would I learn of you, Received ye the Spirit by the works of the law, or by the hearing of faith?
3. Are ye so foolish? having begun in the Spirit, are ye now made perfect by the flesh?
4. Have ye suffered so many things in vain? if it be yet in vain.
5. He therefore that ministereth to you the Spirit, and worketh miracles among you, doeth he it by the works of the law, or by the hearing of faith?
6. Even as Abraham believed God, and it was accounted to him for righteousness.
7. Know ye therefore that they which are of faith, the same are the children of Abraham.
8. And the scripture, foreseeing that God would justify the heathen through faith, preached before the gospel unto Abraham, saying, In thee shall all nations be blessed.
9. So then they which be of faith are blessed with faithful Abraham.
10. For as many as are of the works of the law are under the curse: for it is written, Cursed is every one that continueth not in all things which are written in the book of the law to do them.
11. But that no man is justified by the law in the sight of God, it is evident: for, The just shall live by faith.
12. And the law is not of faith: but, the man that doeth them shall live in them.
13. Christ hath redeemed us from the curse of the law, being made a curse for us: for it is written, Cursed is every one that hangeth on a tree:
14. That the blessing of Abraham might come on the Gentiles through Jesus Christ; that we might receive the promise of the Spirit through faith.

22. But the scripture hath concluded all under sin, that the promise by faith of Jesus Christ might be given to them that believe.
23. But before faith came, we were kept under the law, shut up unto the faith which should afterwards be revealed.
24. Wherefore the law was our schoolmaster to bring us unto Christ, that we might be justified by faith.
25. But after that faith is come, we are no longer under a schoolmaster.
26. For ye are all the children of God by faith in Christ Jesus.
27. For as many of you as have been baptized into Christ have put on Christ.
28. There is neither Jew nor Greek, there is neither bond nor free, there is neither male nor female: for ye are all one in Christ Jesus.
29. And if ye be Christ's, then are ye Abraham's seed, and heirs according to the promise.

Paul wrote this to the church, so listen very carefully. When you believed in your heart that God actually did raise Jesus Christ from the dead and you confessed with your own mouth that belief from your heart, you received what Christ himself called power from on high. This power, or spirit, filled you, sealed you, and began a process inside you that will continue the rest of your natural life. The question is: did you receive this spirit by your unswerving obedience to the law or by the hearing of faith? Are you so foolish to believe for one tiny second that, having begun this process by the power God himself has given you, you can now perfect yourself in the flesh and present yourself before God a completed work?

Have you experienced so many things without any effect at all? That is, if it is yet to be in vain. Therefore, he that ministers this spirit to you, and works miracles among you, does he do this by perfectly keeping the law, or by the hearing of faith? Even as Abraham believed God, it was accounted unto him as righteousness by God himself.

The law wasn't given until Moses, who was a descendant of Abraham generations later. Know most assuredly therefore, that they which are of faith, the very same ones are the children of Abraham regardless of their physical lineage.

The scripture foreseeing, that God himself would justify the heathen through faith, preached even before the gospel unto Abraham, In thee shall all nations be blessed. Then those who are of faith are blessed with faithful Abraham. For as many as are under the works of the law to be righteous before God are under a curse: for it is written, Cursed is everyone that perseveres not in all things written in the book of the law to do them. This says all the law, not just the ten commandments or whatever other laws you want to pick out to observe. It means all the law period.

It is clearly evident that no man is justified by the law in the sight of God because no man today can keep all the law unto righteousness. Church, we can't even keep the ones we pick out to keep, much less all of it. That's why the just shall live by faith. The law is not of faith, but the man that can do all the things written in the law shall live (have Eternal Life) by them. This is what Jesus Christ alone accomplished. No one before or since has ever done that.

Christ himself bought us from the curse of the law in two ways. First, he fulfilled all the law and the prophets and was perfectly obedient to all the law. Second, he was caused to become a curse for us to pay the price: for it is written, Cursed is every man that hangeth on a tree. Because of this, the blessings of Abraham could then come on the Gentiles through Jesus Christ, that we might receive the promise of the spirit through faith—not through the working of the law.

The scripture has concluded that all are under sin for the express purpose that the promise of Eternal Life by faith of Jesus Christ might be given to all that believe. Believe what? By faith, Jesus Christ himself fulfilled all the law and the prophets. Jesus died (was crucified) and arose again the third day after he was buried. He was seen and heard by eyewitnesses to the events. In order to believe these things, any person will have to turn away (repent) from his or her own self serving ways and ideas of self righteousness and self worth. This is the utter limit of human belief.

However, before faith came, the law kept and protected those who had it, teaching them constantly what righteousness is and how far any of them were from it. Those who had the law and those who didn't have the law were shut up unto what faith was at all. Faith wasn't revealed in it's working form in anyone until after Christ had lived, died, was resurrected, witnessed to his apostles and disciples, ascended, and finally the spirit of God himself was poured out on the day of Pentecost.

The law then served as our schoolmaster to bring us to Christ himself, that we may stand before God himself justified in his presence by faith, not by keeping of the law. Since the time that faith itself has come, we are no longer under a schoolmaster. This leads us to a startling revelation hidden right in front of our eyes for nearly 1900 years. The scriptures say: (1) Abraham believed God and it was accounted to him for righteousness; (2) the law kept and protected those under it before faith itself came; (3) those under the law were shut up unto faith that would afterward be revealed; (4) Jesus Christ perfectly fulfilled all the law and the prophets... not all except... all the law and prophets; (5) Christ's mind (his intellect, reasonings, and thoughts) were perfect and therefore perfectly aligned with the mind of God himself. While Christ didn't know everything God knew, he knew perfectly everything God revealed to him. Christ could think and reason exactly the way God did. That's how he was able to perfectly obey God and fulfill all the law and prophets; (6) faith then refers to the perfect mind of Christ himself who was perfectly obedient to God—even unto death; (7) Christ, then, was the living personification of faith itself—the walking, talking, breathing person who had the ability to think, reason, and perfectly understand God himself.

Church, you are all children of God by faith in Christ Jesus because, as many of you as were baptized into Christ have put on Christ (become like he is). In this state, there is neither Jew nor Greek, neither bond nor free. and neither male nor female. In this state, you are all one in Christ Jesus himself. If you are Christ's, then you are Abraham's seed, and heirs according to the promise.

Romans 10

> 8. But what saith it? The word is nigh thee, even in thy mouth, and in thy heart: that is, the word of faith, which we preach;
> 9. That if thou shalt confess with thy mouth the Lord Jesus, and shalt believe in thine heart that God hath raised him from the dead, thou shalt be saved.
> 10. For with the heart man believeth unto righteousness; and with the mouth confession is made unto salvation.
> 11. For the scripture saith, Whosoever believeth on him shall not be ashamed.
> 12. For there is no difference between the Jew and the Greek: for the same Lord over all is rich unto all that call upon him.
> 13. For whosoever shall call upon the name of the Lord shall be saved.
> 17. So then faith cometh by hearing, and hearing by the word of God.

What are we saying here? The word is very near you. It is in your mouth and your heart. It is the word of faith itself, which we are preaching to you. If you shall confess with your mouth the Lord Jesus (not every sin you ever committed) and believe in your own heart that God actually raised Jesus from the dead, you shall be saved. With the heart man believes unto righteousness, not by keeping laws. With the mouth confession of the person who fulfilled all the law (not your own failures) is made unto salvation. The scriptures tell us that whosoever believeth on him shall not be ashamed. The is no difference between the Jew and the Greek because the same Lord over all is rich unto all that call upon him. If he makes no difference, why do we? Don't you realize that putting any differences between people and seeking to qualify righteousness in ourselves or others is in direct disobedience to what the scriptures tell us to do? The scriptures say whosoever shall call upon the name of the Lord shall be saved—whosoever—without exception. We see then that faith comes by understanding what we hear and understanding comes by the word of God. Therefore, faith can only come to us by understanding what the word of God says, not what we believe it says or doesn't say.

Ephesians 2

8. For by grace are ye saved through faith; and that not of yourselves: it is the gift of God:
9. Not of works, lest any man should boast.
10. For we are his workmanship, created in Christ Jesus unto good works, which God hath before ordained that we should walk in them.

Church, each one of you is saved through a faith that none of you have at all and could not possibly earn no matter what you did. It is a gift from God himself to each one of you. It doesn't require any type of good works to receive it—that way none of you will be able to boast of your own accomplishments. What we become is the workmanship of God himself, created in Christ Jesus unto good works, which God himself has before ordained that we should walk in them. Notice that the good works that result from faith follow salvation. Salvation is not the result of doing enough good works to earn salvation.

Philippians 3

8. Yea doubtless, and I count all things but loss for the excellency of the knowledge of Christ Jesus my Lord: for whom I have suffered the loss of all things, and do count them but dung, that I may win Christ,
9. And be found in him, not having mine ow n righteousness, which is of the law, but that which is through the faith of Christ, the righteousness which is of God by faith:

Church, Paul could not have been more blunt about the righteousness he had and the righteousness he was teaching. Paul counted everything as loss when compared to the excellency of the knowledge of Jesus Christ. All the things he suffered as a result of his knowledge of Christ, he counted as waste anyway so he could win Christ. He wanted to be found in Christ, not through keeping the law that would lead him to self glorification and self righteousness, but rather through the faith of Christ himself—the righteousness which is of God by faith. Did Paul say—faith in Christ, or was it faith of Christ? God gave Paul the very same ability Christ himself had. God gave Paul an absolutely perfect mind—just like Christ's is. That is what God gives to whosoever. That is the faith we don't have. That is the gift of God to anyone who believes that God raised Christ from the dead. Will it make us perfect? Did it make Paul, Peter, James, or John perfect? No. It will, however, help us to perfect ourselves from within so we can each reflect the image of the risen Christ himself in our lives. That is, if we are willing to use and develop this powerful gift and not go about to set up our own form of righteousness by the keeping of whatever laws we decide will make us appear righteous before men.

2 Thessalonians 3

1. **Finally, brethren, pray for us, that the word of the Lord may have free course, and be glorified, even as it is with you:**
2. **And that we may be delivered from unreasonable and wicked men: for all men have not faith.**
3. **But the Lord is faithful, who shall stablish you, and keep you from evil.**

Paul asked the congregation at Thessalonica to pray for them that the word of the Lord would have free reign and be glorified, just as it was in Thessalonica. Paul also wanted them to pray for Paul and those with him to be delivered from unreasonable and wicked men because all men do not have faith. Church, burn that into the very depths of your mind. All men do not have faith. Those who don't have faith, even among you, are unreasonable and wicked no matter what they choose to believe. Therefore, Paul is referring to faith as something he got from God—the ability to think, reason, and recognise things the way Christ himself does. Faith and belief are not now nor have they ever been the same thing to God. Why then church, do you teach and believe faith and belief are the same? Do you realize you are perverting the word of God by doing so? Do you care? Whether you care or not, God does. God's judgment is against those who do such things. In all this, be strengthened, God himself is faithful to his own word. He shall stablish and strengthen you in his word if you allow him to do so. He will keep, tend, and protect you from evil—if you allow him to do so. You allow it through the exercise of faith—the ability to think, reason, and recognise things the way Christ does—no matter what you believe to the contrary.

2 Timothy 3

14. But continue thou in the things which thou hast learned and hast been assured of, knowing of whom thou hast learned them;

15. And that from a child thou hast known the holy scriptures, which are able to make thee wise unto salvation through faith which is in Christ Jesus.

In this letter, the Apostle Paul was giving instruction to the Pastor Timothy. Apostle Paul told Pastor Timothy to continue in the things he had learned and been assured of, knowing just who it was that taught him. Church, was Pastor Timothy assured of those things because Apostle Paul told him so, or did Pastor Timothy search the scriptures to see if Apostle Paul was actually telling him the truth? The Bereans searched the scriptures daily to see if the Apostle Paul was telling them the truth. Do you think Apostle Paul expected Pastor Timothy to do anything less? Do you think Pastor Timothy expected his congregation to do any less when he taught them? Church, look at this closely. Neither of these men lorded his position over others or expected to be treated any differently than any other person. Why then, do we have titles, officers, places of honor in congregations, etc.? These things don't make anyone greater or lesser in God's service until we start honoring people and positions above the word of God. Got the message?

Paul also reminded Timothy that he had known the holy scriptures from his childhood. The scriptures themselves are able to make you wise unto salvation through faith—not keeping laws for righteousness—which is in Christ Jesus. Church, does that say faith in Christ Jesus, as in belief in Christ Jesus? Or, does that say through faith which is (itself) in Christ Jesus? The faith which is in Christ Jesus refers to the perfect way Jesus himself thought, reasoned, and recognized everything around himself. This is the thing that Paul says that God has given us as a gift. It is time for us to start using and developing this gift from God instead of struggling to believe whatever it is we believe about faith.

James 1

5. If any of you lack wisdom, let him ask of God, that giveth to all men liberally, and upbraideth not; and it shall be given him.
6. But let him ask in faith, nothing wavering. For he that wavereth is like a wave of the sea driven with the wind and tossed.
7. For let not that man think that he shall receive any thing of the Lord.
8. A double minded man is unstable in all his ways.

Church, if any of you lack wisdom, let him ask of God—the God that gives liberally to all men and doesn't scold, fuss, berate, or go on and on about why you want wisdom in the first place—and it shall be given to you. If the God you worship isn't like that, then you are either looking at him the wrong way, or you are worshipping the wrong God. However, when you ask, ask in faith not wavering at all, because a person who wavers is like a wave in the sea driven with the wind and tossed about.

Don't let any person like that think that he will get anything from God. Such a person is double minded and unstable in all his ways.

Church, let's get this straight. I am not explaining belief, I am explaining faith. This perfect ability Christ himself has does not doubt anything God reveals. This same ability in you struggles with your "belief system" which itself is self centered. When you doubt, make sure that what you doubt is not the result of something you believe. If you ask God for anything you need, and you doubt you are worthy of receiving it, you are already confusing faith and belief. Faith tells you that you are unworthy to begin with. Faith tells you that you receive things from God because he is merciful and full of grace towards you. Belief tells you that somehow you can be good enough to earn what you want and need from God. It is this struggle that causes you to waver back and forth. Do not ask anything from God in that condition and expect to get what you want. You are double minded and unstable. How can you know what you actually want much less if you need what you want?

James 2

1. **My brethren, have not the faith of our Lord Jesus Christ, the Lord of glory, with respect of persons.**
2. **For if there come unto your assembly a man with a gold ring, in goodly apparel, and there come in also a poor man in vile raiment;**
3. **And ye have respect to him that weareth the gay clothing, and say unto him, Sit thou here in a good place; and say to the poor, Stand thou there, or sit here under my footstool:**
4. **Are ye not then partial in yourselves, and are become judges of evil thoughts?**

Church do not dare have the faith that Jesus Christ, the Lord of glory himself has, with respect of persons. That is not a suggestion or an option, nor is it open for discussion or compromise at all. If someone comes into your assembly with gold rings, nice shoes, a good suit and someone else comes in who is obviously poor and really can't afford good clothes, and you tell the sharp dressed man to sit in a good place or a place of honor while you tell the poor man to sit in the back or in a place that is not suitable even for you, are you not partial in yourselves, and become judges of evil thoughts? When you treat people this way, you actually become judges who have evil thoughts. You then justify why you do such detestable things and call that the faith of Christ. If the people you are trying to reach want to be treated that way, they can stay in the world because the world already treats them that way. Christ spent his time with those who were in need and wanted to hear the word of God. Where do you spend your time? Or, do you judge people by their ability to contribute to your wealth? Church, James meant exactly what he said. So did Christ.

James 2

14. **What doth it profit, my brethren, though a man say he hath faith, and have not works? can faith save him?**
15. **If a brother or sister be naked, and destitute of daily food,**
16. **And one of you say unto them, Depart in peace, be ye warmed and filled; notwithstanding ye give them not those things which are needful to the body; what doth it profit?**
17. **Even so faith, if it hath not works, is dead, being alone.**
18. **Yea, a man may say, Thou hast faith, and I have works: shew me thy faith without thy works, and I will shew thee my faith by my works.**
19. **Thou believest that there is one God; thou doest well: the devils also believe, and tremble.**
20. **But wilt thou know, O vain man, that faith without works is dead?**
21. **Was not Abraham our father justified by works, when he had offered Isaac his son upon the altar?**

22. **Seest thou how faith wrought with his works, and by works was faith made perfect?**
23. **And the scripture was fulfilled which saith, Abraham believed God, and it was imputed unto him for righteousness: and he was called the Friend of God.**
24. **Ye see then how that by works a man is justified, and not by faith only.**
25. **Likewise also was not Rahab the harlot justified by works, when she had received the messengers, and had sent them out another way?**
26. **For as the body without the spirit is dead, so faith without works is dead also.**

What profit is there for a man to say he has faith and yet has not one single work to go with it? Can faith save this man by itself? If a brother or sister be naked and without food to eat, and one of you say to them, go in peace; be warmed and filled; just believe God and you'll receive the things you need; yet you give them nothing they need just to stay alive; what good have you done? Church, this is serious. Too many of you today think this way. You actually believe that people are in need because they don't believe God as much as you do. You also believe that God is punishing these people in need for their lack of belief. You are indeed judges with evil thoughts. Even so, this faith that you claim to have, if it is not accompanied by works, is dead, because it is alone. You yourselves know this, yet you search for new ways not to help those in need by finding a way to judge them with scriptures. You then dare to call this faith.

 A man may say, you have faith, and I have works: show me the faith you have without works, and I will show you the faith I have by the very works I do. You believe that there is one God (that is if that is what you really believe); you do well. The devils also believe there is one God, and they tremble. Will you allow yourself to know, O vain and self centered man, that faith without works is dead? Wasn't Abraham justified by works, when he offered his only son Isaac upon the altar? Regardless of whether God just arbitrarily ordered Abraham to sacrifice Isaac on the altar, or whether Abraham thought that was what God meant because Abraham grew up in a Chaldean society that practised child sacrifice is an irrelevant point to argue. The fact is that Abraham put his only son on the altar and was preparing to kill him when an angel from God himself intervened. He was doing exactly what he understood that God wanted him to do.

Do you see how faith was revealed and cooperated with works, and by Abraham's works faith was made complete? What Abraham did was beyond belief. As a result, the scripture that says, Abraham believed God, and it was imputed unto him for righteousness was fulfilled: and he was called the Friend of God. Do you now see that a man is justified by works, and not by faith only?

In the same manner, wasn't Rahab the harlot justified by her works, when she had received the messengers, and sent them out another way? She did not just entertain guests. She received two men who were spies, hid them from the soldiers looking for them, and then sent them out another way so they would not be discovered. She not only risked her own life, but also the lives of her entire family to do what she did. As the body without the spirit (this refers to the spirit of God, not just to mere breath) is dead, so faith itself without works is dead.

1 Peter 1

3. **Blessed be the God and Father of our Lord Jesus Christ, which according to his abundant mercy hath begotten us again unto a lively hope by the resurrection of Jesus Christ from the dead,**
4. **To an inheritance incorruptible, and undefiled, and that fadeth not away, reserved in heaven for you,**
5. **Who are kept by the power of God through faith unto salvation ready to be revealed in the last time.**

Peter said that the God and Father of our Lord Jesus Christ is to be blessed. By his abundant mercy, he himself has birthed us again unto a living hope by the resurrection of Jesus Christ, his only begotten son, from the dead. We have been reborn into an incorruptible and undefiled inheritance that will never fade away. It is reserved in heaven for each one of us who are reserved and protected by the power of God himself through faith (the way Christ recognized, reasoned, and thought) unto the completion of the process of salvation ready to be revealed in each one of us in the last time.

1 Corinthians 12

7. But the manifestation of the Spirit is given to every man to profit withal.
8. For to one is given by the Spirit the word of wisdom; to another the word of knowledge by the same Spirit;
9. To another faith by the same Spirit; to another the gifts of healing by the same Spirit;
10. To another the working of miracles; to another prophecy; to another discerning of spirits; to another divers kinds of tongues; to another the interpretation of tongues:
11. But all these worketh that one and the selfsame Spirit, dividing to every man severally as he will.
12. For as the body is one, and hath many members, and all the members of that one body, being many, are one body: so also is Christ.
13. For by one Spirit are we all baptized into one body, whether we be Jews or Gentiles, whether we be bond or free; and have been all made to drink into one Spirit.

The clear demonstration of the spirit (what Christ himself called power from on high) is given to every man to profit withal from the using. One, by the power of the spirit in him, manifests the word of wisdom. Another manifests the word of knowledge by the power of the very same spirit. Another manifests faith itself by the same spirit. Yet another manifests the gifts of healing by the very same spirit. Another can work miracles; another prophesies; still another is able to discern the presence and types of spirits around him. Another is able to speak in various tongues totally unknown to himself; yet another is able to interpret tongues that are totally unknown to himself. All these things are clear demonstrations of the one and very selfsame spirit, dividing to every man individually as he wills. As our own bodies are one body composed of many parts, and all those parts, being many, are still one body; so also is Christ. We are all baptized into one body by the very same spirit of God. It doesn't matter if we are Jew or gentile. It makes no difference if we are bond or free. Whether we are male or female, what educational level we are, what color we are, what our cultural heritage is, mean absolutely nothing to God. Each and every one of us have been made to drink into the one and very same spirit of God. God gave each one of us the very same spirit. How we manifest that spirit to serve one another; however, is up to each one of us individually.

Church, the scriptures cannot be any plainer than they are. The spirit in us is the very same spirit that filled Jesus Christ when he was baptized. This is the very same spirit God gave to the prophets of old when he sent them with messages to the children of Israel. This is the very same power that God used to raise Christ from the dead and create Eternal Life in him. There is only one spirit of God. The choice of manifestation rests completely with the person who has this power. If God himself were to determine how anyone manifested this power, then He himself would be a respecter of persons. The scriptures say that God is no respecter of persons. Do not dare contradict the scriptures with your traditions and commandments.

Galatians 5

22. But the fruit of the Spirit is love , joy, peace , longsuffering, gentleness, goodness, faith,
23. Meekness, temperance: against such there is no law.

Learning to demonstrate the power of God in your life produces changes in you. These changes together produce a new person referred to in the scriptures as the new man. These changes together are referred to as the fruit of the spirit—not fruits as many but fruit as one. This fruit can be seen in you as love, joy, peace, longsuffering, gentleness, goodness, faith, meekness, and temperance. There is no law against such a fruit at all. The one thing to pay attention to here is that the manifestation of faith produces faith as part of the fruit of the spirit. What that means is that by manifesting faith, you produce faith. God does not give you any more faith than you have through the power of the spirit to begin with.

Learning to recognise things the way Christ does, reason the way he does, and think the very same thoughts he does produces in your own mind the ability to do the same thing. Your mind begins to change and you become more and more like Christ until you can reflect his very image in your life in spite of your natural flaws and shortcomings. As this ability grows in your mind, you are able to manifest faith even greater, which produces an even greater faith in your own mind. This is truly beyond anything the human mind can conceive, much less believe, or ever hope to achieve. This is the power of God working in you both to will and to do of his good pleasure which is to be conformed to the image of His only begotten son, that he may be the firstborn of many brethren and revealing a whole new creation of God.

Church, the only way anyone can have and develop this faith is to have the spirit of God in them because faith is a manifestation of the spirit of God. The only way to have this spirit of God is to confess with your own mouth the Lord Jesus, the savior from sin, and believe in your heart that God raised him from the dead. The power in us is mighty to the overthrowing of strongholds in our minds. It overthrows vain imaginations and things that would exalt themselves above all that is called God. As this way of thinking grows in us, we develop a love that is pure and unfeigned. We develop an abiding joy within ourselves. We develop a true peace that others can sense even if they don't know what it is. We become patient and longsuffering. We show a gentleness that just can't be described or understood by people who are worldly. We exhibit true goodness to others. We grow stronger in our own faith; we are willing to learn and accept instruction. We become moderate in all things. There is no law against becoming this way at all.

2 Corinthians 1

21. Now he which stablisheth us with you in Christ, and hath anointed us, is God;
22. Who hath also sealed us, and given the earnest of the Spirit in our hearts.

God himself has established each one of you with us individually in Christ. He has specifically chosen and anointed each one of us to serve one another. He has individually sealed each one of us with the spirit he has given us. This spirit is the earnest or down payment on the promise of Eternal Life. We received this spirit in our hearts when we believed that God raised Christ from the dead. This is not a group thing, church. This is an individual thing. We should never allow ourselves to think that God prefers one group over another any more than he would show favor to one person over another. Church, this faith that Paul, Peter, and James talk about so much is one of the manifestations of the spirit God has given us. Outside of and without this spirit, there is no faith. Belief exists regardless; however, faith only exists as a manifestation of the spirit God gives those who accept his only begotten son. No spirit—no faith. That is why Paul said that not all men have faith. That is why Paul considered men without faith to be wicked and unreasonable, no matter what they believed.

2 Corinthians 5

1. For we know that if our earthly house of this tabernacle were dissolved, we have a building of God, an house not made with hands, eternal in the heavens.
2. For in this we groan, earnestly desiring to be clothed upon with our house which is from heaven:
3. If so be that being clothed we shall not be found naked.
4. For we that are in this tabernacle do groan, being burdened: not for that we would be unclothed, but

> **clothed upon, that mortality might be swallowed up of life.**
> **5. Now he that hath wrought us for the selfsame thing is God, who also hath given unto us the earnest of the Spirit.**

Church, each one of you listen to this very carefully. Each one of us knows by the power of the spirit dwelling in us, that if our earthly house of this tabernacle—our body—were dissolved, we each have a building of God, made without hands, eternal in the heavens. That does not mean that we have two bodies, one on earth and one in heaven. It means that we have the promise of a new body reserved for each one of us in the heavens. It is for our new body we groan, earnestly desiring to have this body as opposed to the one we have now that is flawed and corrupt.

We that are in this earthly body do groan and are burdened by its corrupt nature. We do not desire to be freed from this body and float around in the heavens, as some believe. Rather, we desire to have this new body, that our own mortality might be swallowed up of Eternal Life that goes with the new body. He that wrought us for the very same thing that is his son right now is God. It is he that has given us the earnest of his own spirit as a guaranteed down payment on the Eternal Life and new body we will receive at the completion of the process of salvation and not until.

> **Ephesians 1**
>
> **12. That we should be to the praise of his glory, who first trusted in Christ.**
> **13. In whom ye also trusted, after that ye heard the word of truth, the gospel of your salvation: in whom also after that ye believed, ye were sealed with that holy Spirit of promise,**
> **14. Which is the earnest of our inheritance until the redemption of the purchased possession, unto the praise of his glory.**

Paul said that the apostles should be the first to the praise of his glory because they first trusted Christ. Each one of us also trusted, after we each heard the word of truth, the gospel of our salvation: in whom we also believed and were sealed with the holy spirit of promise (of Eternal Life). This spirit serves as the earnest (down payment) of our inheritance through Christ himself until the redemption of the purchased possession. Redemption is a legal recovery process that can only be performed by a near kinsman. By his own blood, Christ paid the debt that is required for disobedience and rebellion against God. We will not receive our inheritance (Eternal Life) until this process is complete. Until then, we have the promise and the earnest of the spirit in our hearts. All this is to the praise of the glory of Christ, who died for us while we were yet sinners—without God and without hope in this world.

Hebrews 11

1. **Now faith is the substance of things hoped for, the evidence of things not seen.**
2. **For by it the elders obtained a good report.**
3. **Through faith we understand that the worlds were framed by the word of God, so that things which are seen were not made of things which do appear.**

Faith is the essence—the absolute assurance—of things hoped for, the evidence of things not seen. The question is, what things are we talking about? First, faith is one of nine different manifestations of the spirit of God that is in a Christian. Of the nine, faith is the only one that cannot be physically demonstrated. The hope for a Christian is to reach a point where each of us can reflect the image of Christ himself in our lives despite our natural flaws and weaknesses. In order for that to occur, each of us must learn to think, reason, and recognise things the exact same way as Christ himself. Faith is that ability. While faith cannot itself be seen, the effects of faith can be seen as we each change the way we conduct ourselves in everyday life.

While the elders did not have the ability to think, reason, and recognise things the way Christ does, they did believe God. God counted that as righteousness for them. It is through the manifestation of faith that we can understand that the ages were framed by the word of God. For that reason, the things we see are not made of things that appear. In other words, things are not necessarily what they appear to be. Faith allows us to look closer at everything around us, giving us a deeper understanding of who and what we are as well as where we are going in life.

Romans 3

> **21. But now the righteousness of God without the law is manifested, being witnessed by the law and the prophets;**
> **22. Even the righteousness of God which is by faith of Jesus Christ unto all and upon all them that believe: for there is no difference:**
> **23. For all have sinned, and come short of the glory of God;**
> **24. Being justif ied freely by his grace through the redemption that is in Christ Jesus:**
> **25. Whom God hath set forth to be a propitiation through faith in his blood, to declare his righteousness for the remission of sins that are past, through the forbearance of God;**
> **26. To declare, I say, at this time his righteousness: that he might be just, and the justifier of him which believeth in Jesus.**
> **27. Where is boasting then? It is excluded. By what law? of works? Nay: but by the law of faith.**
> **28. Therefore we conclude that a man is justified by faith without the deeds of the law.**
> **29. Is he the God of the Jews only? is he not also of the Gentiles? Yes, of the Gentiles also:**

> **30. Seeing it is one God, which shall justify the circumcision by faith, and uncircumcision through faith.**
> **31. Do we then make void the law through faith? God forbid: yea, we establish the law.**

In ages past, the law defined the righteousness of God. Now the righteousness of God without the law is manifested, with the law itself and the prophets standing as witnesses; even the righteousness of God which is by faith of Jesus Christ unto all and upon all them that believe that God raised Christ Jesus from the dead. There is no difference to God because all have sinned and come short of the glory of God. They are freely justified by God's own grace through the redemption that is in Christ Jesus. God set Christ Jesus forth to be a propitiation—a payment—through faith in his blood, to declare his righteousness for the remission of sins that are past, through God's own forbearance.

I declare now the righteousness of God: that he might be both Just and the Justifier of any who believe in his only begotten son. Where is boasting in this? It is excluded. By the law of good works and personal obedience to the law itself? No, rather by the law of faith. We therefore conclude that any man is justified before God by faith without the deeds of the law for righteousness because Christ himself fulfilled all the law and the prophets. Does that mean that we only need faith now and don't have to do good works any more? Not at all. The works we do now are the result of faith that is only one manifestation of the spirit of God in us. Rather than trying to keep a law to be righteous through good works, we do good works through manifesting faith because, through the faith God gives us, we already stand righteous before him.

Is he the God of the Jews only? Isn't he the God of the Gentiles as well? Yes, he is also the God of the Gentiles as well. Since there is one God, He shall justify the circumcision—those who have the law and know what righteousness is—by faith, and uncircumcision—those who don't have the law, don't know God at all, and are totally without God and without hope in this world—through faith. This doesn't sound like a big deal, but it is. It means that the uncircumcised do not have to be circumcised and agree to keep all the law to be righteous enough to receive the promises of God. It also means that those who have the law can't keep it enough to be righteous enough before God to receive his promises either. To God there is no difference.

Are we now saying that, because of faith, the law serves no purpose? God forbid anyone would ever think that way. By exercising the manifestation of faith, we individually develop a new nature within ourselves that does the things that the law defines as righteous. Through faith, we establish the law as defining righteousness itself. Rather than being done away with and disregarded, it stands as a witness to all that faith itself really exists. Our actions through faith prove the law as valid because, even without the law, we do the things from our hearts that the law describes as righteous. Belief follows the letter of the law. Faith follows the intent of the law. The letter of the law brings death because of our disobedience. Faith brings Eternal Life because our obedience becomes the obedience of Christ himself who was obedient even to death on the cross.

Hebrews 12

2. Looking unto Jesus the author and finisher of our faith; who for the joy that was set before him endured the cross, despising the shame, and is set down at the right hand of the throne of God.

Church, each one of us should be looking toward Jesus, the very author and finisher of the faith we have. What God has given us began with Jesus and is complete in him. It is not complete in us and will not be complete in us until he (Jesus) returns for those who are his—both the dead in Christ and those of us who are still alive. Jesus, who for the joy that was set before him endured the unimaginable suffering of the cross, despising the shame, and is now set down at the right hand of the throne of God himself, awaiting the judgment of God.

James 1

5. If any of you lack wisdom, let him ask of God, that giveth to all men liberally, and upbraideth not; and it shall be given him.
6. But let him ask in faith, nothing wavering. For he that wavereth is like a wave of the sea driven with the wind and tossed.
7. For let not that man think that he shall receive any thing of the Lord.
8. A double minded man is unstable in all his ways.

Do any of you lack wisdom? Then ask God. God gives to all men liberally without scolding them or berating them. Ask, and it shall be given to you. However, when you ask, ask through the manifestation of faith, not wavering at all. If you waver, you are like a wave of the sea that is driven with the wind and tossed to and fro. Don't think for a minute that you can receive anything from God in that condition because you have no idea what you want or need. Such people are double minded and, as a result, are unstable in all their ways.

CHAPTER 14

Ephesians 6

14. Stand therefore , having your loins girt about with truth, and having on the breastplate of righteousness;

Church, notice that it says stand and not to go out and fight a pitched battle. The breastplate was a very important piece of any soldier's armor. This piece fit over the shoulders and connected on the sides to protect the soldier's chest and back from deadly blows to his vital organs. It protected his heart. As a Christian, this is a vital piece of equipment to have at all times. In The Mind, I told you that the overlapping functions of the mind produced what the scriptures refer to as the heart, your very essence—the thing that makes you who you are. Pay very close attention as we explore this righteousness because this righteousness is what protects your heart.

2 Corinthians 5

17. Therefore if any man be in Christ, he is a new creature: old things are passed away; behold, all things are become new.
18. And all things are of God, who hath reconciled us to himself by Jesus Christ, and hath given to us the ministry of reconciliation;
19. To wit, that God was in Christ, reconciling the world unto himself, not imputing their trespasses unto them; and hath committed unto us the word of reconciliation.

> **20. Now then we are ambassadors for Christ, as though God did beseech you by us: we pray you in Christ's stead, be ye reconciled to God.**
> **21. For he hath made him to be sin for us, who knew no sin; that we might be made the righteousness of God in him.**

Church, watch this. If any man be in Christ, he is a new creature—literally a new creation—because it is God's will that each one of us be conformed to the image of his only begotten son so Christ can be the firstborn among many brethren. Christ is the firstborn from the dead. He is the firstborn of a whole new creation that never existed until God raised him from the dead and created Eternal Life in him. Old things (our old nature) are passed away: behold all things are become new (our new nature). In order to be in Christ, each of us must manifest the faith I discussed in the previous chapter. It is the ability to have the same mind that is in Christ. This faith is one manifestation of the spirit each of you receive when you believe in your heart—the very essence of who you are—that God raised Jesus Christ from the dead. When you receive this spirit, you have the very spirit of God that was in Christ in you. The apostles called that Christ in you. The people in Antioch ridiculed them by calling these strange people Christians. As you manifest faith, you are in Christ because you begin to see things the way he does, reason the way he does, and think the very same thoughts he does. This is what the psalmist is referring to in Psalms 51:10.

As a new creation, all things are of God who has already reconciled us to himself by the death and resurrection of Jesus Christ, the only begotten son of God. He has given each one of us the ministry of reconciliation; that God was in Christ and his perfect obedience, reconciling the world unto himself, not reckoning their trespasses unto them. God has appointed unto each one of us the word of reconciliation. It is our responsibility to show people what God accomplished for us by the death and resurrection of Christ.

We are ambassadors for Christ himself, as though God himself did call for you by us: we call you in Christ's place, that you be reconciled to God. God has made Christ to pay the penalty for sin, even though Christ himself never sinned; that each one of us might be made the righteousness of God in Christ.

Ephesians 1

> **17. That the God of our Lord Jesus Christ, the Father of glory, may give unto you the spirit of wisdom and revelation in the knowledge of him:**
> **18. The eyes of your understanding being enlightened; that ye may know what is the hope of his calling, and what the riches of the glory of his inheritance in the saints,**
> **19. And what is the exceeding greatness of his power to us-ward who believe, according to the working of his mighty power,**
> **20. Which he wrought in Christ, when he raised him from the dead, and set him at his own right hand in the heavenly places,**

Paul prayed the God of our lord Jesus Christ, the father of glory himself, may give you the spirit of wisdom and revelation in the knowledge of him. He prayed that the eyes of your understanding be enlightened; that you may know what is the hope of his calling, and what the riches of the glory of his inheritance in the saints. He also prayed that you may know the exceeding greatness of his power toward us who believe, according to the working of his mighty power, which he wrought in Christ when he raised Christ from the dead and set him at his own right hand in the heavenly places. Church, don't be confused by these things. To God, all these things Paul spoke about are already completed and finished. He completed all this when he raised Christ from the dead and set him at his right had in the heavens. To us; however, this is not a completed work yet because we are still here on the earth and we still struggle with our own weaknesses. Yet, God himself has given each one of us the very same power he used to raise Christ from the dead and complete the work he accomplished in Christ.

It is God's will that we use this power to conform ourselves to the image of Christ. That way, Christ himself will be the firstborn of many brethren, each of whom will be among a whole new creation of God. God has already given us this power—we do not have to wait until we are sanctified enough, sanctified holy enough, holy enough, or righteous enough for God to give it to us. We need to know and understand this. We need to use this power to perfect ourselves from within so we can reflect the very image of the risen Christ himself in each one of us in spite of the flaws we each have. It is through exercising the manifestation of faith that we accomplish this work in ourselves because faith is just one of the manifestations of this power God has given us.

Romans 5

> **15. But not as the offence, so also is the free gift. For if through the offence of one many be dead, much more the grace of God, and the gift by grace, which is by one man, Jesus Christ, hath abounded unto many.**
> **16. And not as it was by one that sinned, so is the gift: for the judgment was by one to condemnation, but the free gift is of many offences unto justification.**
> **17. For if by one man's offence death reigned by one; much more they which receive abundance of grace and of the gift of righteousness shall reign in life by one, Jesus Christ.)**
> **18. Therefore as by the offence of one judgment came upon all men to condemnation; even so by the righteousness of one the free gift came upon all men unto justification of life.**
> **19. For as by one man's disobedience many were made sinners, so by the obedience of one shall many be made righteous.**

The free gift is not like the offence. Look, if the offence of one man resulted in death for many, even greater is the grace of God, and the gift by grace that has abounded to many by one man—Jesus Christ. The gift is not like the judgment that resulted from the sin and rebellion of one man. His disobedience caused condemnation to be brought upon all men. The gift is for many offenses to be justified in the presence of God.

If by one man's offense, death reigned by one; much more each one which receive abundance of grace and the gift of righteousness that goes with it shall reign in Eternal Life by one—Jesus Christ. The offense of one brought judgment upon all men to condemnation. The righteousness of one brought the free gift upon all men to justification of Eternal Life. By one man's disobedience, many were made sinners even before they were ever born. By one man's obedience, many shall be made righteous, when and if each one of them chooses to accept the gift.

Acts 17

30. And the times of this ignorance God winked at; but now commandeth all men every where to repent:
31. Because he hath appointed a day, in the which he will judge the world in righteousness by that man whom he hath ordained; whereof he hath given assurance unto all men, in that he hath raised him from the dead.

There was a time when men didn't know God and were ignorant of him. During this time, God did not directly punish men for their sins; however, the judgment of death took its natural course in man whether they knew God or not. Now; however, God calls all men everywhere to repent because he has chosen a specific time (a day) when he will judge the whole earth in righteousness by the obedience of one man whom God himself chose and specifically appointed. God has given assurance of this to all men because he raised the obedient man from the dead. The righteousness God will judge everyone alike by is the righteousness he gives as a free gift to all who believe that God himself raised Jesus Christ from the dead. This righteousness was expressed to men by the perfect obedience of Christ.

Romans 8

5. For they that are after the flesh do mind the things of the flesh; but they that are after the Spirit the things of the Spirit.
6. For to be carnally minded is death; but to be spiritually minded is life and peace.
7. Because the carnal mind is enmity against God: for it is not subject to the law of God, neither indeed can be.
8. So then they that are in the flesh cannot please God.
9. But ye are not in the flesh, but in the Spirit, if so be that the Spirit of God dwell in you. Now if any man have not the Spirit of Christ, he is none of his.
10. And if Christ be in you, the body is dead because of sin; but the Spirit is life because of righteousness.

Those who are after the flesh concern themselves with the things that are of the flesh. Those that are after the spirit concern themselves with things of the spirit. To be carnally minded results in death. To be spiritually minded results in Eternal Life and peace. The carnal mind is itself enmity against God. It is not, nor ever can be, subject to the law of God. Therefore, those who are in the flesh cannot please God because they are self serving. You are not in the flesh, but in the spirit, if the spirit of God dwells in you. If any man does not have the spirit of Christ (the spirit of God that dwelled in Christ), he is none of Christ's. If Christ (the spirit of God that dwelled in Christ) is in you, then your body is dead because of sin; but the spirit is Eternal Life because of the righteousness of Christ himself.

Romans 10

8. But what saith it? The word is nigh thee, even in thy mouth, and in thy heart: that is, the word of faith, which we preach;

> 9. That if thou shalt confess with thy mouth the Lord Jesus, and shalt believe in thine heart that God hath raised him from the dead, thou shalt be saved.
> 10. For with the heart man believeth unto righteousness; and with the mouth confession is made unto salvation.
> 11. For the scripture saith, Whosoever believeth on him shall not be ashamed.
> 12. For there is no difference between the Jew and the Greek: for the same Lord over all is rich unto all that call upon him.
> 13. For whosoever shall call upon the name of the Lord shall be saved.

Let's recap and look at what we have been saying here. The word is near you, even in your own mouth and in your own heart: that is the word of faith, which we preach. If you shall confess with your mouth the Lord Jesus, and shall believe in your heart that God has raised him from the dead, you shall be saved. Man believes unto righteousness with the heart. 2Cor 5:17-21 tells us we are made the righteousness of God in Christ through his obedience—not ours. Eph 1:17-20 tells us that this was already a completed work of God when he raised Christ from the dead and set Christ on his right in the heavenlies. Rom 5:15-19 tells us that many were made righteous by the obedience of one man. As a Christian, you are righteous now. This offer is made to whosoever will accept it. God makes no difference between any of us.

Galatians 2

> 16. Knowing that a man is not justified by the works of the law, but by the faith of Jesus Christ, even we have believed in Jesus Christ, that we might be justified by the faith of Christ, and not by the works of the law: for by the works of the law shall no flesh be justified.

> 17. But if, while we seek to be justified by Christ, we ourselves also are found sinners, is therefore Christ the minister of sin? God forbid.
> 18. For if I build again the things which I destroyed, I make myself a transgressor.
> 19. For I through the law am dead to the law, that I might live unto God.
> 20. I am crucified with Christ: nevertheless I live; yet not I, but Christ liveth in me: and the life which I now live in the flesh I live by the faith of the Son of God, who loved me, and gave himself for me.
> 21. I do not frustrate the grace of God: for if righteousness come by the law, then Christ is dead in vain.

Church, pay close attention. Paul said that he knew (and so should each one of us) that no man is justified by the works of the law, but by the faith of Christ. Whose faith are we justified by? The faith of Christ. We have believed in Jesus Christ, that we might justified by the faith of Christ (by whose faith? the faith of Christ), and not by the works of the law: for by the law shall no flesh be justified.

If, while we seek to be justified by Christ, we ourselves also are found sinners, can we therefore conclude that Christ is the minister of sin itself? God forbid we should ever think in those terms at all. If any of us builds again the things each of us destroyed to follow Christ in the first place, each one of us makes ourself a transgressor. Each one of us through the law is dead to the law, that each one of us might Live Eternally to God. Each of us is crucified with Christ: nevertheless each of us Lives Eternally; yet not each of us, rather it is Christ that Lives Eternally in each of us. The Life that each of us Lives in the flesh we each Live Eternally by the faith of the Son of God—whose faith?—the Son of God, who loved each one of us, and gave himself for each one of us individually.

Do not frustrate the grace of God. If righteousness come by the law and all we have to do is keep the law to be righteous, then Christ is dead in vain. Paul himself said this. Paul, the man who was a Pharisee among Pharisees—Paul, who studied at the feet of Gamaliel, the grandson of

Hillel—two of the greatest teachers of the law that had ever been known in their time—Paul meant a lot more by this one statement than most people realize. His choice of "in vain" does not just mean vainly or carelessly. It meant the same thing to Paul that it meant to Isaiah when he told the people that God did not create the earth in vain. It meant the same thing to Paul that it meant to Moses when God said "Thou shalt not take the name of the Lord thy God in vain". It meant the same thing to Paul that it meant to Moses when he wrote that the earth became without form and void. It should mean the very same thing to each and every one of you as well. When any of us goes about to set up any system of laws that are designed to make us righteous, each of us is declaring in a loud clamorous voice that the death and resurrection of Jesus Christ is in vain—totally without form and totally void of any purpose whatsoever. That is why the day will come when many will come to Christ and declare the great things each one did in his name and he will say to each one of them—I don't know you—I never knew you.

Romans 10

4. For Christ is the end of the law for righteousness to every one that believeth.

Christ did not nullify or negate the law in any way. He perfectly and completely fulfilled the law by being perfectly obedient to the law for righteousness. His death and resurrection established the way for the righteousness of the law to live in us through the power of the spirit God gives each one of us when we each believe that God raised his only begotten son from the dead.

Romans 5

15. But not as the offence, so also is the free gift. For if through the offence of one many be dead, much more the grace of God, and the gift by grace, which is by one man, Jesus Christ, hath abounded unto many.

> 16. And not as it was by one that sinned, so is the gift: for the judgment was by one to condemnation, but the free gift is of many offences unto justification.
> 17. For if by one man's offence death reigned by one; much more they which receive abundance of grace and of the gift of righteousness shall reign in life by one, Jesus Christ.)
> 18. Therefore as by the offence of one judgment came upon all men to condemnation; even so by the righteousness of one the free gift came upon all men unto justification of life.
> 19. For as by one man's disobedience many were made sinners, so by the obedience of one shall many be made righteous.

Church, the free gift is not like the offense. If through the offense, many are dead, much more the grace of God, and the gift by the grace of God, which is by only one man, Jesus Christ himself, has abounded unto many. The gift from God is not like it was by the one that sinned. The judgment was by the act of one to condemnation, but the free gift is of many offenses unto justification before God himself. If by one man's offense death itself reigned by one; much more they which receive abundance of grace and the gift of righteousness shall reign in Eternal Life by only one, Jesus Christ himself.

The offense of one brought judgment upon all men to condemnation. The righteousness of only one man brought the free gift upon all men to justification of Eternal Life, if any man will accept the gift. The disobedience of only one man made many sinners. The obedience of only one many shall make many righteous before God.

The perfect obedience of Christ made it possible for God to give each of us the gift of righteousness itself without having to struggle with a law for righteousness when and if each of us believes that God himself raised Christ from the dead. That is why, through the faith of Jesus Christ, each of us is dead to the law. That is also why each of us becomes an abomination to God when we each go about to set up laws of righteousness for ourselves.

Philippians 3

7. But what things were gain to me, those I counted loss for Christ.
8. Yea doubtless, and I count all things but loss for the excellency of the knowledge of Christ Jesus my Lord: for whom I have suffered the loss of all things, and do count them but dung, that I may win Christ,
9. And be found in him, not having mine own righteousness, which is of the law, but that which is through the faith of Christ, the righteousness which is of God by faith:
10. That I may know him, and the power of his resurrection, and the fellowship of his sufferings, being made conformable unto his death;
11. If by any means I might attain unto the resurrection of the dead.

Church, listen to what Paul said; hear and understand his mind. This is the mind each of us should have as a Christian. The things that were important and profitable to me before I accepted the death and resurrection of Christ, I counted as total loss for Christ. Doubtless, I count all things loss for the excellency of the knowledge of Christ Jesus my Lord. This isn't just knowing facts and figures about Christ. This is actually sharing his knowledge Paul is talking about here. How many of us seek to do more than just know about Christ as though that is all there is for each of us to do? For this, Paul not only suffered the loss of all things, but also counted those things as no better than dung itself, that he may win Christ. How many of us think that way today?

Paul wanted to be found in Christ, not having his own righteousness by obeying the law, but rather through the faith of Christ himself, the righteousness which is of God by faith and not through keeping any law for righteousness: that Paul might know him, the power of his resurrection, the fellowship of his sufferings, being made conformable to his death; if by any means actually attain the resurrection of the dead.

How many of us today want to know Christ that well? Would we give up everything, suffer anything, even die if necessary? Would we?

2 Timothy 3

14. But continue thou in the things which thou hast learned and hast been assured of, knowing of whom thou hast learned them;
15. And that from a child thou hast known the holy scriptures, which are able to make thee wise unto salvation through faith which is in Christ Jesus.
16. All scripture is given by inspiration of God, and is profitable for doctrine, for reproof, for correction, for instruction in righteousness:
17. That the man of God may be perfect, throughly furnished unto all good works.

Paul is writing to Timothy, who was a pastor of one of the churches that Paul travelled to and from. Paul told Timothy to continue in the things he had learned and been assured of, knowing of whom he had learned them. Timothy had been assured of the things he learned by comparing the things he was taught with the scriptures to see if what he was being taught was true. How many of us do that today? All of us would do well to remember that Augustine told us that it is not what one scripture says, but rather what all the scriptures say together.

Paul then reminded Timothy that he was taught and had known the scriptures from childhood. The scriptures are able to make you wise unto salvation through faith which is in Christ Jesus (not faith in Christ Jesus)—the same thing as the faith of Christ Jesus.

Paul then said that all scripture (anything that is scripture) is given by the inspiration of God. Anything that is not given by the inspiration of God is not scripture at all, no matter how good or reasonable it may sound when anyone speaks or hears it. The scriptures are beneficial to those who understand them because the scriptures teach a person how to judge and live rightly (doctrine), how to recognize when a person strays from right judgment (reproof), how to return to right judgment (correction), altogether instruction in righteousness itself.

The purpose of this instruction is for the man of God to be perfect—not as without flaws or errors, but as being perfected from within and correcting the flaws and errors—throughly furnished—completely prepared—unto all good works. The expression "throughly furnished" is like preparations that are made before a ship sails on a voyage. All the mechanical equipment must be working properly. The crew itself must be well trained and ready to go. Spare parts must be loaded to repair any possible breakdowns or equipment failures. Plenty of food and water must be stored. Sleeping and eating accommodations must be secured. A proper map with course charted must be included. A constant eye must be on the weather, just in case a course change has to be made to avoid or face a storm. This is a lot of preparation and requires a great deal of effort. The scriptures prepare each of us to live life the same way, but it takes a great deal of effort and constant attention to be completely prepared unto all good works.

The same word translated as "righteous" or as "righteousness" is also translated as "just", "justifies", "justified", "justifier", and "justification". The next part of this chapter looks at this to show the relationship between "just" and "righteousness".

Romans 3

20. **Therefore by the deeds of the law there shall no flesh be justified in his sight: for by the law is the knowledge of sin.**
21. **But now the righteousness of God without the law is manifested, being witnessed by the law and the prophets;**
22. **Even the righteousness of God which is by faith of Jesus Christ unto all and upon all them that believe: for there is no difference:**

23. For all have sinned, and come short of the glory of God;
24. Being justif ied freely by his grace through the redemption that is in Christ Jesus:
25. Whom God hath set forth to be a propitiation through faith in his blood, to declare his righteousness for the remission of sins that are past, through the forbearance of God;
26. To declare, I say, at this time his righteousness: that he might be just, and the justifier of him which believeth in Jesus.
27. Where is boasting then? It is excluded. By what law? of works? Nay: but by the law of faith.
28. Therefore we conclude that a man is justified by faith without the deeds of the law.
29. Is he the God of the Jews only? is he not also of the Gentiles? Yes, of the Gentiles also:
30. Seeing it is one God, which shall justify the circumcision by faith, and uncircumcision through faith.
31. Do we then make void the law through faith? God forbid: yea, we establish the law.

Church, understand this completely. By the deeds of the law shall no flesh be justified in the sight of God because by the law is the knowledge of sin in the first place. Now, however, the righteousness of God without the law is manifested. It is witnessed by both the law itself and by the prophets as well. The righteousness of God without the law is by faith of Jesus Christ unto all and upon all who believe God raised Jesus Christ from the dead. There is no qualifying difference to God because all have sinned and come short of the glory of God. All who believe are justified freely by the grace of God through the redemption that is in Christ Jesus—the very one that God has set forth to be a full payment through faith in the blood of Christ. Here is where you miss it, Church. Most of you assume right here that faith and belief mean the same thing. You fail to realize that the word translated 'in' is also translated 'by'. The law says that without the shedding of blood, there can be no remission of sins. Therefore, the payment for sin is made by the blood of Christ Jesus.

Church, this was done to declare the righteousness of God for the remission of sins that are past, through God's own forbearance that declares the greatness of his righteousness. This way, God himself can be both just and the justifier of any person who believes in Jesus. Where now is the boasting and sense of personal accomplishment? It is totally excluded. What law excludes it? Does the law of works? No, but by the law of faith boasting is excluded. We can therefore conclude that a man is justified by faith without having to perform the works of the law to be righteous before God. Church, before you go berserk at what I am saying here, remember that the man who wrote this was a Pharisee of Pharisees, born of the tribe of Benjamin, circumcised on the 8th day, trained personally by Gamaliel, the grandson of Hillel. When this man began following the risen Christ, he did not forget his training. He used his training to prove the truth of God's word itself.

Is the God of Abraham the God of the Jews only? Is he not also the God of the Gentiles as well? Yes, he is also the God of the Gentiles. Therefore, there is only one God. He shall himself justify the circumcision who have the law and know the righteousness of God by the faith of Christ, and justify the uncircumcision who are without God and without hope in this world through the faith of Christ. Does that mean that faith makes the law null and void? God forbid. Through faith, we establish the law as a witness to the righteousness of God himself.

Romans 5

1. **Therefore being justified by faith, we have peace with God through our Lord Jesus Christ:**
2. **By whom also we have access by faith into this grace wherein we stand, and rejoice in hope of the glory of God.**
3. **And not only so, but we glory in tribulations also: knowing that tribulation worketh patience;**

4. And patience, experience; and experience, hope:
5. And hope maketh not ashamed; because the love of God is shed abroad in our hearts by the Holy Ghost which is given unto us.
6. For when we were yet without strength, in due time Christ died for the ungodly.
7. For scarcely for a righteous man will one die: yet peradventure for a good man some would even dare to die.
8. But God commendeth his love toward us, in that, while we were yet sinners, Christ died for us.
9. Much more then, being now justified by his blood, we shall be saved from wrath through him.
10. For if, when we were enemies, we were reconciled to God by the death of his Son, much more, being reconciled, we shall be saved by his life.

Therefore, being justified by the faith of Christ, we have peace with God himself through our lord Jesus Christ. We also have access by the very same faith into this grace wherein we stand, and rejoice in hope of the glory of God himself. We glory in tribulations also, knowing that tribulation works patience. Patience gives experience. Experience brings hope. Hope does not make anyone ashamed, because the love of God is shed abroad in our hearts by the holy spirit which is given each of us when we believe God raised Christ from the dead. When we were yet without strength, in due time Christ himself died for the ungodly.

It is rare that anyone would die for a righteous man. Maybe for a good man would some dare to die. Yet God declared and demonstrated his love for us because, while we were yet sinners and enemies of God and all the he is, Christ died for us. Even more than that, now that we are justified by the blood of Christ himself, we shall be saved from wrath through this very same Christ. If, when we were enemies, we were reconciled to God by the death of his only begotten son, even more, being reconciled already, we shall be saved by the Eternal Life in the son of God now.

Romans 8

> 28. And we know that all things work together for good to them that love God, to them who are the called according to his purpose.
> 29. For whom he did foreknow, he also did predestinate to be conformed to the image of his Son, that he might be the firstborn among many brethren.
> 30. Moreover whom he did predestinate, them he also called: and whom he called, them he also justified: and whom he justified, them he also glorified.
> 31. What shall we then say to these things? If God be for us, who can be against us?
> 32. He that spared not his own Son, but delivered him up for us all, how shall he not with him also freely give us all things?
> 33. Who shall lay any thing to the charge of God's elect? It is God that justifieth.
> 34. Who is he that condemneth? It is Christ that died, yea rather, that is risen again, who is even at the right hand of God, who also maketh intercession for us.

Church, we know that all things work together for good to them that love God, who are themselves called according to his purpose. However, to them that do not love God, all things don't necessarily work together for good. Those whom God foreknew, he predestinated to be conformed to the image of his son, so his only begotten son might be the firstborn among many brethren who are a whole new creation—just like Christ himself is now.

Church, this is the extent of predestination. God has not planned every second of your existence from before the time you were born. The only thing God has predestined is that those who love him are to be conformed to the image of the son of God rather than being conformed to this world. This is God's will for each and every one of us, so quit asking God what his will is. In addition, those who God predestinated to be conformed to the image of his only begotten son, he also called.

Those who God called, he also justified. Those who God justified, he also glorified. All these things God himself did when he raised his only begotten son from the dead. To God, this is a finished work and it applies to whosoever shall call upon the name of the Lord and believe that GOD HIMSELF raised his only begotten son from the dead.

What can we conclude from these things? If God be for us, who can be against us? Who indeed? God himself, who spared not his own son, but delivered him up for us all, how shall he not with his own son also freely give us all things? Who shall lay anything to the charge of the elect of God? God himself is the one who justifies each and every single one of us. Who has the right or the ability to stand before God himself and accuse or judge any one of us? The only person with the right and the ability to do such a thing is Christ himself who died and is risen. Even now, Christ sits at the right hand of God and makes intercession for each and every single one of us.

Galatians 2

16. Knowing that a man is not justified by the works of the law, but by the faith of Jesus Christ, even we have believed in Jesus Christ, that we might be justified by the faith of Christ, and not by the works of the law: for by the works of the law shall no flesh be justified.
17. But if, while we seek to be justified by Christ, we ourselves also are found sinners, is therefore Christ the minister of sin? God forbid.
18. For if I build again the things which I destroyed, I make myself a transgressor.
19. For I through the law am dead to the law, that I might live unto God.
20. I am crucified with Christ: nevertheless I live; yet not I, but Christ liveth in me: and the life which I now live

> in the flesh I live by the faith of the Son of God, who loved me, and gave himself for me.
> 21. I do not frustrate the grace of God: for if righteousness come by the law, then Christ is dead in vain.

Knowing that a man is not nor can be justified by the works of the law, but by the faith of Jesus Christ—whose faith?—Jesus Christ—, even we have believed in Jesus Christ, that we ourselves might be justified before God himself by the faith of Christ, and not by our own works of the law. Church, get this straight once and for all, by the works of the law shall no flesh be justified before God. If, while we seek to be justified before God by the faith of Christ, we ourselves are at the same time found to be sinners and rebellious, can we then say Christ is the minister of sin in us? God forbid. If we go about to rebuild the things we destroyed by accepting the accomplishment of Christ, we make ourselves transgressors.

Through the law, each one of us is dead to the law, that each one of us may Live unto God. Each one of us is crucified with Christ: nevertheless each of us Lives; yet not each of us, but rather Christ Lives in each one of us. The Life each of us now Lives in the flesh, we each Live by the faith of Christ himself—the son of God—who loved each of us, and gave himself for each and every single one of us. Church, do not frustrate the grace of God. If righteousness comes by keeping the law, or any combination of laws, then the death and resurrection of Christ himself has absolutely no meaning or purpose at all. Setting up your own guidelines, rules, regulations, and laws to determine who is righteous before God is blasphemy and is an abomination to God.

Galatians 3

> 22. But the scripture hath concluded all under sin, that the promise by faith of Jesus Christ might be given to them that believe.
> 23. But before faith came, we were kept under the law, shut up unto the faith which should afterwards be revealed.

> 24. Wherefore the law was our schoolmaster to bring us unto Christ, that we might be justified by faith.
> 25. But after that faith is come, we are no longer under a schoolmaster.
> 26. For ye are all the children of God by faith in Christ Jesus.

The scripture has concluded all under sin—whether they had the law and knew God or not—that the promise by faith of Jesus might be given to them that believe—whether they had the law or not. Before faith came, those who had the law were tended, taught, protected, and guided by the law they had. They were specially sealed and reserved by God himself for the faith that would be revealed after the death and resurrection of Christ as a manifestation of the power (spirit) that would be poured out onto and into those who accepted the death and resurrection of the only begotten son of God.

Wherefore, the law has served as schoolmaster to bring each of us to Christ—whether we originally had the law to guide us in the beginning or not—that each and every one of us might be justified before God by the faith of Christ himself. However, now that faith itself has come, we are no longer under a schoolmaster. Each of us now is a child of God by faith in Christ Jesus if we accept his death and resurrection because the same faith that is in Christ Jesus now is a manifestation of the spirit God gives each one of us when we accept the death and resurrection of his only begotten son.

1 Timothy 3

> 16. And without controversy great is the mystery of godliness: God was manifest in the flesh, justified in the Spirit, seen of angels, preached unto the Gentiles, believed on in the world, received up into glory.

By putting this together so far, we can see just how great the mystery of godliness really is. God was manifest in the flesh. Manifest means clearly demonstrated. The scriptures say that Christ was the physical image of God. The scriptures also say that Christ was the exact physical copy of God. Neither of these scriptures intimate in any way that Christ was God Almighty himself in the flesh. God was justified in the spirit because the spirit of God himself in all its fulness dwelt in Christ bodily. That means that Christ himself was an absolutely perfect human being for this to even occur. The angels themselves witnessed the birth, life, ministry, death, resurrection, and ascension of Christ himself. The death and resurrection of Christ was preached to the Gentiles and believed on by those in the world who had never known the God of Abraham or his only begotten son. Christ was received up into glory with his apostles as eyewitnesses to the event itself.

CHAPTER 15

Ephesians 6

14. Stand therefore, having your loins girt about with truth, and having on the breastplate of righteousness;

The next piece of armor referred to is the sash or girdle. It is the piece that fits around the waist and protects the loins which contain the reproductive and other vital organs. A blow there can disable or kill if properly struck by an opponent. The girdle or sash was also the piece of armor that all the other pieces around the area tied into to become one complete armored unit that protected the Roman soldier.

1 Peter 1

13. Wherefore gird up the loins of your mind, be sober, and hope to the end for the grace that is to be brought unto you at the revelation of Jesus Christ;

Church, Peter said to gird up the loins of your mind. His reference to the mind is to the area of your understanding. Paul said to have your loins gird about with truth. Putting these two together, we see that we are to wrap our understanding with truth so we can generate thoughts that are themselves true and pure as in pure of heart. We are also to be sober—of a sound mind that comes from truth itself. Our hope is to the end when, at the revelation of Christ himself we each receive Eternal Life by the very grace of God himself.

John 18

> 37. Pilate therefore said unto him, Art thou a king then? Jesus answered, Thou sayest that I am a king. To this end was I born, and for this cause came I into the world, that I should bear witness unto the truth. Every one that is of the truth heareth my voice.
> 38. Pilate saith unto him, What is truth? And when he had said this, he went out again unto the Jews, and saith unto them, I find in him no fault at all.

Christ had been brought before Pilate to be judged because the temple leaders wanted him put to death. When Pilate asked Jesus if he was a king, Jesus answered that Pilate said so—not himself. Jesus then said that the reason he was born in the first place was to bear witness to the truth. Pilate was a Roman—a Gentile. Romans worshipped many different gods for varying reasons. They followed various philosophies. Not one of them had a clue what truth was—it just depended on how they happened to view things based on the information at the time. That is very similar to what psychology teaches us today in that there is no real single or absolute truth. Truth today depends on how much information you have and how you view that information yourself. As such, truth as it is defined today is subject to change constantly. Such was the case with Pilate. When Jesus told Pilate that everyone that is of the truth hears his voice, Pilate was stunned. He then quite sincerely asked Jesus, "What is truth?". When he had said this, he went to the temple leaders and told them that he could find no fault in Jesus at all.

John 17

> 17. Sanctify them through thy truth: thy word is truth.
> 18. As thou hast sent me into the world, even so have I also sent them into the world.
> 19. And for their sakes I sanctify myself, that they also might be sanctified through the truth.

When Jesus was praying as he was walking with his disciples toward the garden to pray, he said these things. He prayed that God would set his disciples apart by his own truth. He then said that the word of God was truth itself. He then said he was sending his disciples into the world the same way God had sent him into the world. He was setting himself apart for their sakes, so they themselves might also be set apart through the truth.

Romans 2

1. **Therefore thou art inexcusable, O man, whosoever thou art that judgest: for wherein thou judgest another, thou condemnest thyself; for thou that judgest doest the same things.**
2. **But we are sure that the judgment of God is according to truth against them which commit such things.**

Church, listen carefully. It is inexcusable for anyone to judge another for any reason whatsoever. The instant you judge someone else, you condemn yourself, because you who judge do the very same things. However, we are sure that the judgment of God himself is according to truth against any who commit such things.

Romans 1

18. **For the wrath of God is revealed from heaven against all ungodliness and unrighteousness of men, who hold the truth in unrighteousness;**
19. **Because that which may be known of God is manifest in them; for God hath shewed it unto them.**
20. **For the invisible things of him from the creation of the world are clearly seen, being understood by the things that are made, even his eternal power and Godhead; so that they are without excuse:**
21. **Because that, when they knew God, they glorified him not as God, neither were thankful; but became**

> **vain in their imaginations, and their foolish heart was darkened.**
> **22. Professing themselves to be wise, they became fools,**
> **23. And changed the glory of the uncorruptible God into an image made like to corruptible man, and to birds, and fourfooted beasts, and creeping things.**
> **24. Wherefore God also gave them up to uncleanness through the lusts of their own hearts, to dishonour their own bodies between themselves:**
> **25. Who changed the truth of God into a lie, and worshipped and served the creature more than the Creator, who is blessed for ever. Amen.**

Paul is addressing the church in Rome. Even though he is speaking in general about mankind, he is presenting a warning to the members of the church to remember what they came from and not lose sight of their goal. The wrath of God himself is revealed from heaven against all ungodliness and unrighteousness of men—specifically those who hold the truth in unrighteousness. Church, that statement applies to all men whether they know God or not. The reason it does is because the things which may be known of God is already manifest in men, for God has shown it to them. The invisible things of God from the creation of the cosmos itself are and can be clearly seen as ordered things that did not and could not have just happened by random chance. These things can be understood by observing and carefully contemplating the order of the entire universe around us, even God's eternal power and Godhead. Therefore mankind has no excuse to offer whether they know God or not.

From the time of Adam to Noah, men knew God, and they turned away. From the time of Noah to Abraham, men knew God, and they turned away. From the time of Abraham to Moses, men knew God, and they turned away. God gave Moses the law that described and defined righteousness itself. Moses gave it to the people, and they turned away. From Moses to Christ himself, God sent prophets to tell the people his message, and they turned away. Christ, the only begotten son of God in the entire history of mankind itself, was the complete, perfect physical image of God himself. All the righteousness, grace, truth, mercy, and judgment of God himself dwelt bodily in his only begotten son, Jesus Christ. People walked and talked with him, they ate with him, they listened to him, and they turned away. After Christ was crucified, God raised him from the dead. His followers saw him personally. God entered into a new relationship with them by giving them his own power to help and guide them. That brings us up to today. Still after all this men turn away—whether they know God or not.

This happens because, when men have known God, they have not nor would not glorify him as God; neither have they been thankful. Instead, men became without reason at all in their own imaginations, and their own foolish hearts became darkened. They professed themselves to be wise and understand great mysteries. In so doing, they became fools. Mankind has changed the glory of the uncorruptible God himself into an image like corruptible man, like birds, like fourfooted beasts, and like creeping things. As a result, God has allowed mankind to become unclean and foul through the uncontrollable desires of their own hearts, whether they know God or not. They dishonor their own bodies between themselves. They have changed the truth of God into a lie, and worshipped and served the creature more than the Creator, who is himself blessed for ever.

Church, this is the nature of man himself, whether he knows God or not. This is the nature Paul refers to as the old man. We must constantly be aware of this nature in ourselves. We are not here to change the nature of others. We are here to change our own nature and then witness that change in us to others. Otherwise, we really are the hypocrites that those who see us claim we are.

John 1

17. For the law was given by Moses, but grace and truth came by Jesus Christ.

Church, God gave Moses the law and Moses gave the law to the people. Jesus Christ gave the people grace and truth itself.

John 4

23. But the hour cometh, and now is, when the true worshippers shall worship the Father in spirit and in truth: for the Father seeketh such to worship him.
24. God is a Spirit: and they that worship him must worship him in spirit and in truth.

The hour comes, and now is, when the true worshippers of God shall worship the Father in spirit (power) and in truth itself: for the Father seeks such to worship him. God himself is a spirit. Those who worship him must worship him in spirit and truth.

John 8

28. Then said Jesus unto them, When ye have lifted up the Son of man, then shall ye know that I am he, and that I do nothing of myself; but as my Father hath taught me, I speak these things.
29. And he that sent me is with me: the Father hath not left me alone; for I do always those things that please him.
30. As he spake these words, many believed on him.
31. Then said Jesus to those Jews which believed on him, If ye continue in my word, then are ye my disciples indeed;
32. And ye shall know the truth, and the truth shall make you free.
33. They answered him, We be Abraham's seed, and were never in bondage to any man: how sayest thou, Ye shall be made free?
34. Jesus answered them, Verily, verily, I say unto you, Whosoever committeth sin is the servant of sin.
35. And the servant abideth not in the house for ever: but the Son abideth ever.
36. If the Son therefore shall make you free, ye shall be free indeed.

37. I know that ye are Abraham's seed; but ye seek to kill me, because my word hath no place in you.
38. I speak that which I have seen with my Father: and ye do that which ye have seen with your father.
39. They answered and said unto him, Abraham is our father. Jesus saith unto them, If ye were Abraham's children, ye would do the works of Abraham.
40. But now ye seek to kill me, a man that hath told you the truth, which I have heard of God: this did not Abraham.
41. Ye do the deeds of your father. Then said they to him, We be not born of fornication; we have one Father, even God.
42. Jesus said unto them, If God were your Father, ye would love me: for I proceeded forth and came from God; neither came I of myself, but he sent me.
43. Why do ye not understand my speech? even because ye cannot hear my word.
44. Ye are of your father the devil, and the lusts of your father ye will do. He was a murderer from the beginning, and abode not in the truth, because there is no truth in him. When he speaketh a lie, he speaketh of his own: for he is a liar, and the father of it.
45. And because I tell you the truth, ye believe me not.
46. Which of you convinceth me of sin? And if I say the truth, why do ye not believe me?
47. He that is of God heareth God's words: ye therefore hear them not, because ye are not of God.
48. Then answered the Jews, and said unto him, Say we not well that thou art a Samaritan, and hast a devil?
49. Jesus answered, I have not a devil; but I honour my Father, and ye do dishonour me.

Jesus was in the temple teaching the Jews (leaders of the people) after he had handled a situation that was supposed to trap him. He told them that when they had lifted up (killed—not praised) the Son of man, then they would know that this very Jesus was the Son of man himself.

He told them he could do nothing of himself. He spoke the things his Father had taught him. His Father had not left him alone because he always did the things that pleased the Father. As he spoke these things, many of the leaders believed on him.

Church, members and leaders alike, wouldn't it be a lot easier for us if we were to do the same thing he did here with these leaders? If we only spoke the things that God himself revealed to us instead of worrying about our creeds, by-laws, denominational (divisive) doctrines, and such like, more people would find it easier to hear and understand what we say to them. It would also be easier for each of us to tell whether people were actually listening to us as well.

Jesus then told those who believed him that, if they continued in the word he had given them, they would indeed be his disciples. He then said you shall know the truth and the truth shall make you free. Church, where is the truth today? There are over 50,000 different respectable divisions among you, each with a 'truth' that is different from the other 'truths'. The truth according to whom? How about just letting God reveal His truth, and you just do and say what He shows you and tells you? Of course, if you did that, you would have to obey His word, not your interpretation of His word adapted to your particular set of beliefs. Let there be no divisions (denominations) among you, at any time, for any reason,—AT ALL. See, you already don't listen to God.

The leaders response was that they were Abraham's seed and never in bondage to anyone. How could Jesus say, you shall be made free? Jesus said that whosoever commits sin is the servant of sin. The servant does not abide in the house forever, but the son does. Jesus told them he knew they were Abraham's seed, but they sought to kill him because his word had no place in them at all. Jesus then told them that he spoke the things that he had seen with his Father and they did the things they had seen with their father. Their response was that Abraham was their father. Jesus told them that if they were Abraham's children, they would do the works of Abraham.

Church, I am going to interrupt this narrative at this point to make things a little clearer for you because this is about to get very ugly. Jesus wasn't talking to the people—he was talking to the temple leaders and teachers. You know, he was talking directly to the clergy of his time—the great men of God who were the models for everyone else to follow. These were the ones who wore the finest robes and would greet each other with long and showy greetings in the market place. These were they ones who would pray long and eloquently worded prayers in the temple in front of the people. These men made a big show of the money they contributed to the temple and sought recognition and respect among the people. These men strictly observed the law and all its attachments for people to see what paradigms of righteousness and virtue they were.

These men were whitewashed tombs. On the outside, they were bright and beautiful. On the inside, they were repulsive, rotting things. These men were very religious, yet they had absolutely no idea what righteousness was at all. They knew the word of God from cover to cover, yet they had no understanding at all. Did Christ hate them? No. Christ told the people to listen to their teachings, but do not do the things they did. Church, in Jesus' time, there was only one temple. Today, there are over 50,000 divisions in the body of Christ, each with their own laws, customs, creeds, by-laws, and traditions. Each division has its own group of houses of God—each with its own pastors, priests, and spiritual leaders. They compete with one another for an audience of listeners. It's even worse today than it was when Christ walked the earth, so pay very close attention to this narrative.

Jesus then told the leaders that they sought to kill him for telling them the truth. That is something Abraham never did. Jesus then told them they did the deeds of their father. Their response was that they were not born of fornication, they had one Father, even God. The leaders tried to destroy Jesus' credibility by accusing him of being illegitimate. He was presented to them at the age of twelve—the age illegitimate boys were presented according to custom. Legitimate boys were presented at thirteen. Since the leaders considered Jesus to be an illegitimate son, they weren't bound to hear anything he claimed because, according to the law and custom, God had no dealings with illegitimate people.

Jesus' response was that, if God was their Father as they claimed, they would love him. He proceeded forth and came from God. He didn't come in and of himself, rather God sent him. He then told the leaders that they couldn't understand his speech because they could not hear his word. Jesus then told the leaders they were of their father the devil, they would do the lusts of their father. The devil was a murderer from the beginning, and abode not in the truth, because there is no truth in him—even now. When the devil speaks a lie, he speaks of his own: he is a liar, and the father of lies. Because I tell you the truth, you do not believe me. Which one of the leaders convicts me of sin? If I speak the truth then, why do you not believe me? He that is of God hears God's words: you do not hear them because you are not of God.

The leaders' response was classic. They then accused Jesus of being a Samaritan and having a devil. Jesus answered, I have not a devil; but I honor my Father, and you do dishonor me.

This is what the burning desire for the truth costs. First, your credibility—a personal attack. If that doesn't work, maybe next will be a threatened accusation of blasphemy or some other charge. In the end, though, demon possession is the strongest and most feared accusation. Whether you are a member of the body or in some leadership position, the attack will be the same. All will be done in the name of protecting the purity of God's word according to whatever "division" you happen to be in. That's a high price to pay for the truth of God's word and it takes a commitment to pay the price even to death if necessary. God is about to judge his house and He will accept His word as the final judge. Be prepared to accept His word yourself because God will only judge by the truth.

John 14

5. **Thomas saith unto him, Lord, we know not whither thou goest; and how can we know the way?**
6. **Jesus saith unto him, I am the way, the truth, and the life: no man cometh unto the Father, but by me.**

7. If ye had known me, ye should have known my Father also: and from henceforth ye know him, and have seen him.
8. Philip saith unto him, Lord, shew us the Father, and it sufficeth us.
9. Jesus saith unto him, have I been so long time with you, and yet hast thou not known me, Philip? he that hath seen me hath seen the Father; and how sayest thou then, Shew us the Father?
10. Believest thou not that I am in the Father, and the Father in me? the words that I speak unto you I speak not of myself: but the Father that dwelleth in me, he doeth the works.
11. Believe me that I am in the Father, and the Father in me: or else believe me for the very works' sake.
12. Verily, verily, I say unto you, He that believeth on me, the works that I do shall he do also; and greater works than these shall he do; because I go unto my Father.
13. And whatsoever ye shall ask in my name, that will I do, that the Father may be glorified in the Son.
14. If ye shall ask any thing in my name, I will do it.
15. If ye love me, keep my commandments.
16. And I will pray the Father, and he shall give you another Comforter, that he may abide with you for ever;
17. Even the Spirit of truth; whom the world cannot receive, because it seeth him not, neither knoweth him: but ye know him; for he dwelleth with you, and shall be in you.

Jesus was preparing his disciples for his death and he was talking to them about going away. Thomas said, we don't know where you are going; and how can we know the way? Jesus' response was 'I am the way, the truth, and the life: no man cometh to the Father, but by me'. Jesus was perfectly obedient to God. Jesus' words were truth itself because he only spoke and did the things he himself saw and heard from his Father. Jesus had the promise of Eternal Life from God himself. The only way for any man to come to the Father is to be obedient to God the way Jesus was, to only speak and do the things that God himself shows him, and accept the promise of Eternal Life God has given him when he accepts the purpose of the death and resurrection of Jesus Christ himself.

Jesus went on to tell his disciples that, if they had known him, they should have known his Father also: and from henceforth, they knew him, and had seen him. Philip responding by saying: Lord, show us the Father, and it sufficeth us.

Jesus' response was to the point. Have I been so long with you, and yet you have not known me? He that has seen me has seen the Father. How can you say, "Show us the Father?' Don't you believe that I am in the Father and the Father in me. The words I speak to you are not in and of myself: rather the Father that dwells in me, he does the works. Believe me that I am in the Father, and the Father in me: or else believe me for the very works' sake.

Jesus then told them that whoever believed on him would do the same works he did and even greater works than he had done because he was going to the Father. He promised them that he himself would do whatsoever they asked in his name, so the Father could be glorified in the Son. He told them he would do anything they asked in his name.

Church, I need to stop here and ask a few questions. If Jesus never said or did anything of himself, why do some of you insist on teaching and believing that God will give you new clothes, a new car, more money, etc. just because you ask in Jesus' name and believe you will receive it? James tells us our prayers aren't answered the way we WANT them answered because we either ask for the wrong things or ask for the wrong reasons. At no time did Jesus tell his followers to become the self serving hypocrites that we have allowed ourselves to become—all in the name of Jesus. Don't misunderstand me, I am not against prayer and asking for things in the name of Christ Jesus—the risen Son of God Almighty himself. However, if we want to become self serving, we should not even mention the name of Jesus in our prayers. Can't any of you see that the power of Jesus and his disciples is stifled by selfishness? Do you realize that God blesses us so we can bless others? We are not to make a show of the blessings we have to entice others to join us. This type of foolish thinking causes people to hate us with good cause, yet we justify the hatred of others by saying that they hated Jesus without cause and they will hate us as well. Church, not many of you have ever seen the type of hatred Jesus was talking about, much less experienced that type of hatred.

Jesus then told his disciples to keep his commandments if they loved him. He said he would pray the Father to send them another Comforter that would abide with them forever. He identified this Comforter as the spirit of truth; whom the world cannot receive; because the world doesn't see him or know him. Yet, the disciples know him because he dwells with them and was promised to be in them.

John 15

20. Remember the word that I said unto you, The servant is not greater than his lord. If they have persecuted me, they will also persecute you; if they have kept my saying, they will keep yours also.
21. But all these things will they do unto you for my name's sake, because they know not him that sent me.
22. If I had not come and spoken unto them, they had not had sin: but now they have no cloke for their sin.
23. He that hateth me hateth my Father also.
24. If I had not done among them the works which none other man did, they had not had sin: but now have they both seen and hated both me and my Father.
25. But this cometh to pass, that the word might be fulfilled that is written in their law, They hated me without a cause.
26. But when the Comforter is come, whom I will send unto you from the Father, even the Spirit of truth, which proceedeth from the Father, he shall testify of me:
27. And ye also shall bear witness, because ye have been with me from the beginning.

Jesus told his disciples to REMEMBER. The servant is not greater than his lord no matter how much authority his lord may give him. If they have persecuted me, they will also persecute you; if they have kept my saying, they will keep yours also. They will do all these things to you for my name's sake, because they do not know him that sent me. He then said that, if he had not come and spoken to them, they had not had sin. However, since Jesus did speak the truth to them, they no longer had a way to cloke their sin by misusing the law by following the letter and not the intent of the law. He that hates Jesus also hates the Father. Had Jesus not done among them the miracles that no man had ever done or even been able to do before, they had not had sin. However, since Jesus did these miracles, they saw what he did and hated him and his Father. He then told his disciples that all these things happened that the word of their own law might be fulfilled in them, They hated me without cause.

Church, let's stop here for a few minutes. How many Christians today consistently do and say the things that are revealed to them by the spirit of God? How many Christians today consistently do the works Jesus did and greater as he promised us? Come now, there are over 50,000 divisions among you. Surely there are many of you who do these things. Where are you? How many of you today are a servant to those you teach? People outside the church see selfish, judgmental, narrow minded hypocrites trying to force their lifestyle on others. Why do they see that from us? Christ wasn't that way and neither did he or his disciples teach us to be that way. Until Christians learn to desire the truth of God's word above everything else, including their own divisions, they will never do the things Jesus did or say the things he said with any meaning at all. Today Christians are hated mainly because they as a group—not necessarily individually—are seen by others as arrogant, self centered, hypocrites who are willingly defiant of the very God they claim to worship so much. Don't be offended. It is the way we have been taught to be for over 1900 years. It's time to look at ourselves in the light of God's word and transform ourselves into the image of the son of God himself as God intended for us to be in the first place. But, how can we do that?

Jesus then said that, when the Comforter is come, whom he himself would send from the Father, which proceeds from the Father himself, even the spirit of truth itself, he shall testify of Jesus to each one of you. He then told his disciples that they would also bear witness, because they had been with Jesus from the time he began to do and teach the things concerning the kingdom of God until the day he ascended while they watched.

Church, there's how we transform ourselves. The same spirit of truth that filled the apostles on the day of Pentecost is the same holy spirit that fills each one of us today. While we can't give eyewitness testimony to Jesus' life, death, resurrection, and ascension, we are able to recount the records made by those who did witness these things. However, these records have no meaning unless others actually see a change in us. The spirit in us shows us how to change, encourages us to change, and gives us the strength, power, and patience to change ourselves. It is up to each one of us to accept and allow that change to occur in us. As others see the changes in us, the words we speak concerning the record of Jesus literally come alive with power. Those who desire the truth will accept it when they hear it.

John 16

12. I have yet many things to say unto you, but ye cannot bear them now.
13. Howbeit when he, the Spirit of truth, is come, he will guide you into all truth: for he shall not speak of himself; but whatsoever he shall hear, that shall he speak: and he will shew you things to come.
14. He shall glorify me: for he shall receive of mine, and shall shew it unto you.
15. All things that the Father hath are mine: therefore said I, that he shall take of mine, and shall shew it unto you.

Jesus is still talking to his disciples when he tells them that he still had much to say, but they would not be able to bear those things at that time.

He did promise them that the spirit of truth, that was yet to come, would guide them into all truth. The spirit of truth would not speak of himself; but whatsoever he shall hear, that shall he speak. In addition, the spirit of truth will show you things that are yet to come. Jesus then told them that the spirit of truth shall glorify him: for he shall receive of mine, and shall show it to you. Jesus then said all things the Father has are mine: therefore said I, that he shall take of mine, and shall show it to you.

See church, the spirit only speaks what it hears. It never speaks in and of itself. It glorifies Christ himself. If we truly listen to the spirit that God has given each one of us, we can only speak and do the things we have seen and heard of the Father himself through Christ. How simple, yet how much discipline it will take for us to allow the spirit to operate that way in us. We can't try to impress others. We can't brag. We can't look down on others. Gee, that means we would have to learn to be a totally different person than we used to be. That's exactly what the scriptures tell us to do by putting off the old man and putting on the new man that is created in righteousness and true holiness.

Romans 15

5. Now the God of patience and consolation grant you to be likeminded one toward another according to Christ Jesus:
6. That ye may with one mind and one mouth glorify God, even the Father of our Lord Jesus Christ.
7. Wherefore receive ye one another, as Christ also received us to the glory of God.
8. Now I say that Jesus Christ was a minister of the circumcision for the truth of God, to confirm the promises made unto the fathers:
9. And that the Gentiles might glorify God for his mercy; as it is written, For this cause I will confess to thee among the Gentiles, and sing unto thy name.

Paul is talking to the church in Rome. He said that the God of patience and consolation give you the ability to be likeminded one toward another according to Christ Jesus. We are to with one unified mind and one unified voice glorify God himself, the Father of our lord Jesus Christ. This is the same thing he said to the church of Corinth. We are to receive one another just as Christ himself has received each of us to the glory of God. Church, how do you expect to obey these instructions when you are split into so many different divisions (denominations)? Do you honestly think that you are obedient to the word of God by being unified inside your own division? Are you obedient by accepting yourselves, but not others of different divisions? Do you try to work out some type of compromise with other divisions so you can agree to disagree? Just how far will you go to appear unified to others as you continually pervert the word of God?

Jesus Christ was a minister of the circumcision for the truth of God, to confirm the promises made unto the fathers of the children of Israel, not to the Gentiles. He was a light to the Gentiles, that the Gentiles themselves might glorify God for his great mercy. It is written, for this cause I will confess to thee among the Gentiles, and sing unto thy name. Church, we did not come from the children of Israel directly. We came from the Gentile nations. We have no right to the promises God made to the fathers. We have no business trying to claim them or teaching God took them from Israel and gave them to us instead. When we take things that are prophesied to Israel and try to claim them for ourselves, we are perverting God's word. Beware what you teach and believe in your assemblies.

2 Corinthians 4

1. **Therefore seeing we have this ministry, as we have received mercy, we faint not;**
2. **But have renounced the hidden things of dishonesty, not walking in craftiness, nor handling the word of God deceitfully; but by manifestation of the truth**

> **commending ourselves to every man's conscience in the sight of God.**
> **3. But if our gospel be hid, it is hid to them that are lost:**
> **4. In whom the god of this world hath blinded the minds of them which believe not, lest the light of the glorious gospel of Christ, who is the image of God, should shine unto them.**

Since we have this ministry-this same ministry of truth Christ himself had-and, as we ourselves have received mercy, we faint not nor give up. Instead, we have renounced the hidden things of dishonesty, not walking in craftiness, nor handling the word of God deceitfully; but by manifestation (clear demonstration) of the truth commending ourselves to every man's conscience in the sight of God. Church, how do we manifest the truth for every man to see? Do we quote scripture? Do we judge others publicly and loudly? Do we become political and back candidates? Do we have special laws passed?

Church, Christ himself told us how to do this. Peter and John told us how to do this. Paul told us how to do this. Each one of us must bring our own thoughts captive to the obedience of Christ himself. When each of us becomes obedient to God the same way Christ was, each of us will only do and say the things we see and hear from the Father. Then, like Peter and John, we can look anyone right in the face and say that we can't help but to say and do the things we have seen and heard. We ourselves will turn from deceitful craftiness and the hidden things of dishonesty. We will no longer try to justify flattery, compromise, or anything else that opposes the truth in ourselves. It is then that we will see clearly how to help those around us who are in need.

However, if our gospel is hidden at that point, it is hidden only to those who are lost. These are the ones who do not have the love of the truth in their hearts, nor do they desire to have such a thing. The god of this world has blinded their minds to keep the light of the glorious gospel of Christ from shining through to them. Church, make no mistake, such people are both inside and outside your assemblies. That's one of the contributing factors to the great number of divisions among you. Remember, these letters to the churches were focusing on things inside the church that were attacking the congregations.

Ephesians 1

9. Having made known unto us the mystery of his will, according to his good pleasure which he hath purposed in himself:
10. That in the dispensation of the fulness of times he might gather together in one all things in Christ, both which are in heaven, and which are on earth; even in him:
11. In whom also we have obtained an inheritance, being predestinated according to the purpose of him who worketh all things after the counsel of his own will:
12. That we should be to the praise of his glory, who first trusted in Christ.
13. In whom ye also trusted, after that ye heard the word of truth, the gospel of your salvation: in whom also after that ye believed, ye were sealed with that holy Spirit of promise,
14. Which is the earnest of our inheritance until the redemption of the purchased possession, unto the praise of his glory.

Church, Paul is writing to the Ephesian assembly about God and his will. Paul was referring to himself and the other apostles when he spoke to the Ephesians and then explained to them the importance of God's will. God revealed the mystery of his will, according to his good pleasure which he has purposed totally in himself. In the fulness of time God plans to gather together in one (unity) all things in Christ; both which are in heaven, which are on earth; even in him. Paul said the apostles have obtained an inheritance, being predestinated according to the purpose of him who works all things after his own will. This was for the apostles to themselves be to the praise of his glory, who themselves first trusted in Christ. After that, it was for those who trusted also once they heard the word of truth from the apostles, the very gospel of their salvation. What gospel are we talking about here? Are we referring to a gospel of some new social order? Perhaps we are talking about the life and times of some great teacher or prophet. Maybe it is a new self improvement program Paul was referring to here. Don't laugh, some of you teach these very things in your congregations.

Church, the gospel of your salvation is the death and resurrection of Jesus Christ himself to Eternal Life, physically demonstrated to the apostles and to over 500 brethren at once, according to the scriptures. There is no other method of salvation offered for this age. Once you have heard the word of truth and believe what you have heard, you are sealed with the holy spirit of promise, the spirit itself being the earnest—down payment—of our inheritance until the redemption of the purchased possession and not until. This is all to the glory of God himself who purposed this in his own will.

2 Thessalonians 2

7. **For the mystery of iniquity doth already work: only he who now letteth will let, until he be taken out of the way.**
8. **And then shall that Wicked be revealed, whom the Lord shall consume with the spirit of his mouth, and shall destroy with the brightness of his coming:**
9. **Even him, whose coming is after the working of Satan with all power and signs and lying wonders,**
10. **And with all deceivableness of unrighteousness in them that perish; because they received not the love of the truth, that they might be saved.**
11. **And for this cause God shall send them strong delusion, that they should believe a lie:**
12. **That they all might be damned who believed not the truth, but had pleasure in unrighteousness.**
13. **But we are bound to give thanks alway to God for you, brethren beloved of the Lord, because God hath**

> **from the beginning chosen you to salvation through sanctification of the Spirit and belief of the truth:**
> **14. Whereunto he called you by our gospel, to the obtaining of the glory of our Lord Jesus Christ.**

Church, a great and terrible thing is revealed here, so pay very close attention. This letter is written to one particular congregation in the church, but it is directed to the entire church—not the world. Therefore, the subject matter discussed applies to the church itself.

At the time Paul wrote this, the mystery of iniquity was already at work inside some of the congregations of the church. Iniquity is an interesting word. It comes from a root that means "to twist" or "to bend". Therefore, even from the time of Paul, there were those inside the congregations of the church that were bending and twisting the word of truth. This process has been relentless inside the church for over 1900 years. The only thing stopping the church from completely turning away from God is the presence of those among them who hold fast and keep the word of truth. Their presence will continue to keep the church from completely turning away until they themselves are taken out of the way. When and how this particular event will occur is the subject of much debate among the churches. I will not engage in that debate at all. What I can say is that the event will occur and it will be final. There will be no changing sides once this decision is made and the event occurs.

It is after this separation in the church itself that the wicked one himself shall be revealed, the person whom the lord shall consume with the power of his mouth, and shall destroy with the brightness of his coming: even him, the person whose coming itself is completely after the working of Satan himself with ALL power and signs and lying wonders, and with ALL deceivableness of unrighteousness in them that perish; because they received not the love of the truth, that they might be saved. Church, the only way these people could not receive the love of the truth would be for them to refuse to accept the truth and deliberately choose to believe a lie instead. Remember, church, I am talking about those who walk among you as fellow Christians—not those in the world.

It is for this reason that God will send them strong delusion, that they should believe a lie—the lie told by the wicked one himself—that they all might be damned who believed not the truth, but had pleasure in unrighteousness. The lie the wicked one tells is mentioned earlier in this same chapter, however, I have chosen not to reveal it here. If any of you want to know what the lie is, you will have to read just a little further in the text for yourself. Church, when you read from the beginning of the chapter and see the lie and realize actually what it is, a great many of you will be shocked and declare that you will never believe what the wicked one says. However, those of you without the love of the truth in your hearts will believe him because you have been prepared to accept his lie for over a thousand years generation after generation.

To those of you who have the love of the truth in your heart, we are bound to give thanks to God always for you, beloved of the lord, because from the beginning God has chosen you to salvation by the sanctification of his own spirit and belief of the truth: whereunto he called you by our gospel, to the obtaining the glory of our lord Jesus Christ himself. Church, what a calling. Each one of us is offered the same glory that Jesus Christ himself has. To obtain it, all we have to do is to believe the truth when we hear it. In order to do that, we must have the love of the truth in our hearts. See, so simple a child can understand it. It is not easy, though. In order to actually believe the truth, we also have to follow and do what the truth reveals to us. This is where our struggle is, and this is why we pray for one another. None of us are perfect, but we can be perfected from within if we believe and follow the truth of the word of God.

1 Timothy 2

1. I exhort therefore, that, first of all, supplications, prayers, intercessions, and giving of thanks, be made for all men;

> 2. For kings, and for all that are in authority; that we may lead a quiet and peaceable life in all godliness and honesty.
> 3. For this is good and acceptable in the sight of God our Saviour;
> 4. Who will have all men to be saved, and to come unto the knowledge of the truth.
> 5. For there is one God, and one mediator between God and men, the man Christ Jesus;
> 6. Who gave himself a ransom for all, to be testified in due time.

Church, supplications, prayers, intercessions, and giving of thanks are supposed to be made by us for all men; for kings, and all that are in authority; that we may lead a quiet and peaceable life in all godliness and honesty. This is good and acceptable in the sight of God our savior, who will have all men to be saved, and come to the knowledge of the truth. Church, what we are to pray for is not that these people become Christians. We are to pray that these people receive guidance and wisdom enough to carry out their responsibilities and leave us alone to lead a quiet and peaceable life in all godliness and honesty.

However, for us to live that way, we need to learn to be quiet and peaceable. We need to stop interfering with various governments and groups of people. We need to keep our nose out of their business and tend to ours. Before anyone starts yelling about saving the lost, consider this. When Joseph was in Egypt in prison and Pharaoh had him brought before him to interpret a dream, did Joseph tell Pharaoh he had to stop worshipping his gods before Joseph would interpret the dreams? When Daniel was in Babylon and was asked to interpret writing on a wall, did he tell the king he wouldn't interpret it unless the king worshipped the God of Abraham, Isaac, and Jacob first? Church, if we learn to live peaceable, quiet, honest, and godly lives by participating in the things of society that are godly and simply leaving the ungodly things alone, we, by example, will be able to teach our own children and others how to do the selfsame thing. It is then that the words we speak will have power and not just be an opinion of one group who are trying to force our way of life upon others. We then won't just declare the new man, we will become the new man for all to see. If we would do as the scriptures say here, God could work in the hearts of men and those who seek the truth would come to us and the rest would go about their lives. Then, if people hate us, it would be because they hate the truth. However, until we learn to live this way, we cause people to hate us by the things we say about them and the things we do to them in the name of God.

Church, there is one God, and one mediator between God and men, the man Christ Jesus; who gave himself a ransom for all, to be testified in due time. Church, when we follow the scriptures ourselves, we become the new man that is itself the reflection of Christ Jesus, a living witness to the sacrifice Christ Jesus himself made for all men. It is time to correct the wrong we are doing instead of trying to correct the wrong we see others doing.

1 Timothy 3

> **14. These things write I unto thee, hoping to come unto thee shortly:**
> **15. But if I tarry long, that thou mayest know how thou oughtest to behave thyself in the house of God, which is the church of the living God, the pillar and ground of the truth.**

Paul was writing to Timothy, the pastor of a congregation that was beset with many problems. Paul had been addressing these problems up to this point and instructing Timothy about how we should behave in the house of God. Paul declared the house of God to be the church of the living God, and as such, the very pillar and ground of truth itself. Church, how many of us today can say that we, as the church, the body whose head is Christ himself, are the pillar and ground of the truth? Look at us. We are divided into various groups, each with our own personal interpretations of the truth. We don't agree with one another. We don't respect one another. We lie to one another. We judge one another. We disobey the things written to us by Peter, James, John, and Paul. In doing so, we dishonor the work these men did, we dishonor the God who inspired them to do and say the things they did and said, and we dishonor Christ Jesus, who gave himself a ransom for us all. By our own actions, we have polluted the very pillar and ground of truth itself. We need to change ourselves before we sear our own hearts to the point we won't accept the truth ourselves.

2 Timothy 2

14. Of these things put them in remembrance, charging them before the Lord that they strive not about words to no profit, but to the subverting of the hearers.
15. Study to shew thyself approved unto God, a workman that needeth not to be ashamed, rightly dividing the word of truth.
16. But shun profane and vain babblings: for they will increase unto more ungodliness.
17. And their word will eat as doth a canker: of whom is Hymenaeus and Philetus;
18. Who concerning the truth have erred, saying that the resurrection is past already; and overthrow the faith of some.
19. Nevertheless the foundation of God standeth sure, having this seal, The Lord knoweth them that are his. And, Let every one that nameth the name of Christ depart from iniquity.
20. But in a great house there are not only vessels of gold and of silver, but also of wood and of earth; and some to honour, and some to dishonour.
21. If a man therefore purge himself from these, he shall be a vessel unto honour, sanctified, and meet for the master's use, and prepared unto every good work.
22. Flee also youthful lusts: but follow righteousness, faith, charity, peace, with them that call on the Lord out of a pure heart.

23. But foolish and unlearned questions avoid, knowing that they do gender strifes.

24. And the servant of the Lord must not strive; but be gentle unto all men, apt to teach, patient,

25. In meekness instructing those that oppose themselves; if God peradventure will give them repentance to the acknowledging of the truth;

26. And that they may recover themselves out of the snare of the devil, who are taken captive by him at his will.

Church, do not strive over the meanings and nuances of words as is commonly practiced today in our politically correct society. Striving over shades of meaning serves no benefit to the hearers at all. Such strife only serves to subvert the hearers and turn them from understanding the truth. Instead, each one of you study to show yourself approved unto God, a workman that does not need to be ashamed, rightly dividing the word of truth. At the same time, shun profane and vain babblings: for they will increase to more ungodliness. Church understand this. It is important to study God's Word. It is important to be as systematic as any workman when you study. In ancient times, texts were written either in all upper case letters one after another with no spacing between the letters at all, or in all lower case letters, each connected to the other with no spaces at all between them. There was no division into chapters or verses for convenient reading. The text was read and understood by the flow of thoughts expressed in the text. The inspired written thoughts were the only means of punctuation and understanding.

Church, this is important. All the punctuation, all the chapter divisions, and all the verse divisions were added by men as an aid to studying the text. This was not authorised by God or it would have been written that way from the beginning. God punctuated the text by thoughts. When studying, make sure you understand the complete thought you are reading. Men added punctuation and verse division based on their own understanding and not necessarily on God's thoughts. Men also added capitalization of letters the same way. Rightly dividing means understanding the complete thought of God, not expressing some doctrine based upon man's interpretation of God's thought. There is only one dividing of the truth that is rightly divided and that is the way God himself revealed it to those who wrote it down. Any other division is not rightly divided and is not the word of God. God will judge you church by his expressed thought, not by your interpretation of his thought by your various chapters and verses.

Church, stop arguing about doctrines based on chapter and verse. Your vain babblings will only increase to even more ungodliness. Such words will eat at you like a cancer. Hymenaeus and Philetus were two such men who twisted the words of God and taught that the resurrection of the dead had already passed. Their teaching was in error, yet they left out scripture that didn't agree with what they taught. They obscured the meanings of words in the text. They cited parts of scripture out of context. They did all these things to prove their doctrine was the word of God. Their only purpose was to overthrow the faith of others and they did overthrow the faith of some. Church, these same things are being done in your congregations today as a matter of practice to protect your own individual doctrines in each of your over 50,000 different divisions. Remember, God is about to begin judgement in his house by the truth he himself uttered, not by your interpretation of his truth.

In all this, however, the foundation of God stands sure and certain, having this seal, the Lord himself knows them that are his. Let every one of you who name the name of Christ turn completely away from iniquity with its deceptive words and practices. In a great house there are many vessels. Not only are some made of gold and silver, but also some are made of wood and of earth. Some are honorable and some are dishonorable. If any man purge himself of the words and practices of iniquity and its accompanying dishonor, he himself will be a vessel made unto honor, sanctified, meet for the master's use, and prepared to every good work.

Flee youthful lusts with their uncontrollable desires. Instead, follow righteousness, faith, charity, peace, with them that call on the name of the Lord out of a pure heart. Avoid foolish and unlearned questions, knowing that engaging in such things causes strifes, commotions, confusion, emulations, variances, and divisions among you. The servant of the Lord must not strive. Instead, he must be gentle to all men, able and ready to teach, patient, in meekness instructing those who oppose themselves; allowing God, whose spirit searches their hearts, to give them repentance to the acknowledging of the truth; that they may recover themselves from the snare of the devil, who has taken them captive at his will through strifes, commotions, contentions, confusion, emulations, variances, and divisions.

2 Timothy 3

1. **This know also, that in the last days perilous times shall come.**
2. **For men shall be lovers of their own selves, covetous, boasters, proud, blasphemers, disobedient to parents, unthankful, unholy,**
3. **Without natural affection, trucebreakers, false accusers, incontinent, fierce, despisers of those that are good,**
4. **Traitors, heady, highminded, lovers of pleasures more than lovers of God;**
5. **Having a form of godliness, but denying the power thereof: from such turn away.**
6. **For of this sort are they which creep into houses, and lead captive silly women laden with sins, led away with divers lusts,**
7. **Ever learning, and never able to come to the knowledge of the truth.**

Know this also, church, that in the last days perilous times shall come upon you. Men who are among you shall be lovers of their own selves, covetous, boasters, proud, blasphemers, disobedient to parents, unthankful, unholy, without natural affection, trucebreakers, false accusers, without self control, fierce, despisers of those that are good, traitors, heady, highminded, lovers of pleasures more than lovers of God. These men do have a form of godliness because they sit among you and worship with you. They know the right words to speak, the right prayers to pray, the right songs to sing. They know how to greet others, how much money to give, the right testimonies to give. They know when to shake a hand or to give a pat on the back. They do these things among you to appear godly, yet they deny the very God they claim to worship in your presence. From such, turn away. Do not just turn away from the people as men's wisdom would teach you to do. Instead, look at yourself and turn away from the practices of these men that you yourself practice. It is human nature to do these things. First, change your nature to the new nature God has given you. Then, you will see clearly how to deal with the others, but only when and if you are willing to do and say the things that God tells you and shows you through the spirit he has given you.

Church, these men among you are the sort that creep into houses, and lead captive harmless women laden with sins, led away with divers lusts. These men are ever learning, and never able to come to the knowledge of the truth because they have no desire in them to do so.

2 Timothy 4

1. **I charge thee therefore before God, and the Lord Jesus Christ, who shall judge the quick and the dead at his appearing and his kingdom;**
2. **Preach the word; be instant in season, out of season; reprove, rebuke, exhort with all longsuffering and doctrine.**
3. **For the time will come when they will not endure sound doctrine; but after their own lusts shall they heap to themselves teachers, having itching ears;**
4. **And they shall turn away their ears from the truth, and shall be turned unto fables.**

Church, I show you an even worse thing. Pastors, you are charged before God himself, and before the Lord Jesus Christ, who shall judge both the living and the dead at his appearing and his kingdom; preach the word; be instant in season, out of season; reprove, rebuke, exhort with all longsuffering and doctrine. The time will come when those you teach will not endure sound doctrine. Instead, driven by their own uncontrollable desires, they shall heap to themselves teachers, having itching ears; they shall turn away their ears from the truth, and shall be turned unto fables. That means that pastors, teachers, and elders as well will turn away. Someone will have to teach and guide these people with itching ears. This is a terrible thing to consider, but it is something we must face. It will happen among us.

James 1

13. **Let no man say when he is tempted, I am tempted of God: for God cannot be tempted with evil, neither tempteth he any man:**
14. **But every man is tempted, when he is drawn away of his own lust, and enticed.**
15. **Then when lust hath conceived, it bringeth forth sin: and sin, when it is finished, bringeth forth death.**
16. **Do not err, my beloved brethren.**
17. **Every good gift and every perfect gift is from above, and cometh down from the Father of lights, with whom is no variableness, neither shadow of turning.**
18. **Of his own will begat he us with the word of truth, that we should be a kind of firstfruits of his creatures.**
19. **Wherefore, my beloved brethren, let every man be swift to hear, slow to speak, slow to wrath:**
20. **For the wrath of man worketh not the righteousness of God.**

Let no man say that he is tempted of God when he is tempted. God himself cannot be tempted with evil, neither does he tempt any man at all. Every man is tempted when he is drawn away by his own uncontrollable desire, and enticed. Once lust has conceived, it brings forth sin. When sin is finished, it brings forth death. Church, do not err in this understanding.

Every good gift and every perfect gift is from above, and comes down from the Father of lights, with whom is no variableness, neither shadow of turning. Of his own will, God himself birthed us with the word of truth, that we should be a kind of firstfruits of his creatures. Since this is the case, church, let every man be swift to hear, slow to speak, and slow to wrath. Man's wrath does not work the righteousness of God.

CHAPTER 16

Ephesians 6

17. And take the helmet of salvation, and the sword of the Spirit, which is the word of God:

The next piece of the armor we are going to look at is the sword. Its design was simple and efficient. It's length was from the elbow to to tip of the middle finger, about 19 to 22 inches from haft to sword tip. It had a razor sharp edge on each side of the blade. It was designed for slicing from either direction. Its small length made it ideal for fighting in small or cluttered places. It was designed for up close hand to hand combat.

The word of God in this passage refers utterance, specifically to the spoken word of God. Its comparison to the Roman sword is noteworthy. The spoken word should be simple, efficient, as short as possible, and razor sharp. There must be no confusion about what is said. Standing alone, it is not designed for huge pitched battles; however, it is suited very well for in close hand to hand struggles that we face daily within ourselves. It is designed to overthrow strongholds and vain imaginations in our minds.

Matthew 4

1. Then was Jesus led up of the Spirit into the wilderness to be tempted of the devil.
2. And when he had fasted forty days and forty nights, he was afterward an hungred.

> 3. And when the tempter came to him, he said, If thou be the Son of God, command that these stones be made bread.
> 4. But he answered and said, It is written, Man shall not live by bread alone, but by every word that proceedeth out of the mouth of God.

Right after Jesus was baptized by John, Matthew states that the spirit led him into the wilderness to be tempted of the devil himself. After Jesus had been there 40 days and fasted, he was hungry. Then the tempter came to him and suggested that, if Jesus truly were the son of God, he could just command the stones to become bread and just simply eat until he was filled. There was no need for such an important person to be hungry. Jesus' reply was, it is written, Man shall not live by bread alone, but by every word that proceeds out of the mouth of God. Did you get that, church?

The verb live he used is the verb form of the noun LIFE, as in Eternal Life. Yes, man lives on the earth by eating substances that, to him, are food. However, he can only have Eternal Life through consuming the utterances of God. Church, Jesus referred to the written word of God that expressed the utterances that God himself had inspired men to write down and speak themselves.

Matthew 12

> 34. O generation of vipers, how can ye, being evil, speak good things? for out of the abundance of the heart the mouth speaketh.
> 35. A good man out of the good treasure of the heart bringeth forth good things: and an evil man out of the evil treasure bringeth forth evil things.
> 36. But I say unto you, That every idle word that men shall speak, they shall give account thereof in the day of judgment.

Church, out of the abundance of the heart the mouth speaks. Out of the good treasure of his own heart, a good man brings forth good things.

Out of the evil treasure of his own heart, an evil man brings forth evil things. The treasures of your heart are the things you think about and value most. Every idle word that men shall speak, they shall give an account thereof in the day of judgment. Church, we know that, as Christians, we have the spirit of God in us. That spirit reveals to God the thoughts of our hearts that we are unable to utter. That same spirits reveals to us the thoughts of God. Therefore even our thoughts are lifted to God as a prayer, whether we realize it or not. Some of our thoughts are a sweet smelling savor to God. Others, however, assault his nostrils like the rotten garbage they are.

Church, this is why we are instructed to bring every thought captive to the obedience of Christ himself. When we do that, we become like Christ, Peter, and John. We can only say and do the things we have seen and heard from the Father through the spirit that is in us.

Matthew 18

15. Moreover if thy brother shall trespass against thee, go and tell him his fault between thee and him alone: if he shall hear thee, thou hast gained thy brother.
16. But if he will not hear thee, then take with thee one or two more, that in the mouth of two or three witnesses every word may be established.

If your brother offends you by something he says or does, go to him in private and tell him what he has done. If he hears you, he will do what he can to correct the offense, and you have gained your brother. However, if he will not hear you, take one or two others with you and approach him again. Church, that does not mean take a couple of your friends over to set him straight. It means for you to take one or two others with you who have no side or no benefit from this other than simply being a witness. Once you approach your brother in their presence, it is out of their mouths the witness will be established as who is being reasonable and who is not.

Luke 1

35. And the angel answered and said unto her, The Holy Ghost shall come upon thee, and the power of the Highest shall overshadow thee: therefore also that holy thing which shall be born of thee shall be called the Son of God.

36. And, behold, thy cousin Elisabeth, she hath also conceived a son in her old age: and this is the sixth month with her, who was called barren.

37. For with God nothing shall be impossible.

38. And Mary said, Behold the handmaid of the Lord; be it unto me according to thy word. And the angel departed from her.

Mary was talking to an angel. The angel said to her, the Holy Ghost shall come upon thee, and the power of the Highest shall overshadow thee: therefore also that holy thing which shall be born of thee shall be called the Son of God. Behold, thy cousin Elizabeth, she has also conceived a son in her old age: and this is the sixth month with her, who was called barren. For with God nothing shall be impossible.

Church, think about this for a minute. An angel appeared to a woman in Galilee and told her that she would conceive totally in herself because the power of God himself would come on her and cause this to happen. This same angel told the woman that her barren cousin beyond child bearing age was six months pregnant. In today's enlightened age, superstition has no place. People today are intelligent and understand psychology of the human mind. People today look at the people in the past as unenlightened and superstitious. They view God and religious belief as superstitions. Even some among us have these same views. What happened then would be difficult today because no self respecting enlightened young woman of today would accept such a story in the first place.

How did Mary respond? Mary said, Behold the handmaid of the Lord; be it unto me according to thy word. Church, the power of the spoken word is illustrated in that statement. Both the word from

God delivered by the angel and the word spoken by Mary herself are necessary in this case. Mary could have just as easily have said, I don't want any part of this. If she had been unwilling, God could not have forced his power upon her and made her conceive anyway. That is why Paul later said that the power of salvation is near you, even in your mouth. We don't realize the power of the words that come out of our own mouths.

Luke 2

> 25. And, behold, there was a man in Jerusalem, whose name was Simeon; and the same man was just and devout, waiting for the consolation of Israel: and the Holy Ghost was upon him.
> 26. And it was revealed unto him by the Holy Ghost, that he should not see death, before he had seen the Lord's Christ.
> 27. And he came by the Spirit into the temple: and when the parents brought in the child Jesus, to do for him after the custom of the law,
> 28. Then took he him up in his arms, and blessed God, and said,
> 29. Lord, now lettest thou thy servant depart in peace, according to thy word:
> 30. For mine eyes have seen thy salvation,
> 31. Which thou hast prepared before the face of all people;
> 32. A light to lighten the Gentiles, and the glory of thy people Israel.

Simeon was a just and devout man in Jerusalem who was waiting for the consolation of Israel: and the Holy Ghost was upon him. The Holy Ghost revealed to Simeon that he should not see death before he himself had seen the Lord's Christ. The spirit led Simeon to the temple and he waited. He had no idea who the Messiah was, so he waited for the spirit to show him. When Mary and Joseph brought Jesus into the temple to offer the sacrifice for the first born male, Simeon went to them took the baby. He held the baby up, blessed God, and said, Lord, now lettest thou thy servant depart in peace, according to thy word: for mine eyes have seen thy salvation, which thou hast prepared before the face of all people; a light to lighten the Gentiles, and the glory of thy people Israel.

Church, the holy spirit itself came on Simeon and revealed to him that he would not die until he had seen the promised Messiah. This same spirit led Simeon to the temple and Simeon waited. The spirit showed Simeon which person in the temple was the Messiah as he was brought in. It never once said that God spoke to Simeon, yet it does say that the spirit revealed to Simeon. Church, that means that revelation through holy spirit is the same thing as the uttered word of God. It also means that the thoughts we have are revealed to God through the spirit of God in us are our utterances whether we actually speak them aloud or not. Just because you think a thought, and don't say it doesn't mean you haven't uttered it. This is why Paul instructed each one of us to bring our own thoughts captive to the obedience of Christ. When we have the obedience he had, we will be able to speak and do the things we see and hear from the Father, just like Christ did. Will we be perfect like he is? Not as long as we are in this body. But, we will be able to overcome our own flaws enough to reflect the image of Christ himself in spite of our own flawed nature.

Luke 3

1. **Now in the fifteenth year of the reign of Tiberius Caesar, Pontius Pilate being governor of Judaea, and Herod being tetrarch of Galilee, and his brother Philip tetrarch of Ituraea and of the region of Trachonitis, and Lysanias the tetrarch of Abilene,**
2. **Annas and Caiaphas being the high priests, the word of God came unto John the son of Zacharias in the wilderness.**
3. **And he came into all the country about Jordan, preaching the baptism of repentance for the remission of sins;**

The word of God came to John the son of Zacharias in the wilderness. How did this happen? The spirit that was on John from birth revealed the word of God to him. John then went and preached the baptism of repentance for remission of sins in the country all about Jordan.

John 3

> **27. John answered and said, A man can receive nothing, except it be given him from heaven.**
>
> **28. Ye yourselves bear me witness, that I said, I am not the Christ, but that I am sent before him.**
>
> **29. He that hath the bride is the bridegroom: but the friend of the bridegroom, which standeth and heareth him, rejoiceth greatly because of the bridegroom's voice: this my joy therefore is fulfilled.**
>
> **30. He must increase, but I must decrease.**
>
> **31. He that cometh from above is above all: he that is of the earth is earthly, and speaketh of the earth: he that cometh from heaven is above all.**
>
> **32. And what he hath seen and heard, that he testifieth; and no man receiveth his testimony.**
>
> **33. He that hath received his testimony hath set to his seal that God is true.**
>
> **34. For he whom God hath sent speaketh the words of God: for God giveth not the Spirit by measure unto him.**

There were some who came to John and asked him about Jesus. John said, a man can receive nothing, except it be given him from heaven. He then told them they they themselves already bore witness to the fact that John himself had declared that he was not the Christ. John declared that he was sent before Christ. John then referred to Christ as the bridegroom and to himself as the friend of the bridegroom. As a friend, he was content and joyful just to stand and hear the words of the bridegroom. John said that Christ must increase, but he himself must decrease.

John went on to tell them that he that comes from above is above all: he that is of the earth is earthly, and speaks of the earth: he that comes from heaven is above all. He that comes from heaven is above all. What exactly is John saying here? How is he representing Christ? He has just compared himself as the friend of the bridegroom and Christ as the bridegroom. What comparison is he making here? He is comparing his birth to Christ's birth. John was miraculously conceived by a woman who was past child bearing age. John's father was an old man. Never happened before? Sarah had Isaac by Abraham when both of them were too old to have children. John's situation was the same as that. Even though his conception and birth was miraculous, he was earthy because both his parents were of the earth. He referred to Christ's birth as being from above and from heaven. The same power that allowed Elizabeth to conceive in her barren state caused her cousin Mary to conceive in her own womb even though she had never known a man. Therefore Christ's miraculous birth was from heaven and not of the earth. Christ's father then was God himself through the working of his power.

What he that is from heaven has seen and heard, that he testifies; and no man receives his testimony. He that receives his testimony has set his seal that God is true. He whom God has sent speaks the utterances of God: for God does not measure or restrict the spirit he has given him.

John 6

63. It is the spirit that quickeneth; the flesh profiteth nothing: the words that I speak unto you, they are spirit, and they are life.
64. But there are some of you that believe not. For Jesus knew from the beginning who they were that believed not, and who should betray him.
65. And he said, Therefore said I unto you, that no man can come unto me, except it were given unto him of my Father.

> 66. From that time many of his disciples went back, and walked no more with him.
> 67. Then said Jesus unto the twelve, Will ye also go away?
> 68. Then Simon Peter answered him, Lord, to whom shall we go? thou hast the words of eternal life.

Jesus was speaking to his disciples when he said it is the spirit (power) that quickens (makes alive); the flesh profits nothing: the words that I speak to you, they are spirit (power), and they are Eternal Life. Church we have that same power in us as Christians. Our words should be the same as his. However, there are some of you who do not believe. Jesus knew from the beginning who didn't believe, and who should betray him. And he said, Therefore I say unto you, that no man can come unto me, except it were given unto him of my Father. From that time, many of his disciples went back, and did not walk with him any more.

Then Jesus said unto the twelve, Will you also go away? Then Simon Peter answered him, Lord, to whom shall we go? you have the words of Eternal Life. Church, if we today spoke the words of Eternal Life the way Jesus did, our young people would not be searching everywhere to find meaning in their lives. We have the power in us, but we are not obedient to God the way Christ was. Our own selfishness and disobedience is turning people away—not the things we are trying to teach. Of course, there are those who walk among us who are teaching anything but what Jesus taught as well. For someone outside, it is hard to tell the difference.

John 5

> 24. Verily, verily, I say unto you, He that heareth my word, and believeth on him that sent me, hath everlasting life, and shall not come into condemnation; but is passed from death unto life.
> 25. Verily, verily, I say unto you, The hour is coming, and now is, when the dead shall hear the voice of the Son of God: and they that hear shall live.

26. For as the Father hath life in himself; so hath he given to the Son to have life in himself;

27. And hath given him authority to execute judgment also, because he is the Son of man.

Church, these four verses contain volumes that have been overlooked and forgotten for a long time. These aren't gold nuggets of truth. This is the main lode itself, so pay close attention as we go through this.

Truly, truly, I say unto you, He that heareth my word, and believes on him that sent me, has everlasting life, and shall not come into condemnation; but is passed from death to life.

Church, let's break this down. Whoever hears (understands) the word Christ spoke, Christ himself said that this was his word, whoever believes on him that sent Christ (God himself), that person has everlasting life. Here is where we miss what is said. Has, not will someday maybe-if-you-are-good-enough-have, but has right now. Since those people all died, they didn't have eternal life at the time. What exactly was Christ talking about then? He was talking about the judgment of the just and the unjust at the end of the age. Those who received Eternal Life as a reward would bypass the judgment and receive Eternal Life instead.

Truly, truly, I say unto you, the hour is coming, and now is, when the dead shall hear the voice of the son of God: and they that hear shall live (have eternal Life).

Who was Christ talking about here? Was he talking about those in the grave? Did the graves open and the dead all come out while he was talking? Church, in case you are wondering, go to Ecclesiastes 9:5 and read for yourself that the living know they are going to die, but the dead know not any thing. The dead in the graves could not have heard his words at that time because the dead are dead—they know not any thing. Christ was talking to those around him. He considered them to be dead already unless they heard (understood) his word and believed on the Father who sent him to them. Those who heard (understood) his word shall have Eternal Life—no one else.

For as the Father has life in himself; so has he given to the son to have life in himself.

News flash! God has eternal Life and that life is contained totally within himself. This is the same God Christ told the Samaritan woman at Jacob's well is a spirit. God is the only person specifically named that has Life in himself, whether spirit or not. It makes him totally unique. God's life is not derived from, nor depends upon any outside source to maintain it. God gave his only begotten son the promise to have that very same life in himself. When Christ said these things, he was full of the spirit of God, yet, he did not have Eternal Life. If Christ had actually had Eternal Life at the time he was speaking, it would have been impossible for him to die—ever. Therefore, Christ had the very same promise of Eternal Life that we have been given.

And has given him the authority to execute judgment also, because he is the son of Man.

Christ's authority to execute judgment does not rest in his being God's only begotten son—it rests in his being the son of Man. Only a man could experience the things that tempt, affect, and, in the end, destroy a man. James said that God does not tempt anyone, nor can he be tempted. John said that Jesus Christ came totally and completely in the flesh—not part man and part God. Hebrews said that Christ was tempted in every way as we are, yet without sin.

Luke 9

59. And he said unto another, Follow me. But he said, Lord, suffer me first to go and bury my father.
60. Jesus said unto him, Let the dead bury their dead: but go thou and preach the kingdom of God.

The two sentences in this exchange have been misunderstood for a long time because we do not look at them in the proper perspective. As we look at these things, let us consider the things we know about Jesus and the things we don't realize we know about the man he was talking to.

When we do this, we shall see one of the most profound things happen right in front of our eyes.

The scriptures tell us that Jesus knew what was in the hearts of men. Jesus knew who would follow him and who would turn away from him. Therefore, none of his decisions were arbitrary. Also, none of the things he said to anyone were at random or coincidental. The man Jesus was talking to was part of a crowd of people following Jesus and listening to his words. That means that, at some point, this man had left his family and was travelling from place to place to hear the teachings of Jesus. Since he knew what was in the man's heart, Jesus said to the man, Follow me. While no one noticed the man, he followed quietly in the crowd because deep down inside he wanted to know the things of the kingdom of God. However, once this man was singled out, something else happened.

Suddenly, he came face to face with self doubt. To be allowed to follow unnoticed is one thing, but to be singled out of a group and specifically told to follow is another thing entirely. One immediately begins to question his own qualifications and abilities. Moses did the same thing. Paul took us through his own experience when he said he wasn't even meet to be called an apostle because he had persecuted the church of God. The man's first response to Jesus was to ask permission to go home and bury his father. He didn't mean that his father had died; he was referring to a custom practiced during that time period whereby the children took care of their parents until their parents died. This was part of honoring your parents and this custom goes all the way back to the time of Abraham. Today we just stick our parents in a home somewhere, pay someone else to look after them, and go about our own selfish lives.

Jesus responded to the man by telling him to let the dead bury the dead. Instead, Jesus told the man to go and preach the kingdom of God. Jesus had no doubt about what was in the heart of this man even though the man doubted himself. Jesus wanted this man to go and preach the kingdom of God, the words of Life itself to others so that many more, even this man's family, could have Eternal Life.

Church, we are called the same way today and we respond the same way this man did. We doubt our qualifications, we doubt the qualifications of others, we doubt our ability to speak. In short, we do almost anything at all to find a way not to be called. So long as we can follow unnoticed, we do well. However, once we are specifically called, we shudder, stutter, duck, and run like Jonah did. We are afraid that the power that God has given us is not enough to overcome our shortcomings, yet we tell others that such power is greater than any in the world. People see this in us, and call us hypocrites. It is time for us to allow the spirit of God in us strengthen us to the point where we both will and do his good pleasure instead of ours.

Acts 2

14. But Peter, standing up with the eleven, lifted up his voice, and said unto them, Ye men of Judaea, and all ye that dwell at Jerusalem, be this known unto you, and hearken to my words:

Church, pay close attention. Acts 2 describes events that took place on the day of Pentecost. The phenomenal events that took place drew a large crowd in the Temple, the house of God, that they all were in. The crowd was confused and wondered. Some even mocked the apostles. However, Peter stood up with the other eleven apostles and lifted his voice loudly and clearly. He addressed the crowd to listen to his words. He did not say . . . "Thus saith the Lord". He did not say . . . "Listen to what Jesus told us". He said "Hearken to MY words". He then launched into one of the most powerful sermons that these people had ever heard. Peter claimed and took responsibility for every single word he uttered from his own mouth. At that point, Peter had been transformed from a headstrong sniveler to a bold man who uttered the words of God from his own mouth.

How did he do that? Peter was filled with the power of God. That power made it possible for the words of God to become the words of Peter himself so long as he himself allowed it and took responsibility for it himself. Are we to believe that such power died when the apostles died? Are we to believe that, today, we have a different spirit in us that can't accomplish the same things in us that were accomplished in Peter, James, John, Paul and even in Ananias, the simple disciple who healed Paul's blindness?

It would require another book entirely to explain this spirit that God has given us. However, I can say that the spirit of God doesn't change because God himself is the same yesterday, today, and forever. In him is no shadow of turning. In him is no darkness at all. Therefore, the power these men had weren't just for a sign of the times then. This power did not die with the apostles. The spirit of God that fills us today is the very one and selfsame spirit that works all in all. When we allow this spirit to strengthen and encourage us to overcome our own vain imaginations, our words will become the words of God. Our utterances will be power itself. Our words will be the words of Life itself. We will speak with the authority of God himself. Until then, we will just repeat words that don't even mean anything to us, much less to anyone else.

Acts 11

11. **And, behold, immediately there were three men already come unto the house where I was, sent from Caesarea unto me.**
12. **And the spirit bade me go with them, nothing doubting. Moreover these six brethren accompanied me, and we entered into the man's house:**
13. **And he shewed us how he had seen an angel in his house, which stood and said unto him, Send men to Joppa, and call for Simon, whose surname is Peter;**
14. **Who shall tell thee words, whereby thou and all thy house shall be saved.**
15. **And as I began to speak, the Holy Ghost fell on them, as on us at the beginning.**

> 16. Then remembered I the word of the Lord, how that he said, John indeed baptized with water; but ye shall be baptized with the Holy Ghost.
> 17. Forasmuch then as God gave them the like gift as he did unto us, who believed on the Lord Jesus Christ; what was I, that I could withstand God?

Church, this part will make some of you very angry, but the scriptures speak very plainly if you let them speak and not try to make them say what you want them to say. Peter had to give an account of his trip to Caesarea before the brethren in Jerusalem. He took six men with him to serve as witnesses of the events that unfolded as the result of his trip. When they entered the man's house, the man himself showed them how he had seen an angel in his house that told him to send to Joppa, and call for Simon whose surname is Peter, who shall tell you words, whereby you and all your house shall be saved. Notice that it did not say that Peter would perform any rituals that would save them—only that he would speak words that would save this man and his whole house.

Peter then said that, as he began to speak—to utter—, the holy spirit fell on them and filled them the exact same way it had done in the house of God—the temple in Jerusalem—on the day of Pentecost. Then, while he was yet speaking, Peter remembered the word—the utterance—of the Lord, how he said John indeed baptized with water; but you shall—absolutely shall—be baptized (immersed in and filled with) holy spirit. Peter then concluded from the evidence he himself had personally witnessed that God had given these heretofore Gentiles the same gift He had given to the apostles and disciples of Christ, who believed on the Lord Jesus Christ, who was he that he could withstand God? Notice that all this happened before Peter finished speaking, before he extended an invitation for acceptance, and before he commanded that these people be baptized in water. Not the way we teach it at all, is it? Ours goes something like . . . first you repent from being this terrible sinner . . . then you believe in your heart God raised

Christ from the dead . . . then you go down to the altar and confess your sins . . . then you cry a lot and people pray over you . . . then you are scheduled to be baptized publicly . . . then you are trained in the creeds of whatever church you join . . . then if you are holy enough, or maybe sanctified enough, or sanctified holy enough according to whatever your church teaches, spiritual elders can lay hands on you and you can receive the holy spirit you have been learning about.

But . . . but . . . but . . . (nice impression of a motorboat) Peter commanded them to be baptized in water. Yes, he did. They were Gentiles and he had to report to the Jewish Christian group in Jerusalem. When the Christian church first started, it was only among the children of Israel. They had the law of God given to them by Moses. They knew what righteousness was. They knew what sin was. Baptism was a public ritual performed to represent repentance or turning away from disobedience and being cleansed. This allowed the person to start over and become obedient. To them, baptism was a sign of being cleansed and of making a new start. To them, the baptism of the unclean Gentiles would be proof that they had been cleansed.

The Gentiles, however, were a whole different matter. Moses didn't give them the law of God. They didn't know what righteousness was. They didn't know what sin was. They didn't know God at all. They were without God and without hope in this world. They were Uncircumcised. They were an Unclean people with no hope of being clean unless they agreed to be circumcised and keep all the law first. Peter personally witnessed these people being cleansed by God himself when they were filled with the very same spirit that filled Peter and those with him in the temple on the day of Pentecost. His command to baptise them was one of declaring their cleansing by God himself. Peter was not going to dare call anything that God himself cleansed unclean or common. Nor was he going to allow the Christians in Jerusalem any pretext to call them Unclean, either. As a result, the brethren in Jerusalem glorified God because the salvation of God had come to the Gentiles as well.

Eternal Life

Romans 10

> 8. But what saith it? The word is nigh thee, even in thy mouth, and in thy heart: that is, the word of faith, which we preach;
> 9. That if thou shalt confess with thy mouth the Lord Jesus, and shalt believe in thine heart that God hath raised him from the dead, thou shalt be saved.
> 10. For with the heart man believeth unto righteousness; and with the mouth confession is made unto salvation.
> 11. For the scripture saith, Whosoever believeth on him shall not be ashamed.
> 12. For there is no difference between the Jew and the Greek: for the same Lord over all is rich unto all that call upon him.
> 13. For whosoever shall call upon the name of the Lord shall be saved.
> 14. How then shall they call on him in whom they have not believed? and how shall they believe in him of whom they have not heard? and how shall they hear without a preacher?
> 15. And how shall they preach, except they be sent? as it is written, How beautiful are the feet of them that preach the gospel of peace, and bring glad tidings of good things!
> 16. But they have not all obeyed the gospel. For Esaias saith, Lord, who hath believed our report?
> 17. So then faith cometh by hearing, and hearing by the word of God.

What are we saying in all this? The utterance is near you. It is in your own mouth and in your own heart. What utterance? The utterance of faith, which we preach. If you shall confess with your own mouth the Lord Jesus—not every sin you have ever committed and are sorry for—and shall believe in your own heart that God himself has raised

Christ from the dead, you shall be saved—you shall have salvation. Man believes unto righteousness with his own heart when he believes God himself raised Jesus Christ from the dead. Man confesses unto salvation with his own mouth by uttering that Jesus is Lord because he is the only man ever to have lived that fulfilled all the law and prophets. He and he alone was perfectly obedient to God and was completely without sin at all. This utterance can only be made once a person believes that God raised his only begotten son from the dead.

This works because the scripture says, whosoever believes on him shall not be ashamed. There is no difference at all between the Jew and the Greek (Gentile). The same Lord over all is rich unto all that call upon him. Whosoever shall call upon the name of the Lord shall be saved. Pastors, make sure your congregations understand that it is impossible to call upon Jesus as lord without first believing in your own heart that God himself raised Jesus from the dead.

How shall anyone call on someone they have not believed in first? How shall anyone believe in someone they have not heard of first? How shall anyone hear and understand without a preacher? How shall anyone preach, except that God himself send him? It is written, how beautiful are the feet of them that preach the gospel of peace—peace between God and man—, and bring glad tidings of good things. However, not all have obeyed the gospel. Isaiah said, Lord, who has believed our report? So then, faith comes by hearing, and hearing comes by listening to the utterances of God. Listening, in this case, means being focused on the utterances of God, not treating them as they were background elevator music.

Galatians 5

14. For all the law is fulfilled in one word, even in this; Thou shalt love thy neighbour as thyself.

For all you hair splitters, nit pickers, and chapter-and-versers out there, there are seven words in that one word that fulfills all the law. However, those seven words together compose one complete thought, one complete word, one complete utterance. If just one word was changed, left out, or added, the resulting collection of words would not fulfill all the law. There are some things we need to examine about this passage.

First of all, Paul was writing to the church in Galatia. These members had been Gentile before becoming Christian. They didn't have the law, they didn't know what righteousness was, and they didn't know the God of Abraham at all. Instead of Paul requiring them to become circumcised, agreeing to keep all the law, and being baptized with the baptism of repentance taught by John, Paul commanded them to love their neighbors as they loved themselves. Jesus himself had distilled all the law and prophets into two basic commands by saying thou shalt love the lord thy god with all thy heart . . . and thou shalt love thy neighbor as thyself. Then the lawyers wanted a definition of 'your neighbor'.

Second, Paul knew that these people would have to learn to love God the way God loved them in order to love themselves the way God intended for them to do. Paul spent a great deal of time and effort explaining how much God loved them as well as how they could learn to love God. Once they grasped this, they could learn to love themselves the same way God loved them in spite of their individual shortcomings and faults.

Finally, once they had reached the point of having a heart filled with the love of God, they then would be able to love their neighbor the same way. This was not a suggestion . . . it was a command. In so doing, each of these people reflected the image of Jesus, the risen son of God in their own lives in spite of their individual flaws and shortcomings. This love in them gave tremendous power to their utterances and stood as a witness to the love of God himself.

Ephesians 1

12. That we should be to the praise of his glory, who first trusted in Christ.
13. In whom ye also trusted, after that ye heard the word of truth, the gospel of your salvation: in whom also

> after that ye believed, ye were sealed with that holy Spirit of promise,
> 14. Which is the earnest of our inheritance until the redemption of the purchased possession, unto the praise of his glory.

Paul is speaking to the church in Ephesus about his purpose and their purpose. Paul stated that he and the other apostles should themselves be to the praise of God's glory because they first trusted in Christ. After that, to the praise of God's glory, the Ephesians also trusted in Christ after they heard the utterance of truth, the gospel of their salvation. After they believed the gospel of the death and resurrection of Christ, they were sealed with the holy spirit of promise. This spirit is the earnest—the down payment—of our inheritance until the redemption of the possession purchased by the blood of Christ himself. This is to the praise of God himself who provided the way for our salvation and to the praise of Christ himself who was completely obedient to God—even unto death itself.

> **1 Peter 1**
>
> 22. Seeing ye have purified your souls in obeying the truth through the spirit unto unfeigned love of the brethren, see that ye love one another with a pure heart fervently:
> 23. Being born again, not of corruptible seed, but of incorruptible, by the word of God, which liveth and abideth for ever.
> 24. For all flesh is as grass, and all the glory of man as the flower of grass. The grass withereth, and the flower thereof falleth away:
> 25. But the word of the Lord endureth for ever. And this is the word which by the gospel is preached unto you.

Again here church, we see groups of strangers (Gentiles) being addressed. The word 'strangers' refers to their origin before they became Christians.

These people originally were alienated from God. They did not have the law. They did not know God at all. Peter then reassures them that now, as Christians, they have the promise of Eternal Life. For us to understand the impact of these few simple statements, we are going to have to break them down into segments and see what is revealed.

Seeing that you have purified your souls in obeying the truth through the spirit unto unfeigned love of the brethren . . . Who purified your souls? You did. How did you do this? . . . in obeying the truth through the spirit . . . What spirit? the holy spirit God himself filled you with when you believed that God himself raised Christ from the dead . . . unto unfeigned love of the brethren . . . unfeigned love . . . not politically correct . . . not pretentious . . . instead, real, genuine, deep abiding love that is kind, patient, gentle, understanding, caring, and forgiving . . . of the brethren . . . those who, like you, are trying to learn to develop this same love within themselves by obeying the truth through the same spirit you have . . . This love is not now, nor has it ever been, unconditional. With this love, you can not love this world or the things in this world because this world, everything of this world, and everything in this world are self centered and self gratifying.

See that you love one another with a pure heart heart fervently . . . a command, not a suggestion . . . Make certain that your love toward one another is from a pure heart not actuated by selfish or corrupt motives . . . fervently . . . unceasingly, intently, earnestly. Again, we do not see the word 'unconditionally' mentioned at all. 'Unconditionally' is a worldly concept that requires acceptance no matter what. That is a totally selfish concept because it allows a person to do or be whatever he wants regardless. That is unscriptural and totally against everything that Christ, Paul, and Peter taught about the love of God.

Being born again, not of corruptible seed, . . . likened to birth . . . becoming a completely new creation that has never existed before . . . a creation not derived from anything that will grow old, wither, and eventually die . . . but of incorruptible, by the word of God . . . rather of something that will never grow old, wither, and die . . . by the very essence of everything God himself is . . . his nature, his mind, his thoughts, his power . . . which lives and abides forever.

For all flesh is as grass, and all the glory of man is as the flower of grass. The grass withers, and the flower thereof falls away . . . Peter didn't say that all flesh is grass. He said it was as grass. Grass grows, it withers, it dies. So does all flesh. The flower of grass is there for a short time, and it falls away. So do the greatest accomplishments of man with all their glory.

But the word of the Lord endures forever . . . However, the utterance of the Lord stays, remains, stands, continues, is present . . . forever. This is because the very essence of God himself lives and abides forever. And this is the utterance which by the gospel is preached unto you.

Revelation 17

15. And he saith unto me, The waters which thou sawest, where the whore sitteth, are peoples, and multitudes, and nations, and tongues.
16. And the ten horns which thou sawest upon the beast, these shall hate the whore, and shall make her desolate and naked, and shall eat her flesh, and burn her with fire.
17. For God hath put in their hearts to fulfil his will, and to agree, and give their kingdom unto the beast, until the words of God shall be fulfilled.
18. And the woman which thou sawest is that great city, which reigneth over the kings of the earth.

This passage is from the book John wrote called Revelations. It is a prophetic book composed of mysteries, symbols, and images that are still not very well understood today, regardless who may claim otherwise. The key to this passage is understanding verse 17. God does not deliberately force people to do things that are against their own individual will, however, he will allow them to do things that they themselves want to do for their own selfish reasons. For instance, God allowed Pharaoh to harden his own heart after nine plagues simply by removing the plague. However, at the end of the ninth plague, when Pharaoh hardened his heart, God would not allow him to change his mind and reconsider. Again, when the children of Israel wouldn't listen to the prophets God sent and repent of their disobedience even under the judgment of captivity by a foreign nation, God allowed false prophets to tell them that God would never allow them to go into captivity. The same way, God will allow these nations to give their combined power over to the beast until the utterances of God shall be fulfilled.

This is the power of the utterance of God. In order for the utterance to work properly, as God intends, we ourselves must reach the point where each of us will only say and do the things which we ourselves have seen and heard from God. These things are revealed to us by the spirit God himself gave us when each one of us believed that God himself raised his only begotten son, Jesus Christ, from the dead and created Eternal Life in him. This is what the apostles witnessed themselves and this is what they taught. This is the utterance of God that brings us salvation.

CHAPTER 17

Ephesians 6

15. And your feet shod with the preparation of the gospel of peace;

We now return to the Roman soldier. A crucial part of the soldier's armor was his shoes. The Romans introduced a revolutionary thing to warfare with the invention of the hobnail sandal. This shoe had a bottom surface than would provide secure footing on basically any type of terrain. This is a very important piece of the armor because, you are at your enemy's mercy if you lose your footing in battle. Having your feet shod with the preparation of the gospel of peace provides you secure and sound footing under any circumstance. Are we talking about peace on earth, good will toward men? Are we talking about everyone disarm and have one big group hug? Or, are we talking about something else entirely?

Matthew 10

1. And when he had called unto him his twelve disciples, he gave them power against unclean spirits, to cast them out, and to heal all manner of sickness and all manner of disease.
2. Now the names of the twelve apostles are these; The first, Simon, who is called Peter, and Andrew his brother; James the son of Zebedee, and John his brother;

Eternal Life

3. Philip, and Bartholomew; Thomas, and Matthew the publican; James the son of Alphaeus, and Lebbaeus, whose surname was Thaddaeus;
4. Simon the Canaanite, and Judas Iscariot, who also betrayed him.
5. These twelve Jesus sent forth, and commanded them, saying, Go not into the way of the Gentiles, and into any city of the Samaritans enter ye not:
6. But go rather to the lost sheep of the house of Israel.
7. And as ye go, preach, saying, The kingdom of heaven is at hand.
8. Heal the sick, cleanse the lepers, raise the dead, cast out devils: freely ye have received, freely give.
9. Provide neither gold, nor silver, nor brass in your purses,
10. Nor scrip for your journey, neither two coats, neither shoes, nor yet staves: for the workman is worthy of his meat.
11. And into whatsoever city or town ye shall enter, inquire who in it is worthy; and there abide till ye go thence.
12. And when ye come into an house, salute it.
13. And if the house be worthy, let your peace come upon it: but if it be not worthy, let your peace return to you.
14. And whosoever shall not receive you, nor hear your words, when ye depart out of that house or city, shake off the dust of your feet.

Jesus called twelve disciples to him that he also called apostles. He gave these 12 men power against unclean spirits, to cast them out, and to heal all manner of sickness and all manner of disease. He sent these 12 men out, and commanded them, saying, Go not into the way of the Gentiles, and into any city of the Samaritans enter ye not: but rather go to the lost sheep of the house of Israel. Notice that Christ told the apostles to only go to the lost sheep of the house of Israel. They were to preach that the kingdom of heaven was at hand. They were to heal the sick, cleanse the lepers, raise the dead, and cast out devils. Because they hadn't earned what was given them, but rather received what was freely given to them, they were to give freely the same way.

The apostles were not to carry gold, nor silver, nor brass in their purses. Nor were they to carry scrip—a leather pouch for food. Neither were they to carry two coats, nor shoes, nor a staff as a sign of royalty or position of authority because a workman is worthy of his meat. Church, look at this. These instructions were for the apostles only when they went to the lost sheep of the house of Israel. Do these instructions apply directly to the church? No, of course they don't. The apostles were teaching that the kingdom of heaven was at hand. They were testifying that they themselves had seen the king himself and were calling others to come see him for themselves. They were not teaching the death and resurrection of Jesus Christ because Jesus had not been crucified yet.

Church, can we learn from what these men were told and from what they did? Yes, we can learn volumes. They were not to give a worldly impression of who they were. They were not to be ostentatious, or regal in their conduct at all. They were to be helpful and worthy of whatever food they received. They were not to present themselves as superior to anyone. They were to be humble, yet when they spoke, they spoke with the power and authority of God himself by the power of the spirit Jesus had freely given them. Today, church, we seem to be preoccupied with how the pastor dresses, what kind of car he drives, who will get to carry his briefcase, how big a building or arena he is appearing for a short time only, whether we can get a satellite uplink to provide worldwide coverage of the next big event. We've lost that humility—that lowliness of mind. We've lost that helpfulness, and we certainly have lost the ability to speak God's word in the fulness of its power and authority. We rely today on worldly appearance and we call that a spiritual blessing from God.

When any of these men entered a town, they were instructed to ask for someone worthy. They were to go to that household and stay there until they left the town or city. They were not to go from house to house. When they came to a worthy household, they were to embrace it with a warm greeting and allow the peace that was in them to flow outward to the household. However, if the household was not worthy, they were to allow their peace to return to themselves. Whoever would not receive them, or hear their words was to be treated in this manner. When they left the household or the city, they were to shake the dust off their feet so that even the dust from the ground they had walked on would not be with them. This was a custom to show that they were leaving and would not be back—ever.

Notice church that these men gave their peace to the worthy household—they did not negotiate a peace with the household. Today we act as though peace is something we have to have by making others happy or satisfied. We have been taught to negotiate and give up things to get some of the things we want ourselves. That is not the peace of God. That is the peace of this world. Agreeing to disagree is not peace, it is merely reaching a point of truce whereby both sides can continue as they always have before.

Matthew 10

> **34. Think not that I am come to send peace on earth: I came not to send peace, but a sword.**
> **35. For I am come to set a man at variance against his father, and the daughter against her mother, and the daughter in law against her mother in law.**
> **36. And a man's foes shall be they of his ow n household.**

Jesus warned us all not to think for a minute that he came to send peace on earth. Jesus was peace on earth. Those who accepted the truth of what he said and did received the peace he gave them. Those who rejected him and his works received nothing from him. That doesn't mean he didn't love them. It means they received nothing from him because they refused his love. So literally, he came not to bring peace, but a sword. To set those who had the love of the truth in their hearts against those who refused to have the love of the truth in their hearts.

Church, this is why you have so many divisions among you today. There are those among you who desperately seek the truth and those among you who just as desperately seek not to have the truth. You are at variance with one another. It is the same way in the world. Those who seek the truth are at variance with those who do not wish to know the truth. Many deceptive 'truths' are being taught today both in the church and in the world. They each try to find a way to blend and reinforce one another because every single one of these deceptive 'truths' opposes the truth that is in Jesus himself. This is why Jesus said that a man's foes shall be they of his own household.

Luke 10

1. After these things the Lord appointed other seventy also, and sent them two and two before his face into every city and place, whither he himself would come.
2. Therefore said he unto them, The harvest truly is great, but the labourers are few: pray ye therefore the Lord of the harvest, that he would send forth labourers into his harvest.
3. Go your ways: behold, I send you forth as lambs among wolves.
4. Carry neither purse, nor scrip, nor shoes: and salute no man by the way.
5. And into whatsoever house ye enter, first say, Peace be to this house.
6. And if the son of peace be there, your peace shall rest upon it: if not, it shall turn to you again.
7. And in the same house remain, eating and drinking such things as they give: for the labourer is worthy of his hire. Go not from house to house.
8. And into whatsoever city ye enter, and they receive you, eat such things as are set before you:
9. And heal the sick that are therein, and say unto them, The kingdom of God is come nigh unto you.
10. But into whatsoever city ye enter, and they receive you not, go your ways out into the streets of the same, and say,

> **11.** Even the very dust of your city, which cleaveth on us, we do wipe off against you: notwithstanding be ye sure of this, that the kingdom of God is come nigh unto you.
>
> **17.** And the seventy returned again with joy, saying, Lord, even the devils are subject unto us through thy name.
>
> **18.** And he said unto them, I beheld Satan as lightning fall from heaven.
>
> **19.** Behold, I give unto you power to tread on serpents and scorpions, and over all the power of the enemy: and nothing shall by any means hurt you.
>
> **20.** Notwithstanding in this rejoice not, that the spirits are subject unto you; but rather rejoice, because your names are written in heaven.

After Jesus had sent out the twelve apostles and they had returned, he taught them privately and he continued teaching others as well. Then, after some time, he appointed another group of seventy (some texts read seventy-two) others to go out like the apostles did. He did not call these men apostles, yet he gave them the very same power that he had given the apostles. He sent this group out two by two into every city he planned to go to himself.

Jesus instructed them before they left. There was truly a great harvest before them, yet the laborers were few in number. He instructed them to pray to the Lord of the harvest that he would send forth laborers into this harvest. He did not tell them to ask for more laborers because they were so few, but rather that those few would be mighty in the power they had been given. They were to become tireless, relentless, dedicated laborers who were preparing the people to meet their king. Church, what do you think would happen today if we quit sniveling about having too few workers and prayed to become tireless, relentless, dedicated laborers filled with the power of God and the power of his might? The fields are already ripe for harvest and we need to introduce people to the resurrected Jesus Christ himself. Time is short, but there is exactly enough time left to do this. How say you?

Jesus gave the seventy simple instructions. Go your ways. I send you forth as lambs among wolves. Just as the apostles, he told them to carry neither purse, nor scrip, nor shoes. They were not to stop and salute anyone in the way. Saluting was a formal customary method of greeting that could take hours of your time if you engaged in it. Whatever household they entered, they were to salute it by saying 'peace be unto this household'. If the household was worthy, and the son of peace (one who had the love of the truth in his heart) was there, the peace from these men would rest on the entire household. Otherwise, the peace would return to those who gave it. When they entered the house, they were to stay there until they left, eating and drinking what was set before them with thankfulness, not going from house to house, for a workman was worthy of his hire. They were to heal the sick therein and say, the kingdom of God is come near you.

However, in whatever city you enter, and they receive you not, go out into the streets of the city and say, even the dust of your city which clings to us, we do wipe off against you. Nevertheless, understand that the kingdom of God has come near you. Church, this is just like the case of the apostles. This was before the death of Jesus, and these men witnessed the king himself to the people. Therefore, these instructions do not apply directly to you because you are to witness the resurrection of Jesus Christ to Eternal Life. Can we learn from the instructions to the seventy? Of course we can, the very same way we learned from the instructions to the twelve apostles. Jesus gave them the same power he had. God gives us the same power and it dwells in us. According to the promises of Jesus, we can do the things he did and even greater things. We need to become laborers in the Lord's harvest instead of members and passengers. How say you?

Church, listen carefully. Later, the seventy returned again with joy, saying, Lord, even the devils are subject to us through your name. Jesus said to them, I beheld Satan as lightning fall from heaven. Heaven here refers to the sky, not the abode of God, therefore, God did not kick Satan out of heaven when these seventy went out. Jesus beheld Satan come from the sky to the ground with the power and force of a bolt of lightning striking the earth from a cloud. Satan, by his own admission, has been walking to and fro on the earth since at least the time of Job.

Satan personally came to tempt Jesus in the wilderness after Jesus had been there fasting among the wild animals for forty days. It is therefore not surprising that Jesus beheld Satan falling from the sky with the power and force of a bolt of lightning.

Church, listen some more. He then said to them, Behold, I give unto you power to tread on serpents and scorpions, and over all the power of the enemy; and nothing by any means shall hurt you. Nevertheless, do not rejoice that the spirits are subject to you. Rejoice instead that your names are written in heaven. Church, this power Jesus gave to these men dwells in us. Dwelling in each of us right now is power from God himself. Through the risen Christ Jesus, we have power over anything and everything the enemy can do. Nevertheless, we should never rejoice in that. We should instead, however, rejoice that we are sons of God through the death and resurrection of Christ Jesus.

John 14

25. These things have I spoken unto you, being yet present with you.
26. But the Comforter, which is the Holy Ghost, whom the Father will send in my name, he shall teach you all things, and bring all things to your remembrance, whatsoever I have said unto you.
27. Peace I leave with you, my peace I give unto you: not as the world giveth, give I unto you. Let not your heart be troubled, neither let it be afraid.
28. Ye have heard how I said unto you, I go away, and come again unto you. If ye loved me, ye would rejoice, because I said, I go unto the Father: for my Father is greater than I.
29. And now I have told you before it come to pass, that, when it is come to pass, ye might believe.

Church, be very careful here. There are things written here that, if they are true, will cause problems with officially approved doctrine.

Jesus knows his time is near and he is preparing his apostles for the events that are about to take place. He told them that he had spoken things to them while he was yet with them, but that the Father himself would send to them the Comforter, the Holy Ghost (spirit) in Jesus' name. He (the Holy Ghost) would teach them all things, and bring all things to their remembrance whatsoever he himself had said unto them. The question right here is whether this Comforter is a person or not. If the Comforter is a person, then the doctrine established by the Christian church hundreds of years and many deaths later is true and God actually exists as three persons. However, if the Comforter is what Jesus said it was—power from on high—then it is not a person at all and the Church has committed a serious doctrinal error. If you go into the Old Testament and bother to look at all you will find that in Proverbs 1:20, wisdom is referred to as 'she'. Proverbs 9:1 refers to wisdom as both 'her' and 'she'. Matthew 11:19 refers to wisdom and 'her children'. Luke 7:35 refers to wisdom and 'her children'. Are we to conclude and establish by Church doctrine that wisdom is also a person—a female person? Or, is there another answer?

Church, the language spoken by the prophets, the children of Israel, and Jesus himself had no word for 'it' the way we do today. Everything, whether animate or not was referred to as either 'he' or 'she'. Therefore wisdom is 'she' and Comforter (Holy Ghost) is 'he'. This spirit from God that Jesus himself called power from on high is no more a person than wisdom is. It took the Church hundreds of years to establish this power as part of a mystical Godhead—each coequal and coeternal. It took many more hundreds of years to establish Mary as the mother of God based on this mystical Godhead, yet if this mystical Godhead is true the way the Church teaches it, then Mary has to be the mother of God, because she is the mother of one of the coequal and coeternal members of the mystical Godhead. Church, you have a serious doctrinal problem here that must be resolved if you are ever going to be the way

God intended you to be. It's time to search the things that Jesus himself said and not what has necessarily been taught that he said.

Jesus then told his apostles he was leaving his peace with them, he was giving his peace to them. He told them to not be troubled in their heart nor to be afraid. Remember, Jesus was peace itself. His death and subsequent resurrection broke down the wall of enmity between God and man, making peace between God and man. He reminded the apostles that he had told them before that he would go away and, if he did, he would return to them again. If they loved him, they would rejoice because he was going to the Father. He then declared the Father to be greater than he himself was. From his own mouth, he declared that he could not possibly be coequal and coeternal with God. Did he lie to his apostles? Hebrews says he was tempted in every way we are, yet without sin. That means he didn't lie—ever. James says God does not tempt, neither can he be tempted. Did James lie? Think carefully about these things—it's a life and death decision.

Romans 4

24. But for us also, to whom it shall be imputed, if we believe on him that raised up Jesus our Lord from the dead;
25. Who was delivered for our offences, and was raised again for our justification.

Romans 5

1. Therefore being justified by faith, we have peace with God through our Lord Jesus Christ:
2. By whom also we have access by faith into this grace wherein we stand, and rejoice in hope of the glory of God.

Justification shall also be imputed to us if we believe on him that raised Jesus Christ from the dead. Jesus himself was delivered for our offences and was raised so we could be justified before God himself. Therefore being justified by faith, we have peace with God himself through our lord Jesus Christ: by whom we also have access by faith into the grace we stand in before God, and rejoice in the hope of the glory of God himself.

Romans 8

2. For the law of the Spirit of life in Christ Jesus hath made me free from the law of sin and death.

3. For what the law could not do, in that it was weak through the flesh, God sending his own Son in the likeness of sinful flesh, and for sin, condemned sin in the flesh:

4. That the righteousness of the law might be fulfilled in us, who walk not after the flesh, but after the Spirit.

5. For they that are after the flesh do mind the things of the flesh; but they that are after the Spirit the things of the Spirit.

6. For to be carnally minded is death; but to be spiritually minded is life and peace.

7. Because the carnal mind is enmity against God: for it is not subject to the law of God, neither indeed can be.

8. So then they that are in the flesh cannot please God.

9. But ye are not in the flesh, but in the Spirit, if so be that the Spirit of God dwell in you. Now if any man have not the Spirit of Christ, he is none of his.

10. And if Christ be in you, the body is dead because of sin; but the Spirit is life because of righteousness.

The law of the Spirit of life in Christ Jesus has made me free from the law of sin and death . . . What an incredibly outrageous statement! Yet, at the same time, that statement is an absolutely amazing truth. Two completely different perspectives are shown here. The spirit in us that was in Christ is our personal guarantee of Eternal Life. The law given to the children of Israel is based on righteousness by obedience. Disobedience (sin) brings only death.

What the law could not do, in that it was weak through the flesh, because men are naturally disobedient in the flesh, God himself accomplished by sending his only begotten son in the likeness of sinful flesh, and for sin itself, completely condemning sin in the flesh: that the righteousness of the law itself might be fulfilled in those of us who walk not after our own selfish fleshly desires, but, instead, walk after the spirit that God himself has given us.

They that are after the flesh and its selfish desires do mind the things of the flesh; but they that are after the spirit, things the spirit reveals to them are the things they say and do. To be carnally (selfishly) minded is death. To be spiritually minded is Eternal Life and peace with God. The carnal mind is enmity against God: it is not subject to, nor can it ever be subject to the law of God because it is selfish. Therefore, those that are led by their own selfish desires cannot ever please God, no matter what they do in the flesh.

You are not in the flesh, but in the spirit, if the power of God himself dwells in you. Now, if any man does not have the spirit that was in Christ himself, he does not belong to Christ at all. If the spirit that was in Christ dwells in you, your body is dead because of your own disobedience; but the spirit in you is Eternal Life because of the obedience of Christ himself.

Romans 14

12. **So then every one of us shall give account of himself to God.**
13. **Let us not therefore judge one another any more: but judge this rather, that no man put a stumblingblock or an occasion to fall in his brother's way.**
14. **I know, and am persuaded by the Lord Jesus, that there is nothing unclean of itself: but to him that esteemeth any thing to be unclean, to him it is unclean.**
15. **But if thy brother be grieved with thy meat, now walkest thou not charitably. Destroy not him with thy meat, for whom Christ died.**
16. **Let not then your good be evil spoken of:**

> **17. For the kingdom of God is not meat and drink; but righteousness, and peace, and joy in the Holy Ghost.**
> **18. For he that in these things served Christ is acceptable to God, and approved of men.**
> **19. Let us therefore follow after the things which make for peace, and things wherewith one may edify another.**
> **20. For meat destroy not the work of God. All things indeed are pure; but it is evil for that man who eateth with offence.**
> **21. It is good neither to eat flesh, nor to drink wine, nor any thing whereby thy brother stumbleth, or is offended, or is made weak.**

Every one of us shall give an account of ourselves before God. Church, this is not the terrible judgement of God here. This is an account of our behavior as followers of Christ.

Since this is the case, it is time for each of us to stop judging and accusing one another. Instead, we should judge ourselves in this manner. None of us should put a stumblingblock or an occasion to fall in front of our brother—ever.

As a Christian, I know and am completely persuaded that there is nothing that is unclean in and of itself. However, I walk among some who regard different things to be unclean. To those who regard any thing to be unclean, to them it is unclean. They do not yet understand that what God himself has cleansed, do not call common or unclean. Therefore, it would be wrong of me to flaunt my freedom in Christ in front of brothers and sisters with less assurance than I myself have. It would be wrong of me to destroy someone Christ himself died for by my choice of food, words, or actions that caused grief in that person rather than strengthening him.

Do not let your good be evil spoken of. The kingdom of God is not composed of, nor is it determined by meat and drink. Instead it is righteousness, and peace with God, and joy in the holy spirit. He that serves Christ in righteousness, peace, and joy is acceptable to God, and approved of men. Therefore let us enthusiastically pursue those things that produce peace, and things that build and strengthen one another.

Do not destroy the work of God by your choice of meat, the words you use, or your own actions. All things are indeed pure; however, it is evil for a man to participate if he is offended by choice of meat, words, or actions because, to him, it is evil to do so. It is good neither to eat meat, nor drink wine, nor do anything else that would cause your own brother to stumble, or be offended, or be weakened. How say you?

Galatians 5

> **16. This I say then, Walk in the Spirit, and ye shall not fulfil the lust of the flesh.**
> **17. For the flesh lusteth against the Spirit, and the Spirit against the flesh: and these are contrary the one to the other: so that ye cannot do the things that ye would.**
> **18. But if ye be led of the Spirit, ye are not under the law.**
> **19. Now the works of the flesh are manifest, which are these; Adultery, fornication, uncleanness, lasciviousness,**
> **20. Idolatry, witchcraft, hatred, variance, emulations, wrath, strife, seditions, heresies,**
> **21. Envyings, murders, drunkenness, revellings, and such like: of the which I tell you before, as I have also told you in time past, that they which do such things shall not inherit the kingdom of God.**
> **22. But the fruit of the Spirit is love , joy, peace , longsuffering, gentleness, goodness, faith,**
> **23. Meekness, temperance: against such there is no law.**
> **24. And they that are Christ's have crucified the flesh with the affections and lusts.**
> **25. If we live in the Spirit, let us also walk in the Spirit.**
> **26. Let us not be desirous of vain glory, provoking one another, envying one another.**

Walk in the spirit, following the inspiration of the power of God himself in you, and you shall not fulfil your own selfish desires. The flesh (selfishness) desires things against and resists the spirit of God. The spirit of God desires things against and resists selfishness. The flesh and the spirit of God are totally contrary to one another. The clearly demonstrated works of the flesh (selfishness) are these; adultery, fornication, uncleanness, lasciviousness, idolatry, witchcraft, hatred, variance, emulations, wrath, strife, seditions, heresies, envyings, murders, drunkenness, revellings, and other such related behaviors: which I have told you before, and have told you in the past, that they which consistently behave this way shall not inherit the kingdom of God—ever—because these things are self indulgent and self gratifying. All these behaviors are the result of idolatry—putting anything or anyone before God.

In contrast, the fruit of the spirit God has given you is love, joy, peace with God himself, longsuffering, gentleness, goodness, faith, meekness, temperance: against such behavior there is no law. They that are Christ's have crucified the flesh (selfishness) with its affections and lusts. If we live in the power of God, let us also walk in the power of God. Let us not be desirous of vain glory, provoking one another, envying one another.

Galatians 6

15. For in Christ Jesus neither circumcision availeth any thing, nor uncircumcision, but a new creature.
16. And as many as walk according to this rule, peace be on them, and mercy, and upon the Israel of God.

Church, remember this. In Christ Jesus neither circumcision matters nor uncircumcision matters. What matters is that each one of us is a new creature—literally a whole new creation of God himself. As many as follow this rule, let the peace of God himself be on them, and mercy, and upon the Israel of God.

Ephesians 2

11. Wherefore remember, that ye being in time past Gentiles in the flesh, who are called Uncircumcision by that which is called the Circumcision in the flesh made by hands;
12. That at that time ye were without Christ, being aliens from the commonwealth of Israel, and strangers from the covenants of promise, having no hope, and without God in the world:
13. But now in Christ Jesus ye who sometimes were far off are made nigh by the blood of Christ.
14. For he is our peace, who hath made both one, and hath broken down the middle wall of partition between us;
15. Having abolished in his flesh the enmity, even the law of commandments contained in ordinances; for to make in himself of twain one new man, so making peace;
16. And that he might reconcile both unto God in one body by the cross, having slain the enmity thereby:
17. And came and preached peace to you which were afar off, and to them that were nigh.
18. For through him we both have access by one Spirit unto the Father.

Church, remember where you came from. There was a time when you were Gentiles in the flesh and called Uncircumcision by those who were called the Circumcision in the flesh made by hands. At that time, you were without Christ, you were aliens to the commonwealth of Israel, and strangers from the covenants of promise made to the children of Israel. You were totally without hope and without God in this world. At that time the only hope you could have was to be willing to be circumcised in the flesh and agree to keep all the law for righteousness given to the children of Israel. Even today, if you are without Christ, those who are of the Circumcision still consider you without God and strangers to the covenants of promise given to their fathers unless you become circumcised and agree to keep all the law for righteousness.

Now, however, in Christ Jesus you who were sometimes far off and aliens to the commonwealth of Israel are made near by the blood of Christ himself. He himself is our peace. He has made both the Circumcision and the Uncircumcision one. He has broken down the middle wall of partition between us; having abolished in his own flesh the hatred, even the law of commandments contained in ordinances; to make in himself of two different groups of people one new man, so making peace between men. In order for him to reconcile both groups to God in one body by the cross, having slain the hatred by enduring the shame and agony until he died, Jesus came and preached peace with God to which were afar off and Uncircumcised, and to them that were near and Circumcised. It is through him and his obedience that both the Circumcision and the Uncircumcision have access by one spirit—the one and very selfsame spirit—unto the Father himself.

Ephesians 4

1. I Therefore, the prisoner of the Lord, beseech you that ye walk worthy of the vocation wherewith ye are called,
2. With all lowliness and meekness, with longsuffering, forbearing one another in love;
3. Endeavouring to keep the unity of the Spirit in the bond of peace.
4. There is one body, and one Spirit, even as ye are called in one hope of your calling;
5. One Lord, one faith, one baptism,
6. One God and Father of all, who is above all, and through all, and in you all.
7. But unto every one of us is given grace according to the measure of the gift of Christ.
8. Wherefore he saith, When he ascended up on high, he led captivity captive, and gave gifts unto men.

> 9. (Now that he ascended, what is it but that he also descended first into the lower parts of the earth?
> 10. He that descended is the same also that ascended up far above all heavens, that he might fill all things.)
> 11. And he gave some, apostles; and some, prophets; and some, evangelists; and some, pastors and teachers;
> 12. For the perfecting of the saints, for the work of the ministry, for the edifying of the body of Christ:
> 13. Till we all come in the unity of the faith, and of the knowledge of the Son of God, unto a perfect man, unto the measure of the stature of the fulness of Christ:
> 14. That we henceforth be no more children, tossed to and fro, and carried about with every wind of doctrine, by the sleight of men, and cunning craftiness, whereby they lie in wait to deceive;

Church, Paul is begging you for your own good to listen to him. Pay close attention to what is said here. I beseech you that you walk worthy of the vocation wherewith you are called. The word 'vocation' does not mean job, Church. 'Vocation' means calling or invitation. God has given each and every single one of you a high calling in Christ—the individual invitation to receive Eternal Life. There is no higher calling than Eternal Life. The things we do inside the body itself, whether we teach, preach, heal, prophecy, cast out spirits, etc. are merely the ways we each serve one another. They are not now nor have they ever been jobs and appointments that require special recognition from God as we perform them.

Therefore, Church, each one of you is to walk with all humbleness of mind and all willingness to receive instruction, with longsuffering and continual patience, forbearing one another in love; endeavoring to keep the unity of the spirit in the bond of peace with God, with one another, and each of us within ourselves. Church, do not be deceived, if you are not at peace with one another, or at peace within yourselves, you are at enmity with God.

There is one body—the body—the group—whose head is Christ himself, and one spirit—the one and selfsame spirit that God gives to each one of us, even as you are called in one hope of your calling—Eternal Life itself; one Lord—Jesus Christ himself, the head of the one body, one faith—a manifestation of the one and selfsame spirit of God in each one of us, one baptism—each one of us individually filled with power from on high, the spirit of God himself, one God and Father of all, who is above all, and through all, and in you all the very same way he was in his only begotten son, Jesus Christ. But unto each and every one of us is given grace according to the gift of Christ and it was given to him without measure at all.

Wherefore he said, when he ascended up on high, he led captivity captive, and gave gifts unto men. (Now he that ascended, was it but that he also descended first into the lower parts of the earth? He that descended is the same also that ascended up far above all heavens, that he might fill all things.) He gave some, apostles to serve; and some prophets to serve; and some evangelists to serve; and some, pastors and teachers to serve. These servants are expressly present for the perfecting of the saints, for the work of the ministry, for the building and strengthening of the body of Christ: till we all come together in the unity of the faith, and of the knowledge of the son of God himself, unto a perfect man, unto the measure of the stature and fulness of Christ himself: that we henceforth be no more children, tossed to and fro, and carried about by every wind of doctrine, by the fraudulent words and actions of men, and cunning craftiness, whereby they lie in wait to deceive.

Church, Paul's instructions and warnings are clear. If we do not walk the way Paul instructed us here, we will be unable to recognise those deceivers and frauds who walk among us. Paul isn't talking to the Church about people on the outside pulling us away from God. Paul is warning us about those inside who walk among us that will LEAD us away from God! Over time, servants of the body have become rulers of the body instead of Christ. We expect our leaders to tell us what God wants from us and what pleases him. We have totally turned away from the way God intended us to be. Instead of instructors who have great patience and wisdom to share with us, we have produced among ourselves rulers who demand of us. While some of these men are truly servants whose only desire is to teach us what Paul said here, others are frauds who, with cunning craftiness seek to move us as far away from God himself as possible. The sad thing is that a great many of us can not see the difference between the two. This places an enormous burden of those who genuinely try to serve the body from the very depths of their heart.

Philippians 4

6. Be careful for nothing; but in every thing by prayer and supplication with thanksgiving let your requests be made known unto God.
7. And the peace of God, which passeth all understanding, shall keep your hearts and minds through Christ Jesus.
8. Finally, brethren, whatsoever things are true , whatsoever things are honest, whatsoever things are just, whatsoever things are pure, whatsoever things are lovely, whatsoever things are of good report; if there be any virtue, and if there be any praise, think on these things.
9. Those things, which ye have both learned, and received, and heard, and seen in me, do: and the God of peace shall be with you.

Do not worry about anything; instead in everything by prayer and supplication with thanksgiving let your requests be known unto God himself. And the peace of God himself, which passes all understanding, shall keep (tend and protect) your hearts and minds through Christ Jesus. There it is. Not only do you have peace with God, you also have the peace of God himself in you protecting you and nurturing your growth into the fulness of the stature of Christ himself.

Finally, brethren, whatsoever things are true, whatsoever things are honest, whatsoever things are just, whatsoever things are pure (to the pure—all things are pure), whatsoever things are lovely, whatsoever things are reputable; if there be any virtue, and if there be any praise, think on these things. Do this and you will not let your good be evil spoken of. Those things, which you have both learned, and received, and heard, and seen in me, do: and the God of peace himself shall be with you.

Colossians 1

12. Giving thanks unto the Father, which hath made us meet to be partakers of the inheritance of the saints in light:
13. Who hath delivered us from the power of darkness, and hath translated us into the kingdom of his dear Son:
14. In whom we have redemption through his blood, even the forgiveness of sins:
15. Who is the image of the invisible God, the firstborn of every creature:
16. For by him were all things created, that are in heaven, and that are in earth, visible and invisible, whether they be thrones, or dominions, or principalities, or powers: all things were created by him, and for him:
17. And he is before all things, and by him all things consist.
18. And he is the head of the body, the church: who is the beginning, the firstborn from the dead; that in all things he might have the preeminence.
19. For it pleased the Father that in him should all fulness dwell;
20. And, having made peace through the blood of his cross, by him to reconcile all things unto himself; by him, I say, whether they be things in earth, or things in heaven.
21. And you, that were sometime alienated and enemies in your mind by wicked works, yet now hath he reconciled

22. In the body of his flesh through death, to present you holy and unblameable and unreproveable in his sight:
23. If ye continue in the faith grounded and settled, and be not moved away from the hope of the gospel, which ye have heard, and which was preached to every creature which is under heaven; whereof I Paul am made a minister;

Giving thanks to the Father, which has made us qualified to be equal sharers of the inheritance of the saints in light: who himself has delivered us from the power of darkness, and has moved us into the kingdom of his dear son: in whom we have redemption through his blood, even the forgiveness of sins; who himself is the image of the invisible God, the firstborn of every creation: for by him (his obedience) were all things created, that are in heaven, and that are in earth, visible and invisible, whether they be thrones, or dominions, or principalities, or powers: all things were created by him (his obedience), and for him: and he himself is before (ahead of) all things, and by him (his obedience) all things consist (are in union with).

Church, this is the most powerful thing that Paul has uttered about the new heaven and new earth to any assembly so far, yet, today, its importance has become so obscured that people have absolutely no idea that such things even are promised. Today, this segment has been parsed from the context and used to prove that Christ himself created Adam. Paul wasn't talking about—in the beginning God, and his only begotten son before he was ever begotten, created . . .—the world that was before Noah, or the world that changed after Noah, or the world during or after Abraham, or Moses. Paul was talking about the new heaven and new earth, the home of the new creation that hasn't been brought into existence yet. The key to that passage is the statement that 'by him all things consist'. All things do not consist by Christ today, and all the way back to Adam all things have not consisted by Christ. Consist means to be in union with. If the world from the time of Adam has been in total union with Christ, then there was never a need for Christ to be crucified and resurrected.

Church, if we are to say that all things today consist by Christ, then we have a serious problem. We are then saying that this world today, as it is right now, consists (is in union) by Christ. That would put people like Marquis de Sade, Vlad the Impaler, Alastaire Crowley, Adolph Hitler, Pol Pot, and many others all in union with Christ as well. If such a case were true, then there was never a need for Christ to come in the first place. There really is no need for redemption at all because we all consist by Christ from the very beginning, as you teach. This is why there are so many atheists who originate from the Church itself. They know the scriptures as well or better than you do, and classify the scriptures as myths and fairy tales used to control the lives of others through fear and guilt. Forgive my apparent foolishness. I am talking to men as a man. These things I have just said are the thoughts of man and not God, but they are triggered by the teachings you teach from the pulpit. Don't act so righteously indignant! I've met people who actually think this way. Their reasonings eventually come back to this parsed section of scripture we are discussing. The only people on this earth today who even have the opportunity to be in union with Christ are those who have accepted his death and resurrection as full payment for their own natural rebellion. Their acceptance is proven by their own willingness to change their lives so they themselves can reflect the very image of Christ himself. Church, the scriptures demand you answer this.

For he (Christ) is the head of the body, the church: who is the beginning; the firstborn from the dead; that in all things he might have preeminence, for it pleased the Father that in him (Christ) all fulness should dwell; and having made peace with God through the blood of his own cross, by him (Christ), God reconciled all things to himself; by him (Christ), I say, whether they be things in earth or in heaven. This reconciliation began with the resurrection of the firstborn from the dead, not with the creation of Adam. This new creation came after the resurrection of the firstborn from the dead. The church—the body whose head is Christ—is to declare this new creation and be a witness of what is to come by willingly changing their own lives so they reflect the image of Christ himself. Church, we do not yet know what we shall be, but we do know, that when he appears, we shall be like him. Until that time, however, the best we can do is grow and develop ourselves to the point where we reflect the image of Christ himself in our own individual lives in spite of each of our own shortcomings.

And you who were sometime alienated and enemies in your mind by wicked works, yet now has he (Christ) reconciled in the body of his own flesh through death, to present you holy and unblameable and unreproveable in his sight: if you continue in the faith grounded and settled, and be not moved away from the hope of the gospel, which you have heard, and which was preached to every creature which is under heaven; whereof I Paul am made a minister.

Paul closed this part to the Colossian church by reminding them that Christ accomplished all these things while they were still alienated from God by the wicked works in their own minds. The same thing holds true today, therefore, all things today do not consist by Christ. Paul warned them that their union with Christ would happen only if they continued in the faith grounded and settled, and not moved away from the hope of the gospel which they had heard. The same thing is true today. Paul did not judge them, he warned them. Likewise, I do not judge you. Instead, I show you the position that you are in right now, and warn you not to be any longer moved away from the hope of the gospel of the death and resurrection of Jesus Christ to Eternal Life—the very hope of your salvation.

Church, God is about to judge us and allow the whole world to witness what is about to happen to them as well. He is raising those among us who will speak his words as they are inspired, not quote his words to suit their own beliefs or desires. They will use sharpness, not to our destruction, but to our building and strengthening. They will be clothed in the power of God. The things they say will happen. Those who have the love of the truth in their hearts will hear them. Those who do not will not hear them and will be bound by their own selfish desires. Be prepared. Time grows short for us.

1 Thessalonians 5

1. But of the times and the seasons, brethren, ye have no need that I write unto you.
2. For yourselves know perfectly that the day of the Lord so cometh as a thief in the night.
3. For when they shall say, Peace and safety; then sudden destruction cometh upon them, as travail upon a woman with child; and they shall not escape.
4. But ye, brethren, are not in darkness, that that day should overtake you as a thief.
5. Ye are all the children of light, and the children of the day: we are not of the night, nor of darkness.
6. Therefore let us not sleep, as do others; but let us watch and be sober.
7. For they that sleep sleep in the night; and they that be drunken are drunken in the night.
8. But let us, who are of the day, be sober, putting on the breastplate of faith and love; and for an helmet, the hope of salvation.
9. For God hath not appointed us to wrath, but to obtain salvation by our Lord Jesus Christ,
10. Who died for us, that, whether we wake or sleep, we should live together with him.

Brethren, there is no need for you to know the times or seasons because you yourself already know that the day of the lord comes as a thief in the night. How many thieves wake people up and announce that they are there to take whatever they want to take? If they did that, wouldn't it be easier just to come by during the day and say, 'I'm stealing your things'? Your focus should be on preparing for that day and not wondering when it is—just be prepared regardless.

When they say, 'peace and safety'; then sudden destruction shall be upon them, as labor pains are with a woman having childbirth; and they shall not escape. The peace and safety they talk about is not the peace of or with God at all. That peace is the result of crafted truces and alliances and treaties among men to guarantee what the English prime minister referred to as 'Peace in our time'. Shortly afterward, Germany invaded Poland and the whole world went to war.

But you, brethren, are not in darkness, that you should be overtaken in that day as a thief comes in the night. You are all the children of the light, and the children of the day: we are not of the night, nor of darkness. Therefore, let us not sleep as others do. Instead, let us watch and be sober. Those who sleep, sleep in the night; and those who are drunken are drunken in the night.

Instead let us, who are of the day, be sober, alert, watchful, putting on the breastplate of faith and love; and for a helmet, the hope of salvation. Remember, God has not appointed us to wrath, but to obtain salvation by our lord Jesus Christ, who himself died for each one of us, that, whether we wake or sleep, we should live eternally together with him.

James 2

15. If a brother or sister be naked, and destitute of daily food,
16. And one of you say unto them, Depart in peace, be ye warmed and filled; notwithstanding ye give them not those things which are needful to the body; what doth it profit?

Church, this is tough. This is talking about fellow Christians, not the disenfranchised of the world. If a fellow Christian, whether a brother or sister in Christ, comes to you and needs help, in this illustration without proper or enough clothing or without food; and you say to them things like 'Go in peace', 'Be warmed and filled', " Believe God and you'll have what you need', or give them a Bible and say something like 'Here, you can find comfort in these pages'; yet you do not give them the things they need physically at the time, what good have you done? It's easy to look at someone who is having a rough time and think that, if they just went to church regularly, or paid their tithe, or participated in the church activities, they would probably not be in that position.

Do not allow yourself to think that way at all. Remember Job? Job lost his children, all his wealth, his health—everything except a wife who nagged him and three friends who accused him of having some secret sin that he wouldn't confess to God.

Church, we have become too materialistic in our judgements to see the light of God when he reveals it to us in our own hearts. We tend today to base our assessment of a good Christian and obedient disciple by the clothes a person wears, the job they have, the car they drive, their house, etc. Obviously, the more a person has, the more God has blessed him for his obedience. It would never occur to a great many of us that someone could be blessed by God and not have all these material things. We must return to the humility, the compassion, the understanding, the tenderness, the patience, the peace God has given us, the willingness to learn, etc. that was originally in the Church when it first began.

James 3

13. **Who is a wise man and endued with knowledge among you? let him shew out of a good conversation his works with meekness of wisdom.**
14. **But if ye have bitter envying and strife in your hearts, glory not, and lie not against the truth.**
15. **This wisdom descendeth not from above, but is earthly, sensual, devilish.**
16. **For where envying and strife is, there is confusion and every evil work.**
17. **But the wisdom that is from above is first pure, then peaceable, gentle, and easy to be intreated, full of mercy and good fruits, without partiality, and without hypocrisy.**
18. **And the fruit of righteousness is sown in peace of them that make peace.**

Who among you is wise and endued with knowledge? If any of you are such, then show your works through good conduct and meekness of wisdom. If you have bitter envyings and strife in your hearts, do not glory in it, and do not lie against the truth. Such wisdom that allows you act in that manner is not from above (heavenly), but is earthly, sensual, devilish. Where you have envying and strife, you have confusion and every evil work.

The wisdom that is itself from above (heavenly) is first pure, then peaceable—not contentious—, gentle, easy to be entreated, full of mercy and good fruits, without partiality, and without hypocrisy. The fruit of righteousness is sown in peace of them that make peace with God—not through negotiations, concessions, or treaties with others.

1 Peter 3

> 8. **Finally, be ye all of one mind, having compassion one of another, love as brethren, be pitiful, be courteous:**
> 9. **Not rendering evil for evil, or railing for railing: but contrariwise blessing; knowing that ye are thereunto called, that ye should inherit a blessing.**
> 10. **For he that will love life, and see good days, let him refrain his tongue from evil, and his lips that they speak no guile:**
> 11. **Let him eschew evil, and do good; let him seek peace, and ensue it.**
> 12. **For the eyes of the Lord are over the righteous, and his ears are open unto their prayers: but the face of the Lord is against them that do evil.**
> 13. **And who is he that will harm you, if ye be followers of that which is good?**

Church, Peter is talking to you—not to those in the world. All—each and every single one—of you be of one mind. Like Paul said, 'be perfectly joined together in one mind' and one spirit. Among yourselves, have compassion one of another, love one another as brothers and sisters in the same family, have pity, be courteous to one another: not returning evil for evil, or railing for railing against one another: instead bless one another; knowing the calling each of you has, that each one of you should inherit a blessing.

Any among you that will love life, and see good days, let him refrain his tongue from evil, and his lips that they speak no guile—through flattery or deception of any kind—: let him turn from and have nothing to do with evil, and do good instead; let him seek peace with God, and follow after it. The eyes of the lord are always over the righteous, and his ears are ever open to their prayers: but the face of the lord is against them that do evil. Peter did not say to treat the world this way because those of the world will not accept being treated this way. They will not treat others this way. This instruction is for you to treat one another who are of God this way.

2 Peter 3

13. **Nevertheless we, according to his promise, look for new heavens and a new earth, wherein dwelleth righteousness.**
14. **Wherefore, beloved, seeing that ye look for such things, be diligent that ye may be found of him in peace, without spot, and blameless.**
15. **And account that the longsuffering of our Lord is salvation; even as our beloved brother Paul also according to the wisdom given unto him hath written unto you;**

Nevertheless we, according to his promise, look for new heavens and a new earth, wherein dwells righteousness. Church, we need to stop here for a minute and dwell on this statement before continuing. The new heavens and new earth are the home (abode) of righteousness—right judgement—itself. Peter didn't say wherein righteousness and unrighteousness dwell. That means that only righteousness will exist in the new heavens and new earth. Not even the memory of unrighteousness will exist at all. Think about that—no deception, no flattery, no guile, no theft, no uncontrollable desires of any kind, no hatred, no jealousy, no one waiting to trap and control any other, etc.

What a place that will be. To be able to live in a place where you can do or have anything you want because there is no form of unrighteousness at all in anything that exists—even in you. Does that sound like a boring place to you? If it does, you are still unrighteous inside yourself.

Beloved, since you look for such things, be especially diligent that you do everything you can to be found of him in peace—peace with God, peace with yourself, peace with others—, without spot, and blameless. Reason this way; the longsuffering—the incomprehensible patience—of our lord is salvation. It allows for us to make mistakes while learning because it is a growing process within each of us over a period of time. These are the same things our beloved brother Paul has written to you according to the wisdom that was given to him.

Revelation 6

1. And I saw when the Lamb opened one of the seals, and I heard, as it were the noise of thunder, one of the four beasts saying, Come and see.
2. And I saw, and behold a white horse: and he that sat on him had a bow; and a crown was given unto him: and he went forth conquering, and to conquer.
3. And when he had opened the second seal, I heard the second beast say, Come and see.
4. And there went out another horse that was red: and power was given to him that sat thereon to take peace from the earth, and that they should kill one another: and there was given unto him a great sword.
5. And when he had opened the third seal, I heard the third beast say, Come and see. And I beheld, and lo a black horse; and he that sat on him had a pair of balances in his hand.
6. And I heard a voice in the midst of the four beasts say, A measure of wheat for a penny, and three measures of barley for a penny; and see thou hurt not the oil and the wine.

Church, I don't spend a great deal of time in the book of Revelations. My subject matter doesn't take me there very much. The book of Revelations is a book of prophecy with symbols used to represent certain things and specific events. There is much debate among the 'experts' on Revelations as to exactly what is said and when it will happen. I, therefore, choose not to enter that debate because the confusion already at work can hide every evil work, whether those who debate it intend to do so or not. However, this particular section describes a set of conditions that we need to look at briefly.

There will come a time when someone will rise up on this earth who will have the power to wage war and conquer everything on the earth. He will be viewed as a great leader and champion by the people, yet he will not be viewed as a true king by these people. No one will be able to make war against him and the power he has. For a short time, he will establish peace by force, attrition, concession, negotiation, and treaty. This will be the crowning jewel of the peace of man. This man will be skilled in the arts of diplomacy and admired throughout the whole world, yet he will be filled with treachery and deceit and every wicked abomination.

After this, even the peace of man will be taken from the earth itself. Men will kill one another on a great scale. Fights and conflicts will break out threatening to destroy the universal peace established by men. No attempt to control this fighting will work—there will be no peace.

After this, food supply will become the greatest weapon on earth. It will get so terrible that a day's labor will produce only enough income to buy a day's supply of food. Many will starve. Many will be killed trying to get more food. There will be no peace. However, the elite, wealthy ruling class who support and follow this champion will not be affected by these events. They will not have a food shortage or a lack of their luxuries. Even though they will live pretty much as before, there will be no peace.

This is only the overall preview of the beginning of things to come during the transition period from the earth that is now to the earth that is yet to come. This is only a small part of things that are to happen.

This is just a warning to each of you. Church, as Christians, you should not desire that anyone should have to go through these things and you should not celebrate the fact that some will. You should instead be showing people how to have peace with God. It is much more effective to show someone peace with God through your own life and conduct than to try to scare them with predictions of things yet to come.

CHAPTER 18

Ephesians 6

11. Put on the whole armour of God, that ye may be able to stand against the wiles of the devil.

Church, Paul instructs you to put on the whole armor of God—not just parts of it. We are going to spend some time here looking at what it means to 'put on' this armor. When Paul saw these soldiers, each of them was in full armor. Each piece not only had a specific purpose, but was fitted perfectly with each other piece to provide a greater overall protection than could be afforded by any single piece alone.

Matthew 6

24. No man can serve two masters: for either he will hate the one, and love the other; or else he will hold to the one, and despise the other. Ye cannot serve God and mammon.
25. Therefore I say unto you, Take no thought for your life, what ye shall eat, or what ye shall drink; nor yet for your body, what ye shall put on. Is not the life more than meat, and the body than raiment?
26. Behold the fowls of the air: for they sow not, neither do they reap, nor gather into barns; yet your heavenly Father feedeth them. Are ye not much better than they?
27. Which of you by taking thought can add one cubit unto his stature?

28. And why take ye thought for raiment? Consider the lilies of the field, how they grow; they toil not, neither do they spin:

29. And yet I say unto you, That even Solomon in all his glory was not arrayed like one of these.

30. Wherefore, if God so clothe the grass of the field, which to day is, and to morrow is cast into the oven, shall he not much more clothe you, O ye of little faith?

31. Therefore take no thought, saying, What shall we eat? or, What shall we drink? or, Wherewithal shall we be clothed?

32. (For after all these things do the Gentiles seek:) for your heavenly Father knoweth that ye have need of all these things.

33. But seek ye first the kingdom of God, and his righteousness; and all these things shall be added unto you.

34. Take therefore no thought for the morrow: for the morrow shall take thought for the things of itself. Sufficient unto the day is the evil thereof.

No man can serve two masters. A servant must submit himself to a single master, either willingly or unwillingly. An unwilling servant is a constant cause for trouble because he is unhappy where he is and is unwilling to serve to begin with. Trying to serve two masters is the sign of an unwilling servant. That servant is the 'just in case' servant who is trying to come out on top regardless of the prevailing side. Such a person is selfish and rebellious. If he decides to favor one master; he will love one, and hate the other; or else he will hold to one, and despise the other. You cannot serve God and mammon—self serving, rapacious, avaricious greed.

Therefore, I say unto you, do not worry for your life, what things you shall eat, or what things you shall drink; nor even worry for your body, what you shall put on. Is not life itself more than food and drink, and the body more than the clothes you wear? Yet today, Church, we are constantly beset with things like 'dressing for success', 'power dressing', 'dressing to intimidate', etc. We are told that 'the clothes make the man'. It has become so much a part of the affluent, materialistic, lifestyle we are surrounded by, that we have adapted forms of it in our congregations. We use these 'standards' to visually judge whether or not God blesses us or not and how much God blesses us. I ask you now, is not your life worth more to you than simply food and drink? Is not your body worth more to you than the latest fashion style? If that is the case, then stop using materialistic standards to define your relationship to God. Be ever thankful for the things you have right now and quit striving to obtain more things as a 'witness' of God's blessings to you.

Observe the birds in the air. They do not plant seeds. They do not harvest crops. They do not store food in barns. Yet, your Father in heaven feeds them. Are you not much better than they? Which one among you by worrying can add one cubit to his own greatness among others? Why do you worry about clothing? Consider the lilies of the field, and how they grow; they don't labor or work at all, neither do they spin or weave. Yet even Solomon himself in all his glory did not have clothing that could match the beauty of a flower. Now, if God could clothe the grass of the field, which is today, and is thrown into the oven tomorrow, with such a magnificent palette of colors and shapes, shall he not clothe you even more, oh, you of little faith?

Therefore, quit worrying about what you will eat, or what you will drink, or how you will be clothed. The Gentiles pursue these things because these things define their whole identity and their whole life. They chase after the latest fashion style, the newest model car, the big house, the country club membership, the corner office with the best view, the best seat in the house, the reserved table at the finest restaurant, the #1 ranking, the championship ring and trophy, etc. These are the things that give their lives meaning. When they achieve these things— it's not enough—, they want more. Don't look too harshly at them, church, you do exactly the same things and call it 'blessings from God'.

You know very well that your heavenly Father himself knows the needs you have. Instead of worrying about the things you need, seek you first the kingdom of God, and his righteousness; and all the things you need shall be added to you as you need them. Therefore, be thankful for the things you have and rejoice with others for the things they have as well. Do not worry about the things you need tomorrow, for tomorrow shall present its needs tomorrow. There is enough evil to deal with today.

Matthew 22

1. And Jesus answered and spake unto them again by parables, and said,
2. The kingdom of heaven is like unto a certain king, which made a marriage for his son,
3. And sent forth his servants to call them that were bidden to the wedding: and they would not come.
4. Again, he sent forth other servants, saying, Tell them which are bidden, Behold, I have prepared my dinner: my oxen and my fatlings are killed, and all things are ready: come unto the marriage.
5. But they made light of it, and went their ways, one to his farm, another to his merchandise:
6. And the remnant took his servants, and entreated them spitefully, and slew them.
7. But when the king heard thereof, he was wroth: and he sent forth his armies, and destroyed those murderers, and burned up their city.
8. Then saith he to his servants, The wedding is ready, but they which were bidden were not worthy.
9. Go ye therefore into the highways, and as many as ye shall find, bid to the marriage.
10. So those servants went out into the highways, and gathered together all as many as they found, both bad and good: and the wedding was furnished with guests.
11. And when the king came in to see the guests, he saw there a man which had not on a wedding garment:

> 12. And he saith unto him, Friend, how camest thou in hither not having a wedding garment? And he was speechless.
> 13. Then said the king to the servants, Bind him hand and foot, and take him away, and cast him into outer darkness; there shall be weeping and gnashing of teeth.
> 14. For many are called, but few are chosen.

Jesus again spoke a parable those listening. While he is talking about a wedding feast given by a king for his son, he is likening it to the kingdom of heaven itself.

The first thing this king did was send his servants to his invited guests with a message to come to the marriage feast of his son. His invited guests refused to come. The king sent his servants out again to those invited. This time the message was that the dinner was prepared for them, the oxen and fatlings had been killed, and all the arrangements were made: come to the wedding. Instead of accepting the invitation, the guests treated the message as though it was unimportant. They went on about their business. One went to his farm. Another went back to his trading business. However, the ones left took the servants, were spiteful to them, and finally killed them.

When the king heard of these horrible events, he was terribly angry: he sent forth his armies, and destroyed the murderers, and burned their city to the ground. The king then told his servants that the wedding and the feast was ready, but there were no guests because the original guests were unworthy. He instructed them to go out into the streets and just invite anyone they happened across. The servants did as they were told. They went out and invited anyone they met to come to the wedding feast the king was giving in honor of his son. They made no distinction—they invited both good and bad alike. It did not matter whether the people knew the king or not. Thus, the feast was filled with guests.

Church, from the first part of this parable, we see that there was a special group of people favored by the king enough to be personally invited to the feast to celebrate the marriage of his son. This was a special social invitation and was exclusive because the only people invited were the ones on the kings' personal social register. When these worthy people refused the king and killed his servants, the king acted against them swiftly. After he declared them unworthy, he sent an inclusive invitation to anyone who would come, both good and bad reputations alike, whether they knew the king or not. This is not unlike the position you are in today. When God first chose Abraham, he promised that he would build from Abraham a great nation. Then God set the line through Abraham's son Isaac. Then God set the line through Isaac's son Jacob, whom God himself later named Israel. The children of Israel were the special guests of the king. You, church, were not even on the list.

After Christ himself came and taught the lost sheep of the House of Israel and he was crucified, God opened a new way to have a relationship with him. First this new way was only actively presented to the children of Israel. The Gentiles—your fathers, church—were still not on the list. Later, this relationship was finally opened actively to the Gentiles— your fathers, church. Therefore, today as with your fathers church, you are invited to the marriage feast as guests. Those of the children of Israel who are still from their hearts continuing to have the relationship with God the way their fathers did, can not be invited to the feast as guests unless they are willing to accept the relationship God established through the death and resurrection of his only begotten son. Once God has completely removed this relationship, those of the children of Israel will then face a much more difficult time—the time of Jacob's trouble. During this time, those who seek God will be purified and prepared as a bride to attend the same marriage feast. Church, make no mistake, you are not the bride of Christ as you teach. You are the the body whose head is Christ—the groom. You are invited guests to the marriage feast. Quit working on your white wedding gown and start working on your wedding garment.

Church, many of you will argue about what I just said—go ahead. There are many references you can point to in the Old Testament where God is speaking through the prophets to the children of Israel in terms of their place as bride. However, the headings of those sections say that these passages refer to the Church. Church, these promises were made to the children of Israel—not to the new spiritual Israel as you call yourself. These promises were made to the people God himself had chosen before you were ever on the list. Christ himself said the scriptures can not be broken; therefore, the promises were made to the children of Israel—not to you. Stop trying to replace Israel as God's chosen people.

When all the guests were gathered, the king himself came in to see those who had come. He saw a man there who did not have on a wedding garment; and the king himself said to the man, Friend, how did you even get in here without having a wedding garment? Of course, the man was speechless. The king then told his servants to bind the man hand and foot, take him away, and cast him into outer darkness. There shall be weeping and gnashing of teeth because many are called, but few are chosen.

Just exactly what is this wedding garment? What is it made of? What does it look like? That takes us back to what kind of kingdom is this? The scriptures tell us that when all the work is complete, there will be a new earth and new heavens wherein dwells righteousness (only righteousness). That means that, in the end, this kingdom will cover all the heavens and the earth. Therefore, this kingdom is even from its beginning the kingdom of righteousness itself. To attend a wedding feast in such a kingdom would require every single guest to wear a garment made of righteousness itself. No? You don't think or believe so? Let's see, shall we?

In the third chapter of Philippians, Paul made a peculiar statement in the 8th and 9th verses. He wanted to be found in Christ, 'not having mine own righteousness, which is of the law, but that which is through the faith of Christ, the righteousness which is of God by faith:'. Why would Paul, a Pharisee of Pharisees make such a statement? Paul just described two distinctly different kinds of righteousness. He personally wanted to live in such a way that he would be found clothed in the righteousness that is through the faith of Christ, the righteousness of God himself which is by faith. Why did Paul, a Pharisee of Pharisees make that personal choice?

Paul knew what Isaiah said. Isaiah said in the 64th chapter and 6th verse of his book 'But we are all as an unclean thing, and all our righteousnesses are as filthy rags; and we all do fade as a leaf; and our iniquities, like the wind, have taken us away'. Paul knew that his own righteousness, which is of the law, were just filthy rags—not the beautiful wedding garment that it might appear to be to himself and to others. The man in the parable may have had a garment that appeared acceptable to others, but to the king what this man had on was an odoriferous abomination that had no place at that feast or in the kingdom at all.

Church, each one of you now have to make the very same choice. You can choose to accept the accomplishment of Christ and accept the righteousness through the faith of Christ himself to clothe yourself in the righteousness which is of God by faith, or you can go about to clothe yourself in the righteousness which is by keeping the law. If you choose the latter, you indeed will appear righteous to many, but to God you will be an odoriferous and self righteous abomination.

Matthew 27

26. Then released he Barabbas unto them: and when he had scourged Jesus, he delivered him to be crucified.
27. Then the soldiers of the governor took Jesus into the common hall, and gathered unto him the whole band of soldiers.
28. And they stripped him, and put on him a scarlet robe.
29. And when they had platted a crown of thorns, they put it upon his head, and a reed in his right hand: and they bowed the knee before him, and mocked him, saying, Hail, King of the Jews!
30. And they spit upon him, and took the reed, and smote him on the head.
31. And after that they had mocked him, they took the robe off from him, and put his own raiment on him, and led him away to crucify him.

Matthew is describing Jesus' death sentence being carried out on Pilate's orders. Pilate first freed Barabbas. He then had Jesus scourged and turned him over to the governor's soldiers to be crucified. The soldiers took Jesus to the common hall and gathered the whole band of soldiers together.

Next the soldiers stripped Jesus of his clothes and put a scarlet robe on him. They platted a crown of thorns and put it on his head, and put a reed in his right hand: and they bowed the knee before him in mockery, saying, Hail, King of the Jews! They spit on him, took the reed from him, and hit him over the head with it. When they had finished mocking Jesus, they snatched the robe off him, put his own clothes back on him, and led him out to be crucified.

Paul instructs you to put on the whole armor of God from the standpoint that it is yours personally to put on, just as the soldiers put Jesus' own personal clothing back on him before they led him out to crucify him.

Mark 6

7. **And he called unto him the twelve, and began to send them forth by two and two; and gave them power over unclean spirits;**
8. **And commanded them that they should take nothing for their journey, save a staff only; no scrip, no bread, no money in their purse:**
9. **But be shod with sandals; and not put on two coats.**
10. **And he said unto them, In what place soever ye enter into an house, there abide till ye depart from that place.**
11. **And whosoever shall not receive you, nor hear you, when ye depart thence, shake off the dust under your feet for a testimony against them. Verily I say unto you, It shall be more tolerable for Sodom and Gomorrha in the day of judgment, than for that city.**
12. **And they went out, and preached that men should repent.**
13. **And they cast out many devils, and anointed with oil many that were sick, and healed them.**

Jesus sent the twelve out two by two into the area around them and he gave them power over unclean spirits. He also gave them specific instructions for their journey. They were to take nothing with them except for a simple walking stick—nothing ornate. They were to take no money, no food, no bag to carry food. They were to wear sandals, but they were not to put on two cloaks. They were to stay in whatever house they entered until they left the town they came to. They preached repentance just like John was preaching. They healed the sick and cast out devils.

The reason he told them not to wear two personal cloaks was to keep them from being caught up in custom. The poorer people could only afford one personal cloak. The better off could afford two, the outer cloak would protect against the dirt and dust. Then when they arrived, they could remove the outer cloak and the inner cloak was still presentable. Of course, the better off you were, the more ornate the outer cloak could be. It had become a status symbol. The twelve were not to fall into the trap of social importance. The message they carried was far more important than they were.

Again, we see that this armor is personal—just like the one cloak the twelve each were to wear. We are not to think ourselves more important than anyone else. Our message is far more important than any one of us—just like it was with the twelve. We are to make the entire armor—each piece—a part of ourselves personally.

Luke 12

> 22. And he said unto his disciples, Therefore I say unto you, Take no thought for your life, what ye shall eat; neither for the body, what ye shall put on.
> 23. The life is more than meat, and the body is more than raiment.
> 24. Consider the ravens: for they neither sow nor reap; which neither have storehouse nor barn; and God feedeth them: how much more are ye better than the fowls?

25. And which of you with taking thought can add to his stature one cubit?
26. If ye then be not able to do that thing which is least, why take ye thought for the rest?
27. Consider the lilies how they grow: they toil not, they spin not; and yet I say unto you, that Solomon in all his glory was not arrayed like one of these.
28. If then God so clothe the grass, which is to day in the field, and to morrow is cast into the oven; how much more will he clothe you, O ye of little faith?
29. And seek not ye what ye shall eat, or what ye shall drink, neither be ye of doubtful mind.
30. For all these things do the nations of the world seek after: and your Father knoweth that ye have need of these things.
31. But rather seek ye the kingdom of God; and all these things shall be added unto you.

Jesus was talking to his disciples and reminded them of something he had already told them. He told them not to worry about their life, what they had to eat; neither for their body, what clothing they personally had to put on. there is more to life than food, and there is more to the body than clothing. Just consider for a minute the ravens. They neither plant crops nor harvest crops. They have no granaries or barns, yet God feeds them. Are you not worth more than the fowls of the air? Which among you can by worrying add even one cubit to his greatness? Well . . . ? If you are unable to do the things that matter the least, why do you worry about the rest?

Again, consider the lilies, how they grow. They don't work the ground, they don't spin thread or cloth; and yet I say to you—each of you—, that Solomon in all his greatest glory was not clothed like one of these lilies. If God himself clothes the grass of the field with such dazzling beauty, which today is in the field, and tomorrow is cast into the oven; how much more will he personally clothe you, oh you of little faith?

Do not seek what you shall eat, or what you shall drink, nor be you of doubtful mind. These are the things the nations of the world seek after as a sign of success or status, or to intimidate and control others. Your father knows you have need of these things. Seek instead the kingdom of God, and all these things that others seek after shall be added to you as a matter of course.

Luke 15

11. And he said, A certain man had two sons:
12. And the younger of them said to his father, Father, give me the portion of goods that falleth to me. And he divided unto them his living.
13. And not many days after the younger son gathered all together, and took his journey into a far country, and there wasted his substance with riotous living.
14. And when he had spent all, there arose a mighty famine in that land; and he began to be in want.
15. And he went and joined himself to a citizen of that country; and he sent him into his fields to feed swine.
16. And he would fain have filled his belly with the husks that the swine did eat: and no man gave unto him.
17. And when he came to himself, he said, How many hired servants of my father's have bread enough and to spare, and I perish with hunger!
18. I will arise and go to my father, and will say unto him, Father, I have sinned against heaven, and before thee,
19. And am no more worthy to be called thy son: make me as one of thy hired servants.
20. And he arose, and came to his father. But when he was yet a great way off, his father saw him, and had compassion, and ran, and fell on his neck, and kissed him.
21. And the son said unto him, Father, I have sinned against heaven, and in thy sight, and am no more worthy to be called thy son.

> 22. But the father said to his servants, Bring forth the best robe, and put it on him; and put a ring on his hand, and shoes on his feet:
> 23. And bring hither the fatted calf, and kill it; and let us eat, and be merry:
> 24. For this my son was dead, and is alive again; he was lost, and is found. And they began to be merry.

Christ spent much of his time teaching in parables. These were stories that illustrated the things he was trying to show the people. These stories were taken from things people saw around themselves in everyday life. On the surface, parables may show one or more points to consider; however, the parables of Christ always had much deeper meaning than just surface understanding. That is why a great many who heard his teachings could not understand the things he taught. This parable has multiple parts, but we are going to look only at the part that applies to the section I am writing about. No attempt is made to explain the entire parable or the various lessons it illustrates.

A man had two sons. One day the younger son came to his father and said, give me my share of the inheritance. The father then divided the inheritance between both sons, each receiving his allotted share. A few days later, the younger took all his wealth and left his father's house; however, the older son remained with his father. The younger son travelled far away into another country and spent his wealth foolishly and lavishly.

When the younger son had wasted his entire inheritance, the crops failed and food and jobs became scarce. He began to be in want. He had no friends to give him things he needed. He was alone. He finally found a citizen of that country who hired him to go feed the pigs in his fields. He was so hungry that he would have eaten the husks he was feeding to the pigs. Yet, even though he was working, no one would give him anything. He worked for a pig farmer. He wasn't high enough on the social register to merit recognition or help. Then he began to think very seriously about his position.

He realized that even his father's hired servants had plenty of food with enough to spare, yet he was starving to death. With his arrogance now gone, he decided to go to his father and say, Father, I have sinned against heaven, and before you. I do not deserve to even be or even called your son. Please, just hire me to be one of your servants. He arose from where he was and went to his father. While he was yet a long way off, his father saw him and ran to him with compassion—not judgement—, fell of his neck, and kissed him.

The younger son then said, Father, I have sinned against heaven and before you. I do not deserve to even be called your son. Please, just hire me as one of your servants. But his Father said, Bring out the best robe and put it on him personally. Put a ring on his hand personally that shows he is part of the family. Put shoes on his feet so he can personally stand prepared. Bring the fatted calf and kill it. Let us feast and celebrate. This young man, my son, was dead, and now is alive again; he was lost, and is now found.

Romans 13

12. The night is far spent, the day is at hand: let us therefore cast off the works of darkness, and let us put on the armour of light.
13. Let us walk honestly, as in the day; not in rioting and drunkenness, not in chambering and wantonness, not in strife and envying.
14. But put ye on the Lord Jesus Christ, and make not provision for the flesh, to fulfil the lusts thereof.

Church, the night is far spent, the day is at hand. Time grows short for all of us. Therefore, as the sons of God we claim to be, let us cast off the works of darkness we are still comfortable with. Instead, let us each one personally put on the armor of light just as the parables above illustrate personal clothing or possessions. Let us walk honestly, as in the day; not in rioting and drunkenness, not in chambering and wantonness, not in strife and envyings, instead, each one of you personally put on the Lord Jesus Christ, and make not provision for the flesh, to fulfil the lusts thereof.

How can you do this? Do you wear a cross around your neck? Do you wear a shirt that says 'Jesus Loves You'? Do you constantly ask yourself 'What Would Jesus Do'? Quit thinking such worldly thoughts. Paul said for us not to be conformed to this world, but to be transformed by the renewing of our minds. He did not say for us to put on symbols or slogans to illustrate what we call faith. Paul said that it is God's will for each one of us to be conformed to the image of his only begotten son that he himself might be the firstborn of many brethren. Therefore, personally putting on Jesus Christ is learning to think, reason, and understand the way Christ himself did. This whole armor of God is what helps each one of us individually to accomplish this feat by helping each of us to face and overcome our own individual faults. How can you face the corruption outside of you that is trying to weaken you when you haven't even dealt with your own corrupt nature?

1 Corinthians 15

> **49.** And as we have borne the image of the earthy, we shall also bear the image of the heavenly.
> **50.** Now this I say, brethren, that flesh and blood cannot inherit the kingdom of God; neither doth corruption inherit incorruption.
> **51.** Behold, I shew you a mystery; We shall not all sleep, but we shall all be changed,
> **52.** In a moment, in the twinkling of an eye, at the last trump: for the trumpet shall sound, and the dead shall be raised incorruptible, and we shall be changed.
> **53.** For this corruptible must put on incorruption, and this mortal must put on immortality.
> **54.** So when this corruptible shall have put on incorruption, and this mortal shall have put on immortality, then shall be brought to pass the saying that is written, Death is swallowed up in victory.

Church, Paul is talking about a new body and a new life in this passage. It does not exist on the earth at this point in time, but it is promised to people who do exist on earth at this time. Pay close attention to this and see for yourselves.

The promise tells us that, just as surely as we have borne the image of the earthy, we shall also bear the image of the heavenly. When you go back and read the entire chapter, Paul is talking about a new body. In this context, the promise is that we shall have a body that is heavenly, because we have a body that is earthy. Paul was addressing a conflict that had arisen in Corinth over what kind of body these followers would have in this new kingdom. This conflict still rages today among your many different respectable divisions—denominations. Just exactly what kind of body will we have?

Paul said that flesh and blood can not—can not—inherit the kingdom of God; neither does corruption inherit incorruption. We are earthy—flesh and blood. The results of our lives is death—corruption. We can not inherit the kingdom of God the way we are now. Yet, we are promised to be heavenly just as surely as we are earthy now. Here's a mystery. We shall not all sleep—as in death—but we shall all be changed. This will take place in a moment, in the twinkling of an eye, at the last trump; for the trumpet shall sound, and the dead shall be raised incorruptible, and we shall be changed.

For any of us to inherit the kingdom of God, this corruptible must personally put on—be clothed with, become,—incorruption, and this mortal must personally put on—be clothed with, become,—immortality. When the corruptible shall have put on incorruption and the mortal shall have put on immortality, then and only then, shall be brought to pass the saying that is written, Death is swallowed up in victory.

The whole time here Paul is discussing a physical body. When the body is changed and either becomes incorruptible or immortal, it is still physically some type of body. If it were not so, Paul would have made a difference because, in his context, he is discussing different kinds of physical bodies (flesh). The dilemma we are faced with here is that

Paul himself said that flesh and blood can not inherit the kingdom of God. How can we resolve this condition without knowing what kind of body this really is? Men have never seen this new body—this heavenly body—or have they? The apostles did, over 500 brethren at once did, Paul did. Why can't we just accept their eyewitness report of a person who has such a body? Why do we ignore what Christ himself said in Luke when he appeared to those behind locked doors the evening of the first day of the week?

Christ himself said, I am not a spirit as you suppose, for a spirit has not flesh and bones as you see me having. Did Christ say he was flesh and blood? Did he say he was a spirit that took on a physical form to be seen? He said that he himself was flesh and bones like the people were, but no longer flesh and blood like the people were. He had a new kind of flesh—a flesh that contained Eternal Life itself. John himself said that they had witnessed Eternal Life in someone they could physically touch, walk with, talk with, and eat with. This is the body Paul is referring to in this whole chapter. Even Paul saw this body according to his own account of his meeting with Christ on the road to Damascus. If you disagree here, argue with Paul, John, and Luke.

Galatians 3

22. **But the scripture hath concluded all under sin, that the promise by faith of Jesus Christ might be given to them that believe.**
23. **But before faith came, we were kept under the law, shut up unto the faith which should afterwards be revealed.**
24. **Wherefore the law was our schoolmaster to bring us unto Christ, that we might be justified by faith.**
25. **But after that faith is come, we are no longer under a schoolmaster.**
26. **For ye are all the children of God by faith in Christ Jesus.**
27. **For as many of you as have been baptized into Christ have put on Christ.**

> **28. There is neither Jew nor Greek, there is neither bond nor free, there is neither male nor female: for ye are all one in Christ Jesus.**
> **29. And if ye be Christ's, then are ye Abraham's seed, and heirs according to the promise.**

Church, Paul has said some very exciting things in this passage. Pay close attention as this unfolds.

The scriptures themselves have concluded that all are under sin, whether they know it or not. Is that fair? Of course it is. That way, the promise by faith of Jesus Christ might be given to them that believe—only to them that believe. Is that fair? Of course it is. People still have a choice. People can still believe whatever they want to believe. However, the promise by faith of Jesus Christ is only given to those who believe and accept the death and resurrection of Jesus Christ to Eternal Life as witnessed by those who saw him. This is the power of faith itself.

Church, there was a time when faith did not exist on this earth at all. Otherwise, the scriptures could have never said . . . before faith came. Therefore, faith itself is not what we believe or teach that it is. Those who had the law were protected, nurtured, and taught by it. They were prepared for the faith that would be revealed some time after the law was given.

The law, in effect then, became the schoolmaster to bring those who had the law to Christ, that they might be justified by the faith of Christ instead of the works of the law. Just as well, once the promised faith has come, there is no longer any need for the schoolmaster. This now removes the distinction between those who had the law and those who didn't have the law. Therefore, those who accepted the death and resurrection of Jesus Christ are all become children of God by the faith that is in Christ Jesus himself, whether they had the law and knew God or they didn't have the law and were without God and without hope in this world.

Even today, as many of you as have actually been baptized into Christ have put on Christ himself—whether you realize it or not. That relationship with Christ is personal to and for each and every single one of you—as personal as your own clothing. But how do you put on Christ? Do you carry him about on your shoulders? Do you wear some sort of mask? Do you wear jewelry around your neck? Do you wear WWJD T.-shirts, bracelets, anklets, hats, or such like? Those who think worldly thoughts would . . . do you?

Christ was and still is the physical embodiment of faith itself—a whole new creation with a totally different way to think, reason, and understand everything around himself. He taught people a different way to think, reason, and understand everything. To personally put on Christ Jesus requires each and every one of you to learn to think, reason, and understand the way Christ himself does. There is no other way to personally put on Christ. Once you have actually put on Christ, there is neither Jew nor Greek, there is neither bond nor free, there is neither male nor female: for you are all one in Christ Jesus. This is exactly the same relationship Jesus has with God—exactly what he prayed for in the 17th chapter of the gospel of John when he said he wanted them all to be one the same way he and his Father are one. Through Christ, we have exactly the same relationship with God that he does. That relationship does not make Christ any more God than it makes any one or all of us. However, that relationship allows each of us to think, reason, and understand the thoughts of God exactly the same way Christ himself does.

If you are then in Christ this way, then you are Abraham's seed, and heirs to the promise made to Abraham himself before there was ever a law given by God at all. Quit trying to bring the law into this relationship. Faith—the faith of Jesus Christ—is not the result of obeying the law. However, if you develop this new way of thinking, reasoning, and understanding, you will fulfill the intent expressed in the law from your own hearts. Once you manifest the faith of Jesus Christ, your life changes and you willingly become obedient directly to God himself. Why would anyone want to put a law for righteousness between himself and the righteousness of God when Christ removed that barrier by his own death and resurrection?

Ephesians 4

17. This I say therefore, and testify in the Lord, that ye henceforth walk not as other Gentiles walk, in the vanity of their mind,
18. Having the understanding darkened, being alienated from the life of God through the ignorance that is in them, because of the blindness of their heart:
19. Who being past feeling have given themselves over unto lasciviousness, to work all uncleanness with greediness.
20. But ye have not so learned Christ;
21. If so be that ye have heard him, and have been taught by him, as the truth is in Jesus:
22. That ye put off concerning the former conversation the old man, which is corrupt according to the deceitful lusts;
23. And be renewed in the spirit of your mind;
24. And that ye put on the new man, which after God is created in righteousness and true holiness.
25. Wherefore putting away lying, speak every man truth with his neighbour: for we are members one of another.
26. Be ye angry, and sin not: let not the sun go down upon your wrath:
27. Neither give place to the devil.
28. Let him that stole steal no more: but rather let him labour, working with his hands the thing which is good, that he may have to give to him that needeth.
29. Let no corrupt communication proceed out of your mouth, but that which is good to the use of edifying, that it may minister grace unto the hearers.
30. And grieve not the holy Spirit of God, whereby ye are sealed unto the day of redemption.
31. Let all bitterness, and wrath, and anger, and clamour, and evil speaking, be put away from you, with all malice:
32. And be ye kind one to another, tenderhearted, forgiving one another, even as God for Christ's sake hath forgiven you.

Church, the Pharisee of pharisees is not through with you yet. Get ready. Here it comes.

Paul himself testified in the Lord—in unity with Christ so much so that is was as though Christ himself was speaking—that you from now on walk no more as the Gentiles walk, in the vanity of their own mind, having the understanding darkened, being alienated from the Life of God himself through the ignorance that is in them, because of the blindness of their own hearts: who themselves being past feeling have given themselves over to lasciviousness, to work all forms of uncleanness with insatiable greediness.

Church, you have not learned to be this way from Christ. That is, of course, if you have actually heard him, and have been taught by him, as the truth itself is in Jesus. Put off—do completely away with—the conduct of the old man you once were—which is itself corrupt according to deceitful lusts; and be completely renewed in the spirit of your own mind; and put on personally—become—the new man, which after God himself is created in righteousness and true holiness.

Church, that is not a suggestion—it is direct instruction. Pay attention carefully to see how to become this new man that Paul is talking about. Wherefore, putting away lying of any kind, speak every man truth with his neighbor: for we are all members one of another. If you get angry, be angry, but don't use anger as a pretext to sin against anyone or even yourself. Do not let the sun go down on your wrath—don't hold grudges: neither give place to the devil and resort to progressively destructive retaliation.

Let those among you whole stole, steal no more: rather let those labor, working with their hands the thing which is good, that they may have to give to others who are in need. Let no corrupt communication proceed from your mouth at all, instead speak that which is good to the use of building and strengthening others, that it may minister grace to those who hear your words. This isn't just 'dirty words' or 'foul language'. This covers anything you say for any reason at all. If what you say from your own mouth does not build, strengthen, or encourage others, your communication is corrupt. Grieve not the holy spirit of God, whereby each one of you is sealed unto the day of redemption.

Let all bitterness, and wrath, and anger, and clamor, and evil speaking, be put completely away from you, with all malice: and be each of you kind one to another, tenderhearted, forgiving one another, even as God himself for Christ's sake—not yours—has forgiven you.

Colossians 3

> **8. But now ye also put off all these; anger, wrath, malice, blasphemy, filthy communication out of your mouth.**
> **9. Lie not one to another, seeing that ye have put off the old man with his deeds;**
> **10. And have put on the new man, which is renewed in knowledge after the image of him that created him:**
> **11. Where there is neither Greek nor Jew, circumcision nor uncircumcision, Barbarian, Scythian, bond nor free: but Christ is all, and in all.**
> **12. Put on therefore, as the elect of God, holy and beloved, bowels of mercies, kindness, humbleness of mind, meekness, longsuffering;**
> **13. Forbearing one another, and forgiving one another, if any man have a quarrel against any: even as Christ forgave you, so also do ye.**
> **14. And above all these things put on charity, which is the bond of perfectness.**
> **15. And let the peace of God rule in your hearts, to the which also ye are called in one body; and be ye thankful.**
> **16. Let the word of Christ dwell in you richly in all wisdom; teaching and admonishing one another in psalms and hymns and spiritual songs, singing with grace in your hearts to the Lord.**
> **17. And whatsoever ye do in word or deed, do all in the name of the Lord Jesus, giving thanks to God and the Father by him.**

Church, there is more. Also put off—do away with completely—all these; anger, wrath, malice, filthy communication out of your mouth.

Do not lie to one another, since you have personally put off—completely done away with—the old man with his corrupt deeds; and have put on the new man, which is renewed in knowledge after him that created the new man: where there is neither Greek nor Jew, circumcision nor uncircumcision, Barbarian, Scythian, bond nor free: but Christ himself is all and in all. Paul said let there be no divisions among you because the new man does not recognize divisions of any kind for any reason at all—ever. The new man does not agree to disagree. The new man places truth above even the name of God himself—just like God himself does.

Therefore, as the elect of God, holy and beloved, each of you personally put on bowels of mercies, kindness, humbleness of mind, meekness, longsuffering; forbearing one another, and forgiving one another, if any man have a quarrel against any other: even as Christ forgave you, so you forgive one another. Above all these things personally put on—allow yourselves to be filled with charity—the love of God himself—, which is the bond of perfectness. Let the peace of God himself rule in your hearts individually, to the which your are also called in one body with one head; and be thankful.

Let the word of Christ dwell in you richly in all wisdom; teaching and admonishing one another in psalms and hymns and spiritual songs, singing with grace in your hearts to the Lord himself. Whatsoever you personally do in word or deed, personally do all in the name of the Lord Jesus, giving thanks to God and the Father by him.

1 Thessalonians 5

8. But let us, who are of the day, be sober, putting on the breastplate of faith and love; and for an helmet, the hope of salvation.

9. For God hath not appointed us to wrath, but to obtain salvation by our Lord Jesus Christ,

Let each of us, who are of the day, be sober, personally putting on the breastplate of faith and love; and for a helmet, the hope of salvation.

God has not appointed us to wrath, but to obtain salvation by our Lord Jesus Christ.

Luke 24

45. Then opened he their understanding, that they might understand the scriptures,
46. And said unto them, Thus it is written, and thus it behoved Christ to suffer, and to rise from the dead the third day:
47. And that repentance and remission of sins should be preached in his name among all nations, beginning at Jerusalem.
48. And ye are witnesses of these things.
49. And, behold, I send the promise of my Father upon you: but tarry ye in the city of Jerusalem, until ye be endued with power from on high.

In the 24th chapter of Luke, Christ himself was giving his apostles instruction. Then he opened their understanding that they might understand—not debate—the scriptures. He said to them, thus it is written, and thus it behoved Christ to suffer, and to rise from the dead the third day: and that repentance and remission of sins should be preached in his name among all nations, beginning at Jerusalem. You are witnesses of these things—the suffering, the death, and the resurrection of Christ himself. Behold, I send the promise of my Father upon you: but tarry ye in the city of Jerusalem, until ye be endued—literally clothed—with power from on high.

Christ just told the apostles that they were going to receive something so powerful that they would not be able to contain it within themselves. This power from on high would fill them and overflow them, literally clothing each one of them with itself. Church, the power from on high is still the same today as it was then. We are certainly no greater or stronger than the apostles were. This same power—holy spirit—will fill us to overflowing and clothe us just like it did them—if we each accept it and allow it to occur. Everything written in this book is written to show each of you that. If any of you do not have this power, allow it to enter you and overflow you the way it did the apostles and disciples themselves. If any of you have this power in you already, allow it to quicken you—make you alive—and overflow you the way it did the apostles. Each of you watch your lives change and everything change around you as well. Allow this holy spirit to help you put on the new man that is created in righteousness and true holiness.

John 20

> **19. Then the same day at evening, being the first day of the week, when the doors were shut where the disciples were assembled for fear of the Jews, came Jesus and stood in the midst, and saith unto them, Peace be unto you.**
> **20. And when he had so said, he shewed unto them his hands and his side. Then were the disciples glad, when they saw the Lord.**
> **21. Then said Jesus to them again, Peace be unto you: as my Father hath sent me, even so send I you.**
> **22. And when he had said this, he breathed on them, and saith unto them, Receive ye the Holy Ghost:**
> **23. Whose soever sins ye remit, they are remitted unto them; and whose soever sins ye retain, they are retained.**
> **24. But Thomas, one of the twelve, called Didymus, was not with them when Jesus came.**

Then the same day at evening—before sunset because sunset started a new day—, being the first day of the week, when the doors were shut where the disciples were assembled for fear of the Jews, came Jesus and stood in the midst, and said unto them, Peace be unto you. When he had greeted them in this manner, he showed them his hands and his side. The disciples were glad when they saw the Lord. Church, every single person in that room was a disciple of Jesus—there wasn't one single stranger among them.

Then Jesus said to them again, Peace be unto you: as my Father has sent me, even so send I you. Jesus just told all the disciples in that room that he was sending them to do the same things that God himself had sent Jesus to do before he was crucified. When he had told them this, he breathed on them, and said to each one of them, Receive ye the holy Ghost—what he said was power from on high—: whose so ever sins you remit, they are remitted unto them; and whose so ever sins you retain, they are retained. But Thomas, one of the twelve, called Didymus, was not with them when Jesus came.

Church, take note. Thomas was not just one of the disciples. John called Thomas one of the twelve. These were twelve disciples that Jesus himself chose from among many disciples to personally be with him and learn from him. He also sent them out to prepare for his coming to different areas. Therefore, John made a distinction between the twelve apostles and the other disciples. Mark and Luke did as well. Their accounts of the same event on exactly the same day show that Judas had to be in that room if Thomas wasn't there. Tradition teaches otherwise, but the scriptures speak clearly for themselves. Church, if any of us are to become the new man created after God in righteousness and true holiness, then each one of us must seek the truth of the scriptures themselves and not rely on traditions men have handed down generation after generation.

Acts 1

1. **The former treatise have I made, O Theophilus, of all that Jesus began both to do and teach,**
2. **Until the day in which he was taken up, after that he through the Holy Ghost had given commandments unto the apostles whom he had chosen:**
3. **To whom also he shewed himself alive after his passion by many infallible proofs, being seen of them forty days, and speaking of the things pertaining to the kingdom of God:**

> 4. And, being assembled together with them, commanded them that they should not depart from Jerusalem, but wait for the promise of the Father, which, saith he, ye have heard of me.
> 5. For John truly baptized with water; but ye shall be baptized with the Holy Ghost not many days hence.
> 6. When they therefore were come together, they asked of him, saying, Lord, wilt thou at this time restore again the kingdom to Israel?
> 7. And he said unto them, It is not for you to know the times or the seasons, which the Father hath put in his own power.
> 8. But ye shall receive power, after that the Holy Ghost is come upon you: and ye shall be witnesses unto me both in Jerusalem, and in all Judaea, and in Samaria, and unto the uttermost part of the earth.

Church, pay close attention to what Luke is saying here. Luke is referring to a former book he had written and is giving a synopsis of the material he first wrote before he continues with the account he is giving here. Watch the pronouns very closely in this summary.

In his summary, Luke says he had made an account of all the things Jesus began to both do and teach, until the day he was taken up, after he through the holy ghost—that power from on high he promised—had given commandments unto the apostles whom he himself had specifically chosen—not some, or most of them . . . all of them: to whom he showed himself alive after his passion (death) by many infallible proofs, being seen of them—the very ones he personally chose himself—forty days, and speaking (to them specifically) the things pertaining to the kingdom of God.

Being assembled together with them—the ones he personally chose himself—, Jesus commanded them—the same ones he chose—that they should not depart from Jerusalem, but wait for the promise of the Father, which, said he, you—the ones I chose myself—have heard of me. John truly baptized with water; but you—each one of you—shall be baptized with the holy ghost—power from on high—not many days hence. When they therefore were come together, they—the ones he himself had chosen—asked of him, saying, Lord, will you at this time restore the kingdom to Israel?

He said to them—the ones he chose himself—It is not for you to know the times or the seasons, which the Father himself has put in his own power. But you shall receive power, after the holy ghost has come upon you: and you shall be witnesses unto me both in Jerusalem, and in all Judea, and in Samaria, and unto the uttermost part of the earth.

This passage from verses 1-8 deals with Christ's instructions to the apostles he chose himself—including Judas. Had Judas not been there for any reason—like death—the scriptures would have noted so in this section right here.

Acts 2

1. **And when the day of Pentecost was fully come, they were all with one accord in one place.**
2. **And suddenly there came a sound from heaven as of a rushing mighty wind, and it filled all the house where they were sitting.**
3. **And there appeared unto them cloven tongues like as of fire, and it sat upon each of them.**
4. **And they were all filled with the Holy Ghost, and began to speak with other tongues, as the Spirit gave them utterance.**

Again, pay very close attention. When the day of Pentecost was fully come, they were all with one accord in one place. This event occurred 10 days after Christ ascended from the mount of Olives. During that 10 day period, it suddenly became necessary for the apostles to replace Judas because he was no longer numbered among the apostles—he was dead. Had Judas been dead during the forty day period that Jesus was showing himself to the apostles he personally chose and to the other disciples, it would have been just as necessary for him to replace Judas as it was to Peter. These men were all with one accord in one place. The only place these men could have been together with the other disciples and the women was in the temple—the house of God himself.

Suddenly, there came from heaven a sound like a mighty rushing wind, and it filled the house where they were sitting. there appeared unto them cloven tongues that looked like fire, and it sat upon each one of them personally. They—the apostles—were all filled with the holy ghost—power from on high that Jesus had promised. Each one of them began to personally speak with other tongues, as the power that filled each of them gave them the ability and inspiration to do so.

Church, this is the event that Christ told them would happen. He compared it to the baptism of John so the apostles would recognise it when it happened. They were suddenly changed and began to say and do without question the things the power suddenly within them inspired each one of them to do.

Acts 9

17. And Ananias went his way, and entered into the house; and putting his hands on him said, Brother Saul, the Lord, even Jesus, that appeared unto thee in the way as thou camest, hath sent me, that thou mightest receive thy sight, and be filled with the Holy Ghost.

Ananias went his way, and entered into the house; and putting his hands on him said, Brother Saul, the Lord, even Jesus, that appeared to you personally in the way as you came, has sent me, that you might personally receive your sight, and be personally filled with the holy spirit. Does this mean that the holy spirit can't enter anyone personally without someone laying hands on them? No. No one laid hands on the apostles who were filled with the spirit while they were in the temple on the day of Pentecost. No one laid hands on the Gentiles in the house of Cornelius when Peter began speaking to them. This was a specific case for Saul himself.

Acts 13

> 6. And when they had gone through the isle unto Paphos, they found a certain sorcerer, a false prophet, a Jew, whose name was Barjesus:
> 7. Which was with the deputy of the country, Sergius Paulus, a prudent man; who called for Barnabas and Saul, and desired to hear the word of God.
> 8. But Elymas the sorcerer (for so is his name by interpretation) withstood them, seeking to turn away the deputy from the faith.
> 9. Then Saul, (who also is called Paul,) filled with the Holy Ghost, set his eyes on him,

When Saul and Barnabas had gone through the isle of Paphos, they found a certain sorcerer, a false prophet, a Jew, whose name was Barjesus. This man was with Sergius Paulus, the deputy of the country Saul and Barnabas were passing through. Sergius Paulus was a wise and intelligent ruler. He called for Barnabas and Saul, and desired to hear from them the word of God. But Elymas—the false prophet Barjesus—the sorcerer (for so is his name by interpretation) withstood them—challenged them directly in spirit and power—, seeking to turn away the deputy Sergius Paulus from the faith. Then Saul, (who is also called Paul,) filled with the holy ghost—power from on high—set his eyes upon him—Elymas.

Church, we see here that there walk among us people who are very powerful people. They have great spiritual power that may or may not come from God. Here is a sign. Those who seek to turn people away from the faith that Paul spoke of, that Peter and John spoke of, that James spoke of, do not have the spirit of God in them at all. Such people will challenge you directly with the full force of the power in them. Each of you must be able to set your eyes on such a person and discern (determine) the spirit that is in your challenger. In that instant, the spirit of God in you will reveal to you the exact course of action you must take to deal with the challenge.

If you have allowed this spirit in you to develop and if you have allowed this spirit to personally help you overcome your own corrupt nature, you will be able to set your eyes on your challenger and know exactly what to do and say. That is the importance of this armor Paul is talking about in his letter to the Ephesians. That armor is for you to use first to deal with your own corrupt nature. When you have done that, your eye will become single and you will clearly see how to help those around you who are struggling the same way you are and have been. You will also be able to recognise a true enemy of God when you see one. You will be able to see the thoughts and intentions of men's hearts the very same way Christ himself did.

There is far more to this power God has given to us than we understand; however, each of us can increase our understanding by listening to the spirit of God in us and obeying the things it tells us and shows us to do. The armor we have is to keep each one of us on the proper track. The greatest battle we fight is within ourselves. Overcoming our old nature and becoming our new nature is a lifetime battle of monumental proportions. The armor we develop and use constantly from the power God has given us is the only thing we have that allows us to stand fully prepared to face any challenge. Will we make mistakes? Yes. Will we fail? No, not in the end. Will we ever be able to reflect the image of Christ himself in our own personal lives? The scriptures say we will. How say you?

It is my greatest hope and prayer that each of you personally take the time to study the things I have written to you in this book. However, when you do, remember that these are just the basics. The scriptures cover far greater things than I have discussed here at far greater depths. Our lives are a learning process that will continue as long as we live. God has so much more to show you. May your hearts be touched and your lives be blessed by the words written in this book. May you discover the true power of the word of God and the true freedom you have in Christ.

CONCLUSION

At the end, we have arrived at the same place we started. Eternal Life itself is a question of honor. The scriptures tell us that God promised his only begotten son to have Eternal Life. The scriptures also tell us that, not only did God actually create Eternal Life in his only begotten son, but also that this Life was physically witnessed by men who recorded the things they personally saw and heard. The scriptures also tell us that God promised the very same Eternal Life to those of us who would accept the witness of his son and those who knew his son. Just exactly how then does this make Eternal Life a question of honor and just exactly whose honor have we been discussing in this book?

The scriptures say that the word of God is truth. They also say that God himself will judge by the truth. The scriptures also say that God inspired men to speak and write the things that are recorded in the scriptures. The scriptures also say that God himself magnified his word above his own name. Stop and think about that. God himself honors his word above all that he is or does. Putting it simply, if God does not keep his word, then he is not God any more. What if we were in that position? What if we would not exist any more if we did not honor our own word? Guess what? We are in that position.

How can I or anyone say such a thing? There will come a time according to Peter when there is a new heavens and a new earth. In this place only righteousness will exist. Nothing unrighteous will exist there at all—not even the memory of unrighteousness. Where does that put us? That depends on where we put ourselves. Anything we think, say, or do that does not honor truth is unrighteous before God and has no place at all in the new heavens and earth. This book has explained truth. This book has explained how true worshippers are to worship God. It is now up to each one of us to honor the word we have been given without trying to find new and innovative ways to get around what we have been shown. Honoring truth is to seek it, acknowledge it, and obey it. That narrow gate and straight path is a lot narrower and straighter than any of us have ever imagined, but it begins with each one of us.

If we have truly accepted that we are naturally rebellious and totally unable to be righteous by our own efforts, we can then see that the only way we can ever hope to accomplish the task set before us is to accept completely the work already accomplished for us by Christ himself. To begin that process, we must repent—not feel sorry for, but turn completely away from—our old nature. Anything less dishonors the work accomplished by, through, and in Christ himself. If you dishonor the son of God, you also dishonor the God who sent his only begotten son to pay the price for your disobedience. God has given us everything we need to do this and to conform ourselves to the very image of his only begotten son.

We must learn to honor God's word above his own name the same way he does. Part of that is learning to honor our own word above all that we are as well. When we truly begin to follow the inspiration of the spirit that God himself has given us, then we will only say and do the things we hear and see from the inspiration of that spirit in us. We will see and correct our own faults and weaknesses. In time, our obedience will become more and more like the obedience of Jesus Christ himself. Will we ever be perfect? No, not as long as we live on this earth because we are still corrupt by nature—no matter how much we improve ourselves. However, Paul did promise us that we will be perfected from within so that we can reflect the very image of the risen Christ Jesus in our lives in spite of our own weaknesses and shortcomings.

Now would be a good time to read this book again and see just exactly what honor has been bestowed upon us that we should be called the sons of God. Anything else I could say has already been said by this book and by the Bible which inspired what has been written here.

www.ingramcontent.com/pod-product-compliance
Lightning Source LLC
LaVergne TN
LVHW091527060526
838200LV00036B/514